STUDIES IN BAPTIST HISTORY AND THOUGHT
VOLUME 36

Andrew Fuller and the Evangelical Renewal of Pastoral Theology

STUDIES IN BAPTIST HISTORY AND THOUGHT
VOLUME 36

Andrew Fuller and the Evangelical Renewal of Pastoral Theology

Keith S. Grant

Foreword by Bruce Hindmarsh

Copyright © Keith S. Grant 2013

First published 2013 by Paternoster

Paternoster is an imprint of Authentic Media
52, Presley Way, Crownhill, Milton Keynes, MK8 0ES

09 08 07 06 05 04 03   8 7 6 5 4 3 2 1

The right of Keith S. Grant to be identified as the Editor of this Work
has been asserted by him in accordance with the Copyright, Designs
and Patents Act 1988.

British Library Cataloguing in Publication Data
A catalogue record for this book is available from the British Library

ISBN 978-1-84227-779-9

Typeset by the Author
Printed and bound in Great Britain
for Paternoster by Lightning Source, Milton Keynes

Series Preface

Baptists form one of the largest Christian communities in the world, and while they hold the historic faith in common with other mainstream Christian traditions, they nevertheless have important insights which they can offer to the worldwide church. Studies in Baptist History and Thought will be one means towards this end. It is an international series of academic studies which includes original monographs, revised dissertations, collections of essays and conference papers, and aims to cover any aspect of Baptist history and thought. While not all the authors are themselves Baptists, they nevertheless share an interest in relating Baptist history and thought to the other branches of the Christian church and to the wider life of the world.

The series includes studies in various aspects of Baptist history from the seventeenth century down to the present day, including biographical works, and Baptist thought is understood as covering the subject-matter of theology (including interdisciplinary studies embracing biblical studies, philosophy, sociology, practical theology, liturgy and women's studies). The diverse streams of Baptist life throughout the world are all within the scope of these volumes.

The series editors and consultants believe that the academic disciplines of history and theology are of vital importance to the spiritual vitality of the churches of the Baptist faith and order. The series sets out to discuss, examine and explore the many dimensions of their tradition and so to contribute to their on-going intellectual vigour.

For Joy

CONTENTS

Foreword	**xiii**
Acknowledgements	**xv**
Abbreviations	**xvii**
Figures	**xix**

Introduction   **1**

"Very affecting and evangelical": The language of the affections in
    Fuller's evangelical pastoral theology   9

"Cultivating a garden before you undertake a field":
Andrew Fuller's pastoral ministry at Soham and Kettering   15

    Soham, Cambridgeshire (1754-1782)   16
    Kettering, Northamptonshire (1782-1815)   17

Chapter 1
**"I Perceived This Reasoning Would Affect the Whole Tenor of
My Preaching." Conversion: The *Formation* of an Evangelical
and Affectionate Pastoral Theology**   **23**

Context of Conversion: High Calvinist Preaching   26
Context of Conversion: Puritan and Evangelical Narratives   28
"Scripture impressions": Assurance in Pastoral Theology   31
"Presumption": Conversionism in Pastoral Theology   37
"An aversion to creature power": Spiritual Ability in
    Pastoral Theology   41
"Free offers": Preaching in Pastoral Theology   43
The Gospel Worthy of All Acceptation: An Evangelical
    Pastoral Theology   45
Summary   49

Chapter 2
**"There are no bonds to bring them together, or to keep them
together, but love." Ecclesiology: The *Context* of an Evangelical
and Affectionate Pastoral Theology**   **53**
Called to an Evangelical and Affectionate Ministry   54
The Shape of Ordinations and Aspects of Congregational
    Ecclesiology   58
A *Dissenting* Ecclesiology: Ordination and order in scripture and
    society   62
An *Independent* Ecclesiology: Ordination and order between church
    and association   65
A *Congregational* Ecclesiology: Ordination and order between pastor
    and people   72
Summary: An *Affectionate* and *Evangelical* Ecclesiology   75

Chapter 3
**"Beware that you do not preach an unfelt gospel." Preaching: The
Application of an Evangelical and Affectionate Pastoral Theology** 77
"The Simplicity of the Gospel": Fuller's Plain Style of Preaching   78
    Fuller's application of the "plain style"   79
    The genres of Fuller's sermons   84
        i. Expositions   85
        ii. Doctrinal sermons   85
        iii. Practical exhortations 87
    Fuller's extempore delivery   87
"Preaching Christ": The *evangelical* nature of Fuller's preaching   91
    The centrality of the cross of Christ   92
    Zeal for conversion   94
"Affecting the hearts of the people": The *affectionate* nature of
    Fuller's preaching   95
    *"If you would affect others, you must feel": Affections and
    evangelical* experience   96
    *"An affectionate concern after their salvation": Affections
    and evangelical* concern   100
    *"Enlightening the minds and affecting the hearts": Affections
    and evangelical* doctrine   101
Summary   103

Conclusion **107**
"Very affecting and evangelical" 108
Fuller as a particular kind of evangelical 109
The evangelical experience and affections of the pastor 110

Appendixes **113**
Appendix 1: Sermon: "The qualifications and encouragement of a
    faithful minister illustrated by the character and success
    of Barnabas" 113
Appendix 2: Sermon: "Spiritual knowledge and love necessary
    for the ministry" 126
Appendix 3: Letter to John Ryland, jun., with advice to
    ministerial students 131
Appendix 4: Letter to a young minister in prospect of ordination 132

Bibliography **135**

Index **151**

FOREWORD

Keith Grant has done in this book what few historians manage to do at all or to do very well. He tells the story of his subject's life as a pastor not from the outside but from the inside. The outward dimension of Andrew Fuller's career is well known, especially the role he played in the life of William Carey and the rise of the modern missionary movement and his legacy as the leading Baptist theologian and champion of evangelical Calvinism ("Fullerism") in the last third of the eighteenth century as the Particular Baptists moved away from the high Calvinism of an earlier generation to embrace a more evangelical outlook. He was a central figure in the transition of a younger generation of Calvinistic Baptists into the "New Dissent" of the later Evangelical Revival with its reinvigorated associational life, itinerant preaching, educational initiatives, overseas missionary enterprise, and so on. Grant knows this history well and appreciates Fuller's intellectual and practical influence in all these spheres, but the story he has to tell here is of the way the *ordinary* tasks of the pastor were transformed from the inside-out through Fuller's embrace of a thoughtful evangelical religion of the heart. Preaching, pastoral care, leading worship, governance—these were the tasks of any pastor time past or time present, but each one of these ordinary pastoral responsibilities took on new meaning and were directed toward new ends as Fuller's own spiritual life was renewed by a fresh appreciation for the gospel. By closely observing Fuller's spiritual biography and his pastoral work at Soham and then at Kettering, and by paying attention to under-utilized sources such as ordination sermons, Grant is able to show how Fuller's pastoral work found a new centre. As a pastor, Fuller focused upon the way men and women's lives could be transformed by the gospel message (conversion), the manner in which congregational life could express both the freedom of the gospel and the new bonds of affection created by it (ecclesiology), and the need to communicate the gospel to one's congregation with both clarity and depth of feeling (preaching). The theme in all of this was a faith that was "very affecting and evangelical".

Though Grant has done a depth and breadth of original research, including time in the archives, he writes with a clarity and grace that suits his subject and makes the book a pleasure to read for the professional historian or the lay reader, for the pastor or the student. The book makes a significant contribution to the biography of Fuller and to the history of the Baptists in England, but it does much more than this: it provides one of the best accounts available of evangelical pastoral theology among English Dissenters in the eighteenth century. Moreover, it illuminates the history of evangelicalism more generally by demonstrating the way congregational polity was renewed as an expression of evangelical voluntary religion in a way distinct from, but parallel to, the religious societies of Methodism and the evangelical parishes in the Church of England.

Finally, Fuller was very aware of the efforts by Lord Shaftesbury and other moral philosophers in the period to understand human psychology and especially the "moral sense" without recourse to theology. However, as Grant shows, Fuller could only approach these very modern questions in light of the need he felt for the mercy of God and the trust he had in the saving work of Christ. In the end he found a kind of evangelical balance between head and heart that was neither a sentimental pietism nor a rationalist Calvinism but a thoughtful, "affectionate" faith in Christ in the eighteenth-century sense of the term explored so carefully by his theological mentor, Jonathan Edwards. There is a wisdom in this hard-won balance in Fuller's life and thought that makes him an attractive figure in his own times and a model for us today.

Bruce Hindmarsh
Regent College, Vancouver

ACKNOWLEDGEMENTS

A sculpture is shaped by chipping away pieces of the marble. This was how Professor Bruce Hindmarsh often described the process of research, writing, and revising, as he supervised this project, which began as a Master of Theology thesis at Regent College. I am indebted to the craftsmanship of Bruce's own scholarship, and his patient guidance of this apprentice by his enthusiasm, advice, challenges, generosity, and friendship.

I would also like to thank Professor Don Lewis for reading and interacting with the manuscript, and similarly, Professor Michael Haykin, who, for the duration of the project has encouraged me with an interested and helpful correspondence.

At the outset of my research, I was given the gift of three weeks in England to spend time in Fuller's churches and personal papers. During this time, I was the recipient of unexpected and generous hospitality in the homes of Norma and Eric Butlin of Kettering, Ted and Iris Wilson of Soham, and Greg and Eydie Cowley in Oxford.

Of the many librarians and archivists who have helped me solve puzzles and track down scarce titles, I would particularly like to thank Joan Pries, then at the Regent Carey Library, Vancouver; Keith Noseworthy at the Atlantic School of Theology Library, Halifax; and Sue Mills, then at the Angus Library, Regent's Park College, Oxford.

I am grateful to Anthony Cross, Mike Parsons, and Derek Tidball for shepherding me through the publication process, and for combining the personal and professional. Cindy Aalders has been a gracious friend throughout, and generously helped with proofreading and typesetting.

This book on pastoral theology was written while being tutored in pastoral ministry by the people of Eastern Passage Baptist Church in Nova Scotia. Their support, especially that of Elders Mavis Dixon, Perry Horne, and Barbara Bennett, was a gift of love. I would also like to thank friends Rob Nylen, Gordon Dickinson, and Leslie McCurdy, as well as my parents, Shepherd and Doris Grant, and parents-in-law Chad and Nancy Stretch, for their companionship and practical support on this journey.

My greatest thanks and love is to my Joy, and our daughters, Abigail, Lily, and Hannah. For the last few years, Joy has been patient with eighteenth-century dinner conversation, has been steadily supportive through discouragement and adjustments to family life, and has enthusiastically celebrated every milestone, really understanding that it was, finally, not only the book being sculpted, but also its author.

Keith S. Grant
Eastern Passage, Nova Scotia
Advent 2010

ABBREVIATIONS

Fuller, *Diary*   Andrew Fuller, *The Diary of Andrew Fuller*, edited by Michael M. McMullen.

Fuller, *Remains*   Andrew Fuller, *The Last Remains of the Rev. Andrew Fuller*, edited by Joseph Belcher.

Fuller, *Works*   Andrew Fuller, *The Complete Works of Rev. Andrew Fuller with a Memoir of His Life by Andrew Gunton Fuller*, edited by Joseph Belcher, 3 vols. (Philadelphia: American Baptist Publications, 1845). [*Note*: The widely-available reprint by Sprinkle Publications (1988) has the same pagination.]

Morris, *Memoirs*   J.W. Morris, *Memoirs of the Life and Writings of the Rev. Andrew Fuller*.

Ryland, *Life of Fuller*   John Ryland, *The Work of Faith, the Labour of Love, and the Patience of Hope, Illustrated; in the Life and Death of the Rev. Andrew Fuller*, 2nd edition.

FIGURES

Figure 1   Portrait of Andrew Fuller from Ryland, *Life of Fuller*   xx

Figure 2   First page of George Wallis, "Memoirs"   11

Figure 3   Interior of Kettering Baptist Church   19

Figure 4   Portrait of Andrew Fuller from *The Baptist Magazine*
(July 1815)   22

Figure 5   Title page of *The Gospel Worthy of All Acceptation*   46

Figure 6   Portrait of Andrew Fuller from Morris, *Memoirs*   52

Figure 7   Portrait of Andrew Fuller from *The Baptist Magazine*
(October 1815)   76

Figure 8   A page from Fuller's sermon notebook   89

Figure 9   Silhouette portrait of Andrew Fuller from Ryland, *Life
of Fuller*   106

Figure 10   Title page of published ordination service   112

Engraved by J. Sartain

Figure 1: Portrait of Andrew Fuller from Ryland, *Life of Fuller*

INTRODUCTION

"Very Affecting and Evangelical": Andrew Fuller and the Evangelical Renewal of Pastoral Theology

At the end of the eighteenth century, there was a profound transformation of English dissenting churches, as the Particular Baptists, among others, embraced the emphases of evangelicalism. The expansionist and activist signs of that evangelical renewal have been well catalogued: reinvigorated associational life, the promotion of international missions, voluntary societies for spiritual growth and cooperative activity, widespread itinerancy and lay ministry, and initiatives in education and social engagement.[1] Andrew Fuller's (1754-1815) contribution to this evangelical transformation of the church is also well known: his participation in the Northamptonshire Association's cooperative ventures in prayer, itinerancy, education, and social reform; his role in founding, and then as an administrator and advocate for, the Baptist Missionary Society; and especially his articulation of an evangelical and moderate Calvinism, which came to be known as "Fullerism", seen as enabling, even obligating, this more activist and expansionist view of the church's ministry.[2]

---

[1] W.R. Ward, "The Baptists and the Transformation of the Church, 1780-1830", *Baptist Quarterly* 25 (October 1973): 167-184; L.G. Champion, "Evangelical Calvinism and the Structures of Baptist Church Life", *Baptist Quarterly* 28 (January 1980): 196-208; Deryck Lovegrove, *Established Church, Sectarian People: Itinerancy and the Transformation of English Dissent, 1780-1830* (Cambridge: Cambridge University Press, 1988); Olin Robison, "The Particular Baptists in England, 1760-1820" (D. Phil. diss., Oxford University, 1963); Michael Haykin, "The Baptist Identity: A View from the Eighteenth Century", *Evangelical Quarterly* 67, no. 2 (1995): 137-152.

[2] Geoffrey Nuttall, "Northamptonshire and the Modern Question: A Turning Point in Eighteenth-Century Dissent", *Journal of Theological Studies* n.s. 16, no. 1 (1965): 101-123; E.F. Clipsham, "Andrew Fuller and Fullerism: A Study in Evangelical Calvinism", *Baptist Quarterly* 20, no. 1-4 (1963-1964): 99-114, 147-54, 215-25, 269-76; Michael Haykin, *One Heart and One Soul: John Sutcliff of Olney, His Friends and His Times* (Darlington, England: Evangelical Press, 1994); Bruce Hindmarsh, *John Newton and the English Evangelical Tradition between the Conversions of Wesley and Wilberforce* (Oxford: Clarendon Press, 1996), 146.

But if the transformed church had these new expressions of outward-focused ministry, what difference did this evangelical renewal have on the *inner life* of congregations, particularly on the regular ministry of pastors, in their weekly preaching, pastoral care, and leadership? What impact did evangelical theology have on pastoral theology? Andrew Fuller was a pastor—of Particular Baptist churches in Soham, Cambridgeshire (1774-1782) and Kettering, Northamptonshire (1782-1815)—as well as a theologian, missionary administrator, and frequent village preacher, and an account of the transformation of the church should include its effects upon that, his primary vocation.

To take itinerancy as an example of how outward transformation may have had a concomitant congregational change, Deryck Lovegrove has argued persuasively that as one of the important indicators and vehicles of the transformation of Dissent, itinerancy entailed "the adaptation of the traditional pastorate".[3] More specifically, he suggests that "within the Dissenting ministry the point of change was marked by a recasting of the pastoral function to suit contemporary evangelistic needs".[4] W.R. Ward has similarly noted that the evangelical transformation of the church, and itinerant evangelism in particular, was compelling a redefinition of pastoral ministry.[5] And indeed, Andrew Fuller's extra-congregational ministry *did* transform and expand his pastoral practice, a change which exerted a kind of personal pressure on his congregational ministry, a tension that he never entirely resolved to his satisfaction. However, when communicating his pastoral theology through his many ordination sermons, his overall focus was still on the basic pastoral tasks in the weekly congregational setting. So the question still remains: Since the transformed church and the redefined pastorate still relied on preaching and pastoral care in the context of the local church, did those congregational acts in any way undergo a corresponding evangelical transformation? And if so, what was the character of its pastoral theology?

The examination of Andrew Fuller's pastoral theology and ministry, as an influential and, in many respects, representative pastor, goes some way toward locating and defining such a renewal. While the transformation of Dissent at the end of the eighteenth century certainly did result in international missions, voluntary societies, and itinerant evangelism, Andrew Fuller's pastoral theology, which was characterized by evangelicalism's emphasis on conversion and affectionate pastoral ministry *as well as* congregationalism's concern for orderly ministry and discipline, demonstrates that there was also an important evangelical renewal of pastoral theology and practice in the local church. Or, in other words, this study of Andrew Fuller's pastoral theology proposes that

---

[3] Lovegrove, *Established Church, Sectarian People*, 14.

[4] Ibid., 162.

[5] Ward, "Baptists and the Transformation of the Church", 174. Cf. Haykin, "The Baptist Identity", 151.

evangelical renewal did not only take place *alongside* the local church, but especially in congregational ecclesiology, there was a transformation *within* the existing pastoral office, as it became, in the words of a Kettering deacon and diarist, "very affecting and evangelical".[6]

Andrew Fuller's renewed pastoral theology suggests that he considered pastoral ministry within, as well as, say, itinerancy outside the congregation as an effective vehicle for the accomplishment of the aims of evangelicalism, as it took a more conversionist bearing and was evangelical and affectionate in its exercise.[7] The transformation of the church was expressed and accomplished not only in the promotion of international missions, but, also, through a pastoral theology that emphasized the obligation to use means for conversion at home; not only through the creation of voluntary societies alongside or within the church, but, also, through the recovery of the essentially voluntary nature of the local church's ministry to accomplish its evangelical aims; not only through itinerant preaching, but also through the renewal of evangelical and affectionate preaching on a weekly basis in settled pulpits. It is not the intention of this study to gainsay the importance of international missions, voluntary societies, or itinerant preaching as expressions and agents of the new face of Dissent, for indeed, Andrew Fuller was, as we have noted, an advocate for them; rather, the renewal of existing means was as much a part of the transformation of the church as the creation of new means. It is the character of Andrew Fuller's pastoral theology as *evangelical* and *affectionate* which signals its renewal.

Fuller is often noted by historians as an evangelical because of the nature of his theological project and his participation in the revitalization of the Calvinistic Baptists.[8] In his recent biographical study, Peter Morden explores the extent to which Fuller's thought and ministry reflect the quadrilateral of characteristics—crucicentrism, conversionism, biblicism, and activism—which David Bebbington has identified as the essence of evangelicalism.[9] With regard

---

[6] George Wallis (1775-1869), "Memoirs, etc, of State of Mind, continued", mss diary (15 March 1805 - 1 June 1817), Fuller Baptist Church, Kettering, 14 July 1811.

[7] Lovegrove, *Established Church, Sectarian People*, 17, frames itinerancy in these terms.

[8] For example, Gordon Rupp, *Religion in England, 1688-1791*, Oxford History of the Christian Church, ed. Henry Chadwick and Owen Chadwick (Oxford: Clarendon Press, 1986), 487; David Bebbington, *Evangelicalism in Modern Britain: A History from the 1730s to the 1980s* (Grand Rapids: Baker Book House, 1989), 64-65; Hindmarsh, *John Newton*, 122-123, 146; Mark Noll, *The Rise of Evangelicalism: The Age of Edwards, Whitefield and the Wesleys*, vol. 1 of *A History of Evangelicalism: People, Movements and Ideas in the English-Speaking World* (Downers Grove: InterVarsity Press, 2003), 193, 207-209.

[9] Peter Morden, *Offering Christ to the World: Andrew Fuller (1754-1815) and the Revival of Eighteenth Century Particular Baptist Life*, Studies in Baptist History and Thought (Carlisle: Paternoster Press, 2003); Bebbington, *Evangelicalism in Modern*

to Fuller's pastoral ministry, Morden draws attention to those features which are specifically evangelistic, indicating Fuller's "clear conversionist agenda", and, therefore, his evangelicalism.[10] The defining of Fuller's evangelicalism, however, could, also, go in the other direction, beginning not with what is generally or essentially "evangelical", but with the unique angle of view Fuller provides as a Calvinistic Baptist.[11] Fuller, himself, defined his pastoral theology, and especially his preaching, as "evangelical", but because of his lively adherence to Baptist and congregational principles, his expression of that evangelical pastoral theology was different from that of, say, an Evangelical clergyman in the Church of England, or of a Methodist preacher. Fuller was, for example, convinced that an orderly and vigorous congregational ecclesiology was not only compatible with, but actually promoted and nurtured, the same evangelical aims that were expressed in Anglican voluntary societies and Methodist connexions. Exploring the nature of Fuller's pastoral theology and his hyphenated definition of "evangelical", then, enriches our understanding of evangelicalism and its varieties.

In a discussion of Anglican pastoralia in the eighteenth century, John Walsh and Stephen Taylor describe an essential continuity of pastoral work and pastoral self-understanding across the theological spectrum of the Church, and remark: "What distinguished the self-consciously 'serious' Evangelical clergy toward the end of the century was less their definition of pastoral duties than their conception of what it was to be a Christian."[12] While Walsh and Taylor are specifically describing clergy within the Church of England, their comment begs the question whether there was, in fact, an impact by evangelical piety upon pastoral theology, or whether we can speak of a distinctively evangelical

---

Britain, esp. 2-17. To David Bebbington's four criteria, George Marsden, "Introduction", in *Evangelicalism and Modern America*, ed. George Marsden (Grand Rapids, MI: Eerdmans, 1984), vii-xvi, adds transdenominationalism; and John G. Stackhouse, Jr., "Defining 'Evangelical'", in *Church & Faith Trends* (The Centre for Research on Canadian Evangelicals) 1, no. 1 (2007): 1-5, expands the set to six by making explicit the criterion of being both orthodox and orthoprax. Compare the four characteristics of evangelical pietism or experiential Protestantism identified by F. Ernest Stoeffler, *The Rise of Evangelical Pietism*, in Studies in the History of Religions (Leiden: E. J. Brill, 1965), 13-23: experiential, idealistic, biblical, and oppositive.

[10] Morden, *Offering Christ to the World*, chap. 5, esp. 103.

[11] See the brief comments on defining evangelicalism by its essence and its various strands, in Hindmarsh, *John Newton*, 8-9. See also John Wolffe, *The Expansion of Evangelicalism: The Age of Wilberforce, More, Chalmers and Finney*, vol. 2 of *A History of Evangelicalism: People, Movements and Ideas in the English-Speaking World* (Downers Grove: InterVarsity Press, 2007), 19-21.

[12] John Walsh and Stephen Taylor, "Introduction", in John Walsh, Colin Haydon, and Stephen Taylor, eds., *The Church of England, c.1689-c.1833: From Toleration to Tractarianism* (Cambridge: Cambridge University Press, 1993), 14.

approach to the main pastoral duties. The literature of pastoralia, broadly considered, tends to express a basic continuity, allowing some scholars to speak of a "classical tradition" of pastoral theology, including reflection on the basic pastoral tasks of preaching, spiritual care, leading worship, or presiding over discipline, as well as themes related to pastoral vocation and piety, such as ordination, self-watch, or the appropriate handling of authority.[13] Within that great continuity of pastoral reflection, however, are significant differences of emphasis and priority, and important variations in defining aspects of pastoral ministry. Historical events, theology, the forms of pastoral literature, and even individual personalities each contribute to the ways pastoral theology is shaped, and which aspects of ministry come to the fore, and which recede.[14] This study of Andrew Fuller will suggest that yes, the evangelical "conception of what it was to be a Christian" did, in fact, have a bearing on pastoral theology and practice. Preaching remained the central activity of pastoral ministry for evangelicals, but there was an important change in their understanding of what preaching was for, and consequently what its main themes, manner of delivery, and intended audience should be. If preaching were for moral education, the reformation of manners, or even social cohesion, then its character would be different in important ways from preaching that was primarily for conversion and communicating affectionate experience. In addition to the basic similarity of pastoral duties across the theological spectrum, there can be identified, in the work of Andrew Fuller, one distinctively evangelical pastoral theology—a specifically evangelical contribution to pastoralia and an underappreciated aspect of how the church was transformed by evangelicalism. The evangelical

---

[13] David Cornick, "Pastoral Care in England: Perkins, Baxter and Burnet", in G.R. Evans, ed., *A History of Pastoral Care* (London and New York: Cassell, 2000), 313; Andrew Purves, *Pastoral Theology in the Classical Tradition* (Louisville: Westminster John Knox Press, 2001); and Thomas Oden, *Pastoral Theology: Essentials of Ministry* (San Francisco: Harper & Row, 1983).

[14] To take but one example, also noted by Walsh and Taylor ("Introduction", 16-17), the pastoral theology of the Church of England in the period after Toleration (1689) was significantly shaped by a widespread perception of competition from Dissenters. Latitudinarian divines such as Bishop Gilbert Burnet felt that the new condition of religious voluntarism required a reformation of the Church's pastoral care, out of which context came Burnet's influential clergy handbook, *Discourse of the Pastoral Care* (1692). Despite the continuities in its definition of pastoral duties, Burnet's pastoral theology did not offer a generic pastoral theology, but rather expressed a specific view of pastoral ministry shaped to a great degree by the new voluntarism and theological convictions about church reform. See also John Walsh, "Religious Societies: Methodist and Evangelical, 1738-1800", in *Voluntary Religion*, ed. W.J. Sheils and Diana Wood, Studies in Church History (Oxford: Basil Blackwell, 1986), 279, 282; Mark Goldie, "John Locke, Jonas Proast and Religious Toleration, 1688-1692", in Walsh, et al, eds., *The Church of England*, 165-166; and W.M. Jacob, *The Clerical Profession in the Long Eighteenth Century, 1680-1840* (Oxford: Oxford University Press, 2007), 203-204.

reformation in what it meant to be a Christian—converted and growing in an assured, affectionate faith—significantly transformed the aims, importance, and manner of the main pastoral duties. Evangelical theology and piety did lead to a transformed pastoral theology, a change which was not primarily in terms of new pastoral duties as much as a renewal of the character of those duties, as it were, from within.

Andrew Fuller was not alone among the Particular Baptists in giving voice to an evangelical pastoral theology, although his articulation of such a theology was perhaps the most complete and certainly the most influential. The story of eighteenth century Particular Baptists has often been dominated—with considerable justification—by the prominence of, and eventual shift from, high Calvinism. Roger Hayden, however, has demonstrated that alongside, and even at times overlapping with, that high Calvinism was a strong current of evangelical Calvinism and a vigorously evangelistic ministry. The centre for that moderate Calvinism through the middle years of the eighteenth century was not London or Northamptonshire, but the Western Baptist Association, particularly associated with Bristol Academy.[15] Hayden's thesis is borne out by, among other pastoral literature, the published sermons which had been preached before the Bristol Education Society, many of which dwelled on ministerial themes, and which emphasized an educated, able, and evangelical ministry, an approach very similar to that articulated by Andrew Fuller.[16] Similarly, an evangelical pastoral theology was urged in a ministerial handbook published by John Ryland, jun., (1753-1825), a close colleague of Fuller, a correspondent with wide evangelical connections, and both a graduate and tutor at Bristol Academy. Ryland's *Christianæ Militiæ Viaticum: Or, A Brief Directory for Evangelical Ministers*[17] is a compilation of selections from Cotton Mather, David Brainerd, John Rogers, Jonathan Edwards, and John Owen, each on maintaining the vitality of the pastor's own spiritual life; Ryland presented an evangelical piety as the basis of an evangelical pastoral ministry. The last words of the book, very representative of the whole, share Andrew Fuller's emphasis on the necessity of the pastor's own affectionate experience for an evangelical ministry; Owen says that a minister who attends to spiritual things chiefly with a thought to what can be said to others will lose the "Power and Efficacy" of his ministry to his hearers, and "he will have little Benefit by

---

[15] Roger Hayden, "Evangelical Calvinism among Eighteenth-Century British Baptists, with Particular Reference to Bernard Foskett, Hugh and Caleb Evans, and the Bristol Baptist Academy, 1690-1791" (Ph.D., University of Keele, 1991). The broader presence of moderate Calvinism had been briefly noted by Robison, "The Particular Baptists in England", 46-55, and Ward, "Baptists and the Transformation of the Church", 167.

[16] See the Bibliography for a large sample of these sermons.

[17] 2nd ed, (London: W. Button, 1799). In at least this edition the directory was printed in miniature (two by three inches), making it a convenient pocket book for regular devotional reading.

his own Ministry, who is not solicitous, in the first place, to enjoy an Experience in his own heart of the Power of the Truths he teaches unto others".[18] Fuller's evangelical pastoral theology finds its place in this context among other evangelical Particular Baptists, but his work provides a unique and important subject for study, in part because of the breadth of source material, including what is probably the largest extant collection of eighteenth century Baptist ordination sermons by a single preacher. Within his larger body of writing, Fuller sets such an evangelical ministry on a firm theological footing. Further, the nature of Fuller's pastoral theology, also, invites examination because, as a prominent leader, his renewed perspective and ministry was influential among his peers and younger contemporaries. Biographer J.W. Morris observed that Fuller's influence was important precisely in those matters which were addressed in his pastoral theology:

> He had a bishopric, without any of its titles or emoluments; and the care of all the churches, within the immediate sphere of his acquaintance, came upon him daily. In their formation, in the ordination of their pastors, and in every case of difficulty, his assistance was required, and in these important services he excelled.[19]

The renewed pastoral theology of Andrew Fuller will be examined from three overlapping aspects or definitions of that discipline. The first of these, perhaps its most basic stance, defines pastoral theology as "the interface between theology and Christian doctrine on the one hand, and pastoral experience and care on the other".[20] From this perspective, pastoral theology describes the pastoral and congregational implications of theological systems, and, conversely, allows Christian experience to influence the formation of doctrine.[21] It is "theology seen from the shepherding perspective".[22] Second, pastoral theology is an expression of ecclesiology and church order, locating the role of the minister in relationship to the church and other officers.[23] Here the focus is determining the essence and aims of ordained ministry, its vocation

---

[18] Ryland, *Christianæ Militiæ Viaticum*, 96.

[19] J.W. Morris, *Memoirs of the Life and Writings of the Rev. Andrew Fuller*, ed. Rufus Babcock, jun. (Boston: Lincoln & Edmands, 1830), 77.

[20] Derek Tidball, *Skilful Shepherds: Explorations in Pastoral Theology* (Leicester: Apollos, 1997), 24.

[21] Ibid., 24; Stephen Pattison and James Woodward, "An Introduction to Pastoral and Practical Theology", in James Woodward and Stephen Pattison, ed., *The Blackwell Reader in Pastoral and Practical Theology* (Oxford: Blackwell, 2000), xiii.

[22] Tidball, *Skilful Shepherds*, 24; Seward Hiltner, "The Meaning and Importance of Pastoral Theology", in *The Blackwell Reader in Pastoral and Practical Theology*, ed. James Woodward and Stephen Pattison (Oxford: Blackwell, 2000), 28.

[23] Tidball, *Skilful Shepherds*, 18-19.

and qualifications, and its boundaries with the general priesthood.[24] And third, pastoral theology is theological reflection on "the office and functions of the pastor", the definition, aims, and guidance for preaching, pastoral care, worship, ordinances, and leadership.[25] As often as possible, Fuller's actual pastoral ministry will be set alongside his theological convictions about that ministry. These three perspectives more or less correspond with the chapters of this study: the *formation* of Fuller's conversionist pastoral theology against the backdrop of the pastoral implications of high and evangelical varieties of Calvinism; the congregational *context* of his pastoral theology examined as an element of his ecclesiology; the *application* of the broader themes to the central pastoral task of preaching.

The argument will proceed by demonstrating, from each of these three angles, that Fuller's pastoral theology was a congregational instance of evangelical renewal, an expression and agent of the transformation of Dissent as vital as those alongside and beyond the local church. More substantively, each chapter will, also, reveal a facet of Fuller's evangelicalism—and especially its character as "affectionate and evangelical"—as seen in precisely this pastoral renewal. Chapter One shows Fuller's manifesto of evangelical Calvinism, *The Gospel Worthy of All Acceptation*, to be centrally concerned with pastoral theology, providing warrants for a more assured approach of spiritual seekers in the process of conversion, and obligating ministers to take a more confidently conversionist stance toward their hearers. Chapter Two sets Fuller's evangelicalism squarely in the context of his congregational ecclesiology. While his ecclesiology, in some ways, serves as a tension with other evangelicals and evangelical impulses, it is one of the important elements in defining the specific nature of Fuller's Baptist and dissenting version of evangelicalism, expressed differently than his Anglican and Methodist counterparts. Even here, though, the renewal of Fuller's pastoral theology is evident, with his emphases on voluntarism, conversionist aims, and affectionate bonds. Chapter Three argues that Fuller's renewed pastoral theology was particularly expressed in his preaching, and that the character of that renewal can be substantiated and defined with reference to his key convictions about preaching: *plain* in composition and delivery, *evangelical* in content and concern, and *affectionate* in feeling and application. Andrew Fuller's pastoral theology is a convincing example of evangelical transformation occurring within, as well as beyond, the Particular Baptist churches of the late eighteenth century.

Throughout the study, the interplay between "evangelical" and "affectionate" is explored, and by way of introduction we will survey the

---

[24] Cf. W.R. Ward, "Pastoral Office and the General Priesthood in the Great Awakening", in *The Ministry: Clerical and Lay*, Studies in Church History, ed. W.J. Sheils and Diana Wood (Oxford: Basil Blackwell, 1989).

[25] Oden, *Pastoral Theology*, x; Tidball, *Skilful Shepherds*, 19.

psychology and vocabulary of the affections which Fuller relied upon to give voice to his evangelical concerns. And while elements of Fuller's biography are developed at various points in the book (particularly his conversion and early ministry in the first chapter), to provide a larger narrative frame, and to get some sense of the congregational context of his pastoral ministry, it will be useful to first sketch the general outlines of his life, ministry, and two churches.

"Very affecting and evangelical":
The language of the affections in Fuller's evangelical pastoral theology

When Kettering diarist and deacon George Wallis described Fuller's ministry as "very affecting and evangelical",[26] he employed the language of a widespread and nuanced religious psychology, he signaled the important pairing of "affectionate" and "evangelical", and he highlighted terms that were among the most characteristic of Andrew Fuller's pastoral theology.

This discourse made use of a vocabulary of the heart: "affections" and "affectionate", "passions", "love", "zeal", "sense", "sentiment", "relish", "inclination", and "feeling". The affections were distinguished, on the one hand, from enthusiasm or mere impulsive passion, and, on the other hand, from speculative or disinterested knowledge. In other terms, the affections could be described as a felt response to truth, personal experience accompanying understanding, the heart's inclination toward revealed facts, or rational desires.[27] While to modern readers "affections" usually connotes emotion and feeling over against reason and intellect, to Fuller and his eighteenth-century contemporaries the use of the language of the affections was more nuanced and comprehensive, and, in fact, quite successfully bridged that gap between heart and mind. Indeed, Thomas Dixon has argued that it was the departure from this psychology of the affections and its subtle intertwining of the cognitive and the affective which led to the more recent invention of the category of emotions, "conceived as a set of morally disengaged, bodily, non-cognitive and involuntary feelings". Affections, or moral sentiments, were understood as "rational and voluntary movements of the soul, while still being subjectively warm and lively psychological states".[28] That organic connection between a considered doctrine and its affective response is nicely expressed by Andrew

---

[26] Wallis, "Memoirs", 14 July 1811.

[27] John E. Smith, "Religious Affections and the 'Sense of the Heart'", in Sang Hyun Lee, ed., *The Princeton Companion to Jonathan Edwards* (Princeton: Princeton University Press, 2005), 105; Thomas Dixon, *From Passions to Emotions: The Creation of a Secular Psychological Category* (Cambridge: Cambridge University Press, 2003), 64-65.

[28] Dixon, *From Passions to Emotions*, 3; see 64-65. See, also, Thomas Dixon, "Theology, Anti-theology and Atheology: From Christian Passions to Secular Emotions" *Modern Theology*, 15 (July 1999) 3, 301-305.

Fuller: "If … we feel and realize the sentiments we deliver, emotions and actions will be the natural expressions of the heart."[29] The language of the affections was used in a way that integrated, rather than set at odds, mind and heart.

The affections figured prominently in the philosophical and moral writings of Lord Shaftesbury (1671-1713), Francis Hutcheson (1694-1746) and David Hume (1711-1776), among others, as moral philosophy and theology in the eighteenth century exhibited a greater concern with human nature and the inner life, including the relationship between reason and the affections.[30] But the language of the affections was, also, quite fully developed and employed to articulate the particular concerns of evangelicals. The roots of this language went, at least, as deep as a strand of Puritan writing which emphasized personal or "experimental" religion, the close application of biblical truth to individual cases, and the role of the heart in sensing and responding to the gospel, appropriately labeled by Terrence Erdt as a "Calvinist psychology of the heart".[31] Evangelicals drew upon these traditions, this language of the heart, to describe and define appropriate kinds of responses to the gospel.

Diarist George Wallis' description of Fuller's pastoral ministry as "very affecting and evangelical", also, suggests the mutual importance of the terms, for the language of the heart was a kind of evangelical accent to accompany evangelical doctrinal content. Affectionate discourse was a mark of evangelicalism and the wider movement of the "religion of the heart".[32] Isabel Rivers has made a penetrating study of the "Affectionate religion" of early evangelical Dissent in the context of eighteenth century moral philosophy. She has argued that while a rationalizing tendency in Dissent led some to tilt toward the heterodox and to marginalize the affections, evangelical Dissenters articulated a faith that was orthodox, experimental (i.e. personal), and affectionate:

---

[29] Fuller, *Works*, i.137.

[30] Norman Fiering, *Jonathan Edwards's Moral Thought and Its British Context* (Chapel Hill: University of North Carolina Press, 1981), 5-6; Dixon, *From Passions to Emotions*, 70-72; Isabel Rivers, *Reason, Grace, and Sentiment: A Study of the Language of Religion and Ethics in England, 1660-1780*, vol. 1, *Whichcote to Wesley* (Cambridge: Cambridge University Press, 1991).

[31] Terrence Erdt, *Jonathan Edwards, Art and the Sense of the Heart* (Amherst: University of Massachusetts Press, 1980), 2; see also Brad Walton, *Jonathan Edwards, Religious Affections and the Puritan Analysis of True Piety, Spiritual Sensation and Heart Religion* in Studies in American Religion, Volume 74, (Lewiston, NY: The Edwin Mellen Press, 2002), and the remarks on continuity and discontinuity at Rivers, *Reason, Grace, and Sentiment*, i.166-168.

[32] Rivers, *Reason, Grace, and Sentiment*, i.167-168, 196-197; Ted A. Campbell, *The Religion of the Heart: A Study of European Religious Life in the Seventeenth and Eighteenth Centuries* (Columbia: University of South Carolina Press, 1991), esp. 2-3.

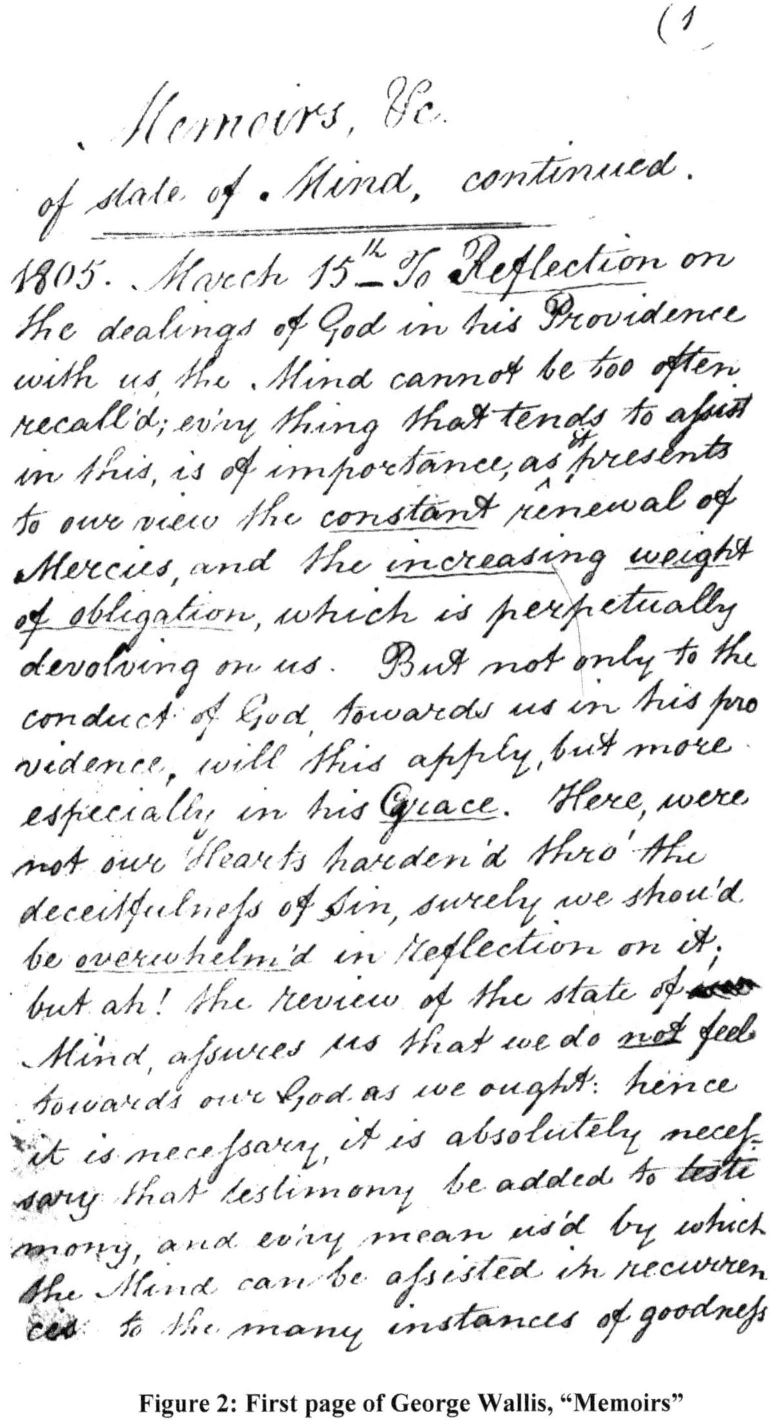

(1

Memoirs, &c.
of state of Mind, continued.

1805. March 15th— To Reflection on
the dealings of God in his Providence
with us, the Mind cannot be too often
recall'd; evry thing that tends to assist
in this, is of importance; as it presents
to our view the constant renewal of
Mercies, and the increasing weight
of obligation, which is perpetually
devolving on us. But not only to the
conduct of God, towards us in his pro
vidence, will this apply, but more
especially in his Grace. Here, were
not our Hearts harden'd thro' the
deceitfulness of Sin, surely we shou'd
be overwhelm'd in Reflection on it;
but ah! the review of the state of
Mind, assures us that we do not feel
towards our God as we ought: hence
it is necessary, it is absolutely necef_
sary that testimony be added to testi
mony, and evry mean us'd by which
the Mind can be assisted in recurren
ces to the many instances of goodness

Figure 2: First page of George Wallis, "Memoirs"

> The evangelical tendency emphasizes the traditional Reformation doctrines of grace, atonement, justification by faith (often covered by the label 'orthodoxy'), the importance of experimental knowledge, meaning both the believer's own experience of religion, and acquaintance with the variety of the experience of others, and the central function of the heart and affections in religion in relation to the will and understanding.[33]

The heart and the affections were emphasized in concert with orthodox doctrine, reflecting a concern for a lively and heartfelt response to the gospel, for a voluntary, sincere, and personal Christianity, as opposed to rationalism, nominalism, or cold orthodoxy. Prominent in Rivers' account of the affectionate nature of early evangelicalism are Isaac Watts (1674-1748) and Philip Doddridge (1702-1751). In a representative quotation, Watts employed the language of the affections and passions to combine evangelical doctrine and personal experience:

> It is the Influence of Religion on the Passions, that doth in a great Measure make the Difference between the true Christian and the mere outward Professor: The mere Professor may know as much of the Doctrines of Religion, and of the Duties of it, as the most religious Man: but he doth not fear and love, and desire and hope, and mourn and rejoice, as the true Christian doth.[34]

The psychology of the affections provided evangelicals and others with a vocabulary which successfully integrated mind and heart, the objective and subjective, and with that vocabulary of the heart, evangelicalism became marked by its union of orthodox doctrine and personal, heart-felt experience.

The most comprehensive evangelical study of the affections—and, certainly, for Andrew Fuller the most influential—was that by Jonathan Edwards (1703–1758), particularly in his *A Treatise Concerning Religious Affections* (1746).[35] Edwards insisted upon the central place of the affections in the spiritual life (against rationalist detractors) and articulated criteria for discerning true from false affections (against the excesses of enthusiasm), all within the context of the evangelical revivals of the Great Awakening.[36] Edwards said that "True

---

[33] Rivers, *Reason, Grace, and Sentiment*, i.167.

[34] Isaac Watts, *Discourses of the Love of God and the Use and Abuse of the Passions in Religion, with a devout Meditation suited to each Discourse. To which is prefix'd, A plain and particular Account of the Natural Passions, with Rules of the Government of them* (London, 1729), 173.

[35] Fuller, *Works*, ii.641 and *Diary*, 3 February 1781; Jonathan Edwards, *A Treatise Concerning Religious Affections* [1746], ed. John E. Smith, in *The Works of Jonathan Edwards*, Volume 2, ed. Perry Miller, (New Haven: Yale University Press, 1959).

[36] Smith, "Religious Affections and the 'Sense of the Heart'", 103 and elsewhere. For discussions of Edwards's psychology of the affections and the sense of the heart, see, in

religion, in great part, consists in holy affections", which he defined as "the more vigorous and sensible exercises of the inclination and will of the soul".[37] He described a "sense of the heart", accompanying regeneration, by which a person perceives the excellency and beauty of God in the gospel of Jesus Christ.[38] Thus being enabled to perceive the gospel with the heart—as well as the mind—the person's whole being is inclined toward that truth, expressed with godly affections. "If the great things of religion are rightly understood," Edwards said, "they will affect the heart."[39] And so he regularly distinguished between two ways of knowing: first, "that which is merely speculative or notional", and second, "that which consists in the sense of the heart: as when there is a sense of the beauty, amiableness, or sweetness of a thing; so that the heart is sensible of pleasure and delight in the presence of the idea of it".[40] Or, again, when there is a unity between head and heart, "the mind don't only speculate and behold, but relishes and feels".[41] Edwards' full treatment of the affections demonstrated their centrality to evangelical faith, and attempting to balance what he perceived as both rationalist and emotional excesses, he insisted on the unity of the mind's understanding of doctrine and the heart's affectionate response.

The dual emphasis upon the "very affecting" and the "evangelical" is arguably the defining characteristic of Andrew Fuller's own pastoral theology. While he drew on the language in relation to other important themes in his theological and polemical writing, his usage of the affections is most concentrated and creative when describing his evangelical approach to pastoral

---

addition to his *Treatise Concerning the Religious Affections*, Edwards' "A Divine and Supernatural Light", in *Sermons and Discourses, 1730-1733*, ed. Mark Valeri, in *The Works of Jonathan Edwards*, vol 17, ed. Harry Stout, (New Haven: Yale University Press, 1999), 405-426; and "Miscellany 782. Ideas. Sense of the Heart. Spiritual Knowledge or Conviction. Faith." in *The "Miscellanies, 501-832*, ed. Ava Chamberlain, in *The Works of Jonathan Edwards*, vol 18, ed. Harry Stout, (New Haven: Yale University Press, 2000), 452-466; and for analysis and discussion: Perry Miller, "Jonathan Edwards on the Sense of the Heart" *Harvard Theological Review*, 41 (April 1948) 2: 123-145; Roland André Delattre, *Beauty and Sensibility in the Thought of Jonathan Edwards: An Essay in Aesthetics and Theological Ethics* (New Haven: Yale University Press, 1968); Erdt, *Jonathan Edwards*; Fiering, *Jonathan Edwards's Moral Thought*; Walton, *Jonathan Edwards*; Louis J. Mitchell, *Jonathan Edwards on the Experience of Beauty*, in Studies in Reformed Theology and History (Princeton: Princeton Theological Seminary, 2003).

[37] Edwards, *Religious Affections*, 95 and 96.

[38] Ibid., 205-6, 208, 260; "Divine and Supernatural Light"; "Miscellany 782", 459.

[39] Edwards, *Religious Affections*, 120.

[40] Edwards, "Divine and Supernatural Light", 413; see also, among other places, *Religious Affections*, 271-272.

[41] Edwards, *Religious Affections*, 272; see Delattre, *Beauty and Sensibility*, 7.

theology.

In a nice summary statement, Fuller affirmed the prominence of the affections and, also, the essence of those affections as a response to orthodox doctrine: "The union of genuine orthodoxy and affection constitutes true religion."[42] The winsomeness and warmth of his addresses and of his pastoral theology are due in great part to this carefully held balance, noted by Wallis, between the affectionate and the evangelical. In the spirit of developing a working psychology of the heart for pastoral ministry, Fuller urged pastors to be students of human nature, to understand "the anatomy of the soul", or the "springs of action" and to know how to distinguish between godly affections and criminal passions.[43] The general outline of Fuller's understanding of the affections bears the influence of Edwards, including the necessity of a sense of the heart to apprehend religious truth and the beauty of God, often drawing on some of Edwards' best-known metaphors. Spiritual truths cannot be known by "mere intellect" or "simple knowledge," wrote Fuller, "any more than the sweetness of honey or the bitterness of wormwood can be ascertained by the sight of the eye". Rather, the gospel can be known only as God imparts a "holy susceptibility and relish for the truth", a new "approbation of the heart", by which one can have a "sense of their Divine excellency" or discern the "Divine beauties".[44]

Fuller made strong assertions about the centrality of the affections in evangelical faith and ministry—"Beware that you do not preach an unfelt gospel"[45]—but was careful to communicate both the subjective and cognitive aspects of evangelical affections. In the sermon, "The Nature and Importance of an Intimate Knowledge of Divine Truth", Fuller said,

> Knowledge and affection have a mutual influence on each other. … We cannot love an unknown gospel, any more than an unknown God. Affection is fed by knowledge, being thereby furnished with grounds, or reasons, for its operations. By the expansion of the mind the heart is supplied with objects which fill it with delight.[46]

Affection joined with knowledge, reason with delight, mind with heart: a fully orbed articulation of the affections. That religious psychology mapped onto his pastoral theology, balancing doctrine and experience, truth and feeling: "The

[42] Fuller, *Works*, i.549.
[43] Ibid., i.480.
[44] Ibid., ii.410, 413, 602. Beginning on the last of these pages, Fuller begins a quotation five pages in length from Edwards' *Religious Affections.* See Chris Chun, "'Sense of the Heart': Jonathan Edwards' Legacy in the Writings of Andrew Fuller", *Eusebeia* (Spring 2008) 9: 117-134, for a discussion of how Fuller adapts Edwards' arguments for his own particular theological ends.
[45] Fuller, *Works*, i.489.
[46] Ibid., i.169.

two main objects to be attained in the work of the Christian ministry," Fuller urged, are "enlightening the minds and affecting the hearts of the people."[47]

As this study of Fuller's pastoral theology unfolds, the language of the affections will come to the forefront at key moments: when responding to a semblance of assurance built on scripture impressions, when articulating the voluntary nature of pastoral relationships, and, particularly, when outlining evangelical pastoral motivations and the dynamics of preaching. In relation to preaching, for example, Fuller especially joined together the affectionate and the evangelical, using those terms together to indicate that the gospel must be felt and experienced by the preacher in his own life to communicate it to others, to insist on the pastor's spiritual concern for the conversion of his hearers, and the pastoral task of attending to both doctrine and affectionate experience, the combination of head and heart. Or, in other words, evangelical doctrine must be communicated with an affectionate manner and arise from affectionate motives.

The perceptive description, by his Kettering congregant, of Fuller's ministry as "very affecting and evangelical" summarizes the main concerns and vocabulary of Andrew Fuller's pastoral theology. The language of the affections was used in the eighteenth century as a nuanced way of describing the heart's response to truth, of a personal and felt inclination toward doctrine, and not merely a distant or speculative knowledge. Rather than highlighting the affective to the exclusion of the rational, affectionate language insisted upon the mutual necessity of head and heart. With their emphasis upon both orthodox doctrine and sincere personal experience of faith, it is not surprising that evangelicals made regular use and thorough study of the affections. Andrew Fuller's use of affectionate language is most pronounced when outlining his evangelical pastoral theology, and he creatively allowed affectionate and evangelical to define each other, so that it can be argued that to the extent that Fuller's pastoral theology is affectionate, it is evangelical.

"Cultivating a garden before you undertake a field": Andrew Fuller's pastoral ministry at Soham and Kettering

In one of his letters to a young minister about to be ordained, Fuller encouragingly suggested, "A young man in your circumstances will have an advantage in beginning a church on a small scale. It will be like cultivating a garden before you undertake a field."[48] It is very likely that he has his own experiences at Soham and Kettering in mind, reflecting on the differences between the two settings, and more significantly, the pastoral and theological transformation he had undergone. Fuller's ministry at Soham could be

---

[47] Ibid., i.479.

[48] Andrew Fuller, letter to a young minister, in *The Baptist Magazine*, 7 (1815), 419-420, as cited in Michael A.G. Haykin, ed., *The Armies of the Lamb: The Spirituality of Andrew Fuller* (Dundas: Joshua Press, 2001), 240.

considered as the period of his theological development, and that at Kettering as the broadening application of that pastoral theology.

Soham, Cambridgeshire (1754-1782)

Andrew Fuller was born at Wicken, Cambridgeshire, in February 1754 to a family who farmed the drained fenlands, and who were of nonconforming principles. His grandmother, Philippa Gunton, was one of the original members of the Particular Baptist church at nearby Soham, established only two years before Fuller's birth.[49] The church had its origins in the Independent church at Isleham, a fruit of the evangelistic ministry of ejected ministers Francis Holcroft (1629?-1693) and David Culy (*d.* 1725?), and which, later, became reorganized as the Pound Lane Particular Baptist Church, from which Charles Spurgeon (1834-1892) would be baptized. At the time, however, the Isleham Independent church declared, contrary to the desires of some of its members, that "a Waterman should never more enter the Pulpit", and so in 1752, a small number embodied themselves as a Particular Baptist church, and, shortly thereafter, invited John Eve (*d.* 1782) to be their pastor.[50] Geoffrey Nuttall notes that the Soham church was firmly within a network of high Calvinism, influenced by Richard Davis (1658-1714) and his successors, and this was, indeed, the case during Fuller's spiritual coming of age under the ministry of John Eve.[51] The socially marginal location of these Baptist dissenters in Soham might be gauged by their necessity, for the first several decades of the church's history, of holding baptisms as secretly as possible. They were, as the Church Book describes them,

> administered in a very private manner, either early in the morning (often as early as 2 or 3 o'clock) or late at Night if moonlight, on account of the great opposition they had to encounter and because the populace behaved so ill that they could not attend to it with sufficient solemnity. None appear to have been allowed to be present except members and friends introduced by them, and concerning whom

---

[49] On the history of the church, see The Church Book (1752-1868), in mss at the Cambridgeshire Record Office, and in Transcript (L. Grimshaw), Angus Library, Regent's Park College, Oxford; Andrew Fuller, "A narration of the dealings of God in a way of Providence with the Baptist Church of Christ at Soham, from the year 1770, as Containing its dissolution, replantation, and progression", mss, Cambridgeshire Record Office; Kenneth A.C. Parsons, ed., *The Church Book of the Independent Church (Now Pound Lane Baptist) Isleham, 1693-1805* (Cambridge: Cambridge Antiquarian Records Society, 1984); Ryland, *Life of Fuller*, 8-10.

[50] Soham Church Book, 2.

[51] Nuttall, "Northamptonshire and The Modern Question", 121.

there was reason to hope there was some good thing in them towards the Lord God of the house of Israel.[52]

And so it was that Andrew Fuller, though a hearer at the church for much of his life, had never witnessed a baptism until his sixteenth year, after his own conversion experience. On seeing the baptism, he recalled, "I was considerably affected by what I saw and heard. The solemn immersion of a person, on a profession of faith in Christ, carried such conviction with it, that I wept like a child, on the occasion", and was himself baptized about a month later, in April of 1770.[53] In the days immediately after his baptism he was derided by a group of young men for having been "dipped".[54] When Fuller was received into membership on the hearing of his religious experience, there were about thirty members who, perhaps reflecting the socio-economic status of that membership, met in a wooden barn which had "nothing but earth for its floor, no ceiling concealed its thatch from the eye. There were no regular pews or seats, but a number of chairs and forms without backs."[55]

Fuller was encouraged by the church to begin preaching occasionally in 1772, and was invited to become their pastor two years later, when he was twenty years old. He was ordained in May 1775. The church joined the Northamptonshire Association in the same year, which provided for Fuller a formative network of friends and colleagues, including Robert Hall, sen. (1728-1791), who delivered the charge at his Soham ordination, John Ryland, jun., and John Sutcliff (1752-1814).[56]

His pastorate at Soham was a time of theological self-education, the formation of his pastoral practice, and a considered and radical conversion to a more evangelical Calvinism, the story of which is told in Chapter One, and which culminated in the drafting of *The Gospel Worthy of All Acceptation*. To support his growing family, Fuller unsuccessfully attempted to supplement his paltry income with a school and a store. He remained at Soham until 1782 when, after a protracted and agonizing period of discernment, a combination of financial pressure, broken affections, and theological differences led to his removal to Kettering in Northamptonshire.

Kettering, Northamptonshire (1782-1815)

The "field" of ministry which Fuller undertook at Kettering shared in Northamptonshire's legacy of Independency. The county was a stronghold of

---

[52] Soham Church Book, 9.

[53] Ryland, *Life of Fuller*, 22.

[54] Ibid.

[55] Soham Church Book, 10.

[56] The nature and import of this network of friends, which was later to include William Carey, is helpfully portrayed by Haykin, *One Heart and One Soul*.

Lollardy in the fourteenth century, and a centre of Puritanism in the sixteenth and seventeenth centuries.[57] Although many of the clergy and laymen compromised their Puritan convictions following the Act of Uniformity in 1662, unwilling to follow that movement "into the wilderness of dissent", there remained in Northamptonshire enough of its legacy of Calvinism, anti-clericalism, personal piety, and a "faithful church", that the county is "closely identified with the rise of Independency or Congregationalism".[58] Northamptonshire had seen the very diverse ministries of Richard Davis of Rothwell, Phillip Doddridge of Northampton, and William Law (1686-1761) of King's Cliffe.

The Particular Baptist church at Kettering, similarly to the Soham church, emerged from an Independent congregation which had been gathered by an ejected Puritan clergyman. Shortly after the founding pastor's death, one of the elders, William Wallis (*d*. 1715), and six others described as "Anabaptist" in their beliefs, withdrew to form their own church in 1696.[59] Wallis became the first pastor of the Particular Baptist church, which met in Bayley's Yard, Newland Street. Wallis was followed in the pastoral office by his son, Thomas, around 1715, and the Wallis family remained instrumental in the church for several generations. It is one of the ironies of church history that the congregation to which Fuller became pastor was the one in which John Gill (1697-1771) was converted, during the ministry of William Wallis, who he considered his "spiritual father"; during the ministry of Thomas Wallis, Gill and John Brine (1703-1765) were baptized and called into ministry.[60] While this congregation was getting established, a second group of dismissed members from the Independent church, including their pastor, had been

---

[57] See R.M. Serjeantson and W. Ryland D. Adkins, "Ecclesiastical History", in *The Victoria History of the County of Northampton*, ed. R.M. Serjeantson and W. Ryland D. Adkins (London: James Street, 1906) 2:1-78; R.L. Greenall, *A History of Northamptonshire*, The Darwen County History Series (London: Phillimore, 1979).

[58] Serjeantson and Adkins, "Ecclesiastical History", 62, 50.

[59] The sources for the history of the Baptist church at Kettering (later called Fuller Baptist) are: The Kettering Baptist Church Book (c.1768-1815); Narrative Notes on the history of the church, in the back of the Church Book, by pastors Brown and Fuller; "A brief history of the Baptist Church at Kettering" (c. 1815-1820), in the Gotch Papers; Gladys M. Barrett, *A Brief History of Fuller Church, Kettering* (St. Albans, Hertfordshire, c. 1945); and Frederick W. Bull, *A Sketch of the History of the Town of Kettering, Together with Some Account of its Worthies* (Kettering: Northamptonshire Printing & Publishing Co., 1891) and *Supplement to the History of the Town of Kettering, Together with a Further Account of its Worthies* (Kettering: Northamptonshire Printing & Publishing Co., 1908).

[60] See Narrative Notes, 6; John Rippon, "A Brief Memoir of the Life and Writings of the Reverend and Learned John Gill, D.D.", in John Gill, *An Exposition of the Old Testament* (London: City Press, 1852), 1:x.

meeting in Goosepasture Lane, and shortly after adopting a Baptist covenant in 1723, were merged with the Bayley's Yard church. The merged church practiced open communion until 1765, when they drew up a new church covenant and confession of faith, which insisted on baptism by immersion "before the admission into a visible church".[61]

At the time of Fuller's settlement at Kettering, there was, in addition to the Baptist church, the parish church of St. Peter and St. Paul, a Methodist chapel, and the Independent church, the minister of which was Thomas Toller (*d.* 1821), a graduate of Doddridge's academy.[62] Kettering was a town of about 3,000 residents during the late eighteenth century, although as a market town, it had many small villages in its orbit. It was the centre of the county's weaving trade around the time of Fuller's arrival in Kettering, and by the time of his death, as that industry was waning, there was just beginning to develop what would become an important shoe production. During Fuller's ministry there was a bread riot in 1795, and the area experienced enclosure in 1803-1804.[63]

Figure 3: The interior of the Kettering Baptist Church, with the pulpit from which Fuller preached. The photo was taken later in the 19th Century.

---

[61] The Kettering Church Book begins with this 1765 covenant and brief confession of faith.

[62] See Robert Hall, jun., "Memoir of the Rev. Thomas Toller" (1821), in *The Works of The Rev Robert Hall, A.M.*, ed. Olinthus Gregory (London: Henry G. Bohn, 1832), 5: 305-346. Hall offers an insightful comparison of the ministry, preaching, and characters of Kettering colleagues Fuller and Toller, 341-344.

[63] Greenall, *History of Northamptonshire*, 80; Bull, *A Sketch of the History of the Town of Kettering*, 1:38-45.

When Andrew Fuller came to the Kettering church in 1782, there were 88 members. By the time of his death in 1815, there were 174 members and about a thousand hearers.[64] The church's meeting-place was converted from a warehouse, provided by deacon Beeby Wallis (1736-1792), and expanded at least twice during Fuller's ministry. The interior was spacious but plain; the high pulpit was set, inconveniently for the congregation, between two tall windows. The square box pews, not all of which were arranged to face the pulpit directly, were assigned on the basis of subscription.[65]

The Kettering church was of a very different character than Fuller's Soham "garden", being larger, having a greater proportion of people of education and financial means, more actively associational, and most importantly, receptive of Fuller's more evangelical Calvinism. To what extent that receptivity represented a change of position is difficult to assess from the records, but it certainly did put the church in some conflict with its high Calvinist neighbours. Reflecting on the difficulty one of their hearers was having to move their membership to Kettering from nearby Rushden, the church recorded,

> That there are some differences in sentiment between us and the church at Rushden, is true. We consider the doctrines of grace as entirely consistent with a free address to every sinner, and with an universal obligation on all men where the gospel is preached, to repent of their sins, and turn to God through Jesus Christ. They think otherwise...[66]

The formation of the Particular Baptist Society for the Propagation of the Gospel Among the Heathen (hereafter, the Baptist Missionary Society) in 1792 was effected in a home near to the Kettering church, and the first meagre donations towards its aims were famously collected in Fuller's snuff box. The event was defining for Fuller's life and ministry, as he became the mission's Secretary—a full-time administrator, in reality—entailing a voluminous correspondence, the selection of new missionaries, political lobbying, and fund-raising and preaching throughout England, as well as five visits to Scotland and one to Ireland. All this, while he engaged in a prolific pattern of writing, particularly concerned with apologetic responses to high Calvinism, Socinianism, Deism, Universalism, and Sandemanianism, as well as regular contributions to dissenting and evangelical periodicals.

While this broader activity had a great impact upon his pastoral ministry, to

---

[64] Kettering Church Book, 145. 232 people were received into membership during Fuller's ministry.

[65] There is a mss record book at the Fuller Baptist Church in which there is a layout of the pews, mapping the assigned places of subscribers, and a record of the funds collected. See, also, A.G. Fuller, *Andrew Fuller, Men Worth Remembering* (London: Hodder and Stoughton, 1882), 76-77.

[66] Kettering Church Book, 93.

say nothing of his domestic life, we are reminded of the significance and effectiveness of that ministry by the words entered into the diary of George Wallis, days before Fuller died in May 1815, a testimony to Fuller's evangelical and affectionate pastoral practice: "Him, that has so long fed us with the bread of life, that has so affectionately, so faithfully, and so fervently Counsel'd, exhorted, reprov'd, and animated by doctrine, by precept, and by example, the people of his charge; him who has <u>liv'd</u> so much for <u>others</u>!"[67]

---

[67] Wallis, "Memoirs", 23 April 1815; emphasis in original.

**Figure 4: Portrait of Andrew Fuller from *The Baptist Magazine*
(July 1815)**

"I Perceived This Reasoning Would Affect the Whole Tenor of My Preaching."

Conversion:
The Formation of an Evangelical and Affectionate Pastoral Theology

In 1769, at the age of fifteen, Andrew Fuller embraced Jesus Christ in conversion. In 1781, then twenty-seven years old and engaged in pastoral ministry, he completed the first draft of *The Gospel Worthy of All Acceptation*, which insisted on the sinner's obligation to believe in Jesus Christ, and the minister's corresponding duty to proclaim the gospel. It is remarkable that this, Fuller's seminal work, should be so evangelical and envision such a conversionist pastoral theology, given that his own experience of seeking conversion in a high Calvinist setting was encumbered by his own overwhelming lack of assurance and the intentional reticence from the pulpit. The difference between first profession of faith and first publication invites an exploration of Fuller's narrative of his spiritual and theological conversions, culminating in the writing of that book. This chapter will assert that the renewal of pastoral theology was a central and instigating rationale for Andrew Fuller's articulation of evangelical Calvinism, as he envisioned a more assured approach of the spiritual seeker to God, and a more assertively conversionist ministry of the preacher toward his hearers. Or, in other words, *The Gospel Worthy of All Acceptation* was essentially concerned with pastoral theology: first, by addressing key pastoral issues of spiritual seekers in the process of conversion, and second, by giving urgent direction for a conversionist pastoral ministry, particularly preaching. We will demonstrate why Fuller's most important book was a *pastoral* document, and how it was an *evangelical* document, and this by setting it against the pastoral background of high Calvinism.

The pastoral concerns of individuals and the obligations of pastors in preaching are indeed at the heart of Fuller's theological project, and particularly

The Gospel Worthy of All Acceptation. Fuller urged a recovery of free offers of
the gospel, emphasizing such conversionism as the central feature of
evangelical preaching. J.W. Morris observed that this important book was the
means "of awakening the attention of several of his brethren to the important
duties of their office, of giving a more practical turn to their preaching, and a
new face to their religious interests".[1] However, the pastoral nature of *The
Gospel Worthy of All Acceptation* is apparent, not only by its strong guidance
for the function of pastors, but, also, by considering Fuller's conversion
narrative as a site for exploring what Ellen Charry has called, "the pastoral
function of doctrine".[2] Charry contends that primary Christian doctrines have
"character-forming intentions", and that in classical theological endeavour,
systems of doctrine were intended to have a salutary or curative effect in the
conforming of persons to the character of God.[3] Andrew Fuller ascribed to such
a view of doctrine's pastoral function, and, perhaps ironically, given Fuller's
experience, so, too, did John Gill: "Doctrine has an influence upon practice,
especially evangelical doctrine, spiritually understood, affectionately embraced,
and powerfully and feelingly experienced."[4] There is unavoidably a pastoral
and practical cast to theological systems. An exposition of Fuller's conversion
narrative provides a better understanding of the pastoral implications of high
Calvinism for the individual seeker and its actual congregational experience
and, by contrast, the renewed pastoral function of *The Gospel Worthy of All
Acceptation*. E.F. Clipsham was surely right when he said of Fuller, "It was
because he was a pastor that he was compelled also to be a theologian", and by
tracing the development of Fuller's conversion, we will demonstrate that a
renewed pastoral theology was central to his first treatise of evangelical
theology.[5]

The evangelical nature of *The Gospel Worthy of All Acceptation* is widely
acknowledged. David Bebbington, for example, referring to it as "the classic
statement of eighteenth-century Evangelical Calvinism", and Mark Noll noting
that its publication marked "the triumph of evangelicalism among England's
Particular Baptists".[6] The work's essential evangelicalism is expressed
precisely in its dual pastoral intent: first, by clearing the way for the individual
seeker's more assured and affectionate approach to God; and second, by
defining for preachers a more direct and unhesitating approach to hearers,

[1] Morris, *Memoir*, 83.
[2] Ellen T. Charry, *By the Renewing of Your Minds: The Pastoral Function of Christian Doctrine* (Oxford: Oxford University Press, 1997).
[3] Ibid., esp. 6, 18-19, and chapter 10. See Tidball, *Skilful Shepherds*, 24; Pattison and Woodward, "Introduction to Pastoral and Practical Theology", xiii.
[4] E.g., Fuller, *Works*, ii.22; iii.339; Gill, *Body of Divinity*, i.vii.
[5] Clipsham, "Andrew Fuller and Fullerism", 100.
[6] Bebbington, *Evangelicalism in Modern Britain*, 64-65; Noll, *Rise of Evangelicalism*, 193.

particularly the unconverted.[7] Both of these pastoral aspects were described in terms of "obligation" and "duty", and so were more urgently conversionist and affectionately evangelical from the perspective of both hearer and preacher.

Fuller relayed his conversion narrative in letters to friends in 1798, 1809, and 1815.[8] The first of these letters begins: "You request the particulars of that change, of which I was the subject near thirty years ago."[9] Fuller's spiritual change in conversion begins his autobiographical reminiscences, but he does not consider them complete until he has, also, narrated his "change of views"— the shift in his theological convictions compelled by reflection on his own conversion experience and early pastoral ministry.[10] Indeed, the climax of Fuller's narrative is neither his own conversion, nor his call to ministry, but rather, the writing of the *Gospel Worthy of All Acceptation.*

The following exposition of Fuller's narrative letters opens up an understanding of the effects of high Calvinism (and the evangelical response) for personal piety and pastoral practice. Beginning with a comparison of high Calvinism with the earlier Puritan conversion narratives, we will see that Fuller experienced these key elements of the pastoral function of high Calvinism: an emphasis on subjective grounds for assurance, a view of justification that invited a fear of presumption, rather than conversionism, a restricted appraisal of spiritual ability, and the well-known denial that free offers of the gospel should be made. The themes of *The Gospel Worthy of All Acceptation* reveal the development of an evangelical pastoral theology that encouraged, rather than frustrated, conversionist and affectionate piety and pastoral practice.

Fuller's theological transformation and particularly his seminal book, *The Gospel Worthy of All Acceptation*, is, rightly, recognized as a crucial contribution to the renewal of the Particular Baptists and the formation of the Baptist Missionary Society. What this chapter will demonstrate is that the personal experiences and specific questions which led to its formulation were essentially pastoral, and that at the heart of the work is the renewal of pastoral theology. That renewed pastoral theology is evangelical in nature: an assured approach of the individual to God, an unhesitating approach of the preacher to the unconverted, and from both perspectives, urgently conversionist and affectionate.

---

[7] Campbell, *Religion of the Heart*, 2-3, 6, 173.

[8] Ryland, *Life of Fuller*, 11-40. The letters, as presented by Ryland, bear the marks of his editorial hand, chiefly evidenced by his weaving of their originally overlapped and repeated content as a single chronological narrative in five letters with some appended material. The first two letters (of five, originally published anonymously in the *Evangelical Magazine*) were addressed to Charles Stuart of Edinburgh, the next two to a "friend in Liverpool", and for the final no recipient is named.

[9] Ibid., 11.

[10] Ibid., 35.

Context of Conversion: High Calvinist Preaching

The very first words of Fuller's narrative establish the high Calvinist worldview of his Soham congregation as the primary background for understanding his conversion, and underline the practical implications of this variety of Calvinism for shaping the practice of pastoral ministry: "My father and mother were dissenters, of the Calvinistic persuasion, who were in the habit of hearing Mr. Eve, a Baptist minister; who, being what is here termed *high* in his sentiments, or tinged with false Calvinism, had little or nothing to say to the unconverted."[11]

Mr. Eve's "high" or "false" Calvinism, also commonly described as hyper Calvinism, was distinguished, in the landscape of eighteenth-century Baptist theology, from "moderate" or Arminian-leaning Baxterian Calvinism, and from the "strict" or evangelical Calvinism to which Fuller himself would later turn.[12] The high Calvinism of John Eve and the Soham church was widespread among Particular Baptists, and as the primary context for Fuller's conversion and later pastoral theology, requires some definition, first, by describing its genealogy and, then, its central emphases.

The genesis of high Calvinism can be located in the Antinomian controversies of the mid-seventeenth century.[13] The Puritan divines of the Westminster Assembly found themselves in opposition to the doctrinal antinomianism of Tobias Crisp (1600-1643), John Saltmarsh (*d.* 1647), and John Eaton (1575-1641), the first of whom became so identified with the position that Fuller would describe it as "Crispism".[14] In the late 1690s, Independent Richard Davis of Rothwell, whose wide-ranging evangelistic and church-planting ministry was centred in Northamptonshire, became the lightning rod for another controversy, charged with antinomianism by moderate Calvinists, including Richard Baxter (1615-1691). Davis' theological indebtedness to Crisp, whose sermons had recently been republished, was particularly obvious from his views on eternal justification.[15] It is important to

---

[11] Ibid., 11. As throughout, unless otherwise noted, italics in quotations are in the original text.

[12] For Fuller's taxonomy of Baptist varieties of Calvinism, see ibid., 368-369; and letters written to John Ryland, defining Fuller's own Calvinism vis-à-vis John Calvin and Richard Baxter, in Fuller, *Works*, ii.711-715. Cf. also Hindmarsh, *John Newton*, 122-125 for a discussion and table comparing the major theological positions of the Evangelical Revival on key points of doctrine.

[13] This account of high Calvinism depends upon Peter Toon, *The Emergence of Hyper-Calvinism in English Nonconformity, 1689-1765* (London: The Olive Tree, 1967); Curt Daniel, "Hyper Calvinism and John Gill" (Ph.D. diss., University of Edinburgh, 1983); John von Rohr, *The Covenant of Grace in Puritan Thought*, American Academy of Religion: Studies in Religion, ed. Charles Hardwick and James O. Duke (Atlanta: Scholars Press, 1986); and Nuttall, "Northamptonshire and the Modern Question".

[14] Fuller, *Works*, ii.713.

[15] Richard Davis, *A Vindication of the Doctrine of Justification and Union Before Faith*

note, however, that like Crisp himself, Davis was in no way restricted from making free offers of the gospel for the greater part of his vigorously evangelistic ministry. It was not until later in his life that Davis had adopted the "no offer" position of Joseph Hussey (1660-1726) and repented of those former free offers of the gospel.[16] But by this time, Davis' network of churches and influence was well established, and was likely one means of spreading a "no offer" brand of high Calvinism among Independent and Baptist churches. By the mid-eighteenth century, this version of high Calvinism was the received orthodoxy among Particular Baptist churches in London and the Northamptonshire Association, chiefly through the systematizing and popularizing influence of John Gill and John Brine, both from Kettering and both in key London pulpits.[17] While the Evangelical Revival was transforming much of the English religious landscape, another theological controversy was preoccupying the Baptists and Independents of Old Dissent; the "Modern Question" posed the query whether or not it was the *duty* of sinners to believe the gospel, and its corollary, whether ministers could make a "free offer" of the gospel.[18] The strong negative answer to this question by Gill, Brine, and others, together with other elements of high Calvinist piety, meant that Particular Baptists were largely, though not entirely, unaffected by the Revival until the late-eighteenth century.

Turning from its personalities and sources to its theological emphases, in high Calvinist thought the carefully-struck balance between divine sovereignty and human responsibility that typified Puritan covenant theology was upset.[19] In common with earlier Calvinists, such as Theodore Beza (1519-1605) and

---

(London, 1698).

[16] Joseph Hussey had earlier testified against Richard Davis on the charge of antinomianism at an inquiry at Kettering, but, later, came to adopt not only similar doctrinal antinomianism, but, also, came to reject "free offers" of the gospel. See his *God's Operations of Grace, but No Offers of His Grace* (London: D. Bridge, 1707). On Davis' disavowal of his earlier offers, see John Gill's preface to Richard Davis, *Hymns composed on several subjects, and on divers occasions*, 7th ed. (London, 1748), v; and Geoffrey Nuttall's analysis, "Northamptonshire and the Modern Question", 113-114.

[17] Hayden, "Evangelical Calvinism", convincingly argues that a more evangelical Calvinism, as expressed in the 1689 Baptist Confession, modeled on the Westminster Confession, had long been maintained in the Western Baptist Association and particularly Bristol's Broadmead Baptist Church and Academy, suggesting that the theological landscape was more varied than is sometimes portrayed.

[18] The Modern Question was posed by Richard Davis' successor at Rothwell, Matthias Maurice, who ironically answered in the affirmative: *A Modern Question Modestly Answered* (London, 1737). This, and pamphlets by Abraham Taylor, Alvery Jackson, John Smalley, and others for the affirmative, were answered in the negative by, among others, John Brine, Lewis Wayman, and in various of his writings, John Gill. See Nuttall, "Northamptonshire and the Modern Question".

[19] Cf. von Rohr, *The Covenant of Grace in Puritan Thought*, 1-10.

William Perkins (1558-1602), high Calvinists adhered to supralapsarianism, which placed God's decrees of election and reprobation prior to God's decrees to create Adam and to permit him the freedom to sin. The high Calvinist innovation on this theme, however, was to emphasize the eternal decrees to the *de facto* neglect of the faith of the individual in history. The most characteristic example was the doctrine of eternal justification, in which the elect were considered to be united with Christ in eternity, rather than in time.[20] Their emphasis on the logic of the eternal decrees led to the denial of free offers of the gospel in preaching, the redrawing of the Puritan conversion narrative, the dependence on more subjective grounds for assurance, a severely introspective piety, and at least in its popular expressions, a tendency to antinomianism. Many of these themes will be explored at greater length in the exposition of Andrew Fuller's conversion experience, for which the other significant context is the pattern of the Puritan (and evangelical) narrative.

Context of Conversion: Puritan and Evangelical Narratives

From the general observation that Mr. Eve, the minister at the Baptist church at Soham, had "little or nothing to say to the unconverted", Fuller proceeds to the first-person import of that studied avoidance, saying, "I, therefore, never considered myself as any way concerned in what I heard from the pulpit. Nevertheless, *by reading and reflection*, I was sometimes strongly impressed in a way of conviction."[21] At the outset of Fuller's recollections, then, he highlights the effects of pastoral theology on his personal spirituality; the principled hesitation from the pulpit proved an early encumbrance to his own conversion. Fuller's remarks, also, refer to the role of reading and reflection in the stages preparatory to conversion, and, particularly, the tension he experienced between high Calvinist preaching and Puritan devotional writing. The overlapping and sometimes contradictory influences of pulpit and books of practical divinity was where, for Fuller and many others, the streams of Puritan and high Calvinist theologies met, and it was left to individuals to sort through the dissonance between the preaching in their churches and the books in their homes—the one emphasizing conversion and assurance, the other offering little pastoral guidance in either.[22] When Fuller was in his early teens, and beginning

---

[20] This was one of the central doctrines of Tobias Crisp and Richard Davis, and was, also, maintained by Gill. See Daniel, "Hyper Calvinism and John Gill", 320; and Toon, *Hyper Calvinism*, 28-29, 60-61, 111.

[21] Ryland, *Life of Fuller*, 11 (emphasis added).

[22] On the functions of books of practical divinity, and particularly the Puritans, see Isabel Rivers, "Dissenting and Methodist Books of Practical Divinity", in *Books and Their Readers in Eighteenth-Century England*, ed. Isabel Rivers (Leicester: Leicester University Press, 1982), 127-164; John Walsh, "Origins of the Evangelical Revival", in *Essays in Modern Church History in Memory of Norman Sykes*, ed. G.V. Bennett and J.D. Walsh (London: Adam and Charles Black, 1966), 159; and Michael Watts, *The*

to have "serious thoughts about futurity", he was reading works by, among others, later Puritan John Bunyan (1628-1688) and Scottish Calvinist Ralph Erskine (1685-1752).[23] Bunyan's autobiographical *Grace Abounding to the Chief of Sinners* and allegorical *Pilgrim's Progress* provided a template for conversion, and Erskine's catechism was designed to offer practical spiritual guidance to young readers during the different stages of that conversion process. Fuller's use of these works is indicative of a widespread eighteenth-century adoption of Puritan theology of salvation, and its personalization in the shape of the conversion narrative.[24] The importance of these narratives as a context for Fuller's own conversion, and particularly the significant alteration of the Puritan model at key points, invites an exploration of their shape.

The Puritans' careful attention to the *ordo salutis* was mapped onto Christian experience in the typical pattern of their conversion narratives, of which John Bunyan's *Grace Abounding to the Chief of Sinners* and *Pilgrim's Progress* were widely-read examples.[25] Elements of these narratives which are preparatory to conversion include early religious impressions, a catalog of the sins of youth, hardness of heart or the searing of conscience, the "alarming" effect of dangerous or life-threatening situations, great conviction of sin, an overwhelming, but legal, fear of deserved damnation, and oscillating periods of self-exertion and despairing of salvation or being included among the elect. The climax of these conversion narratives is an abandonment of any hope of salvation other than the promise of justification by faith in Christ. Having truly apprehended justification in Christ, the convert experiences a true, godly repentance and new obedience, now assured of their salvation. Though this

---

Dissenters, vol. 1, *From the Reformation to the French Revolution* (Oxford: Clarendon Press, 1978), 426.

[23] Ryland, *Life of Fuller*, 12, 13.

[24] Bruce Hindmarsh, *The Evangelical Conversion Narrative: Spiritual Autobiography in Early Modern England* (Oxford: Oxford University Press, 2005), 15; the discussion of the conversion narrative that follows relies significantly on the analysis on pages 15, 37, 51-52, 68-74, and the book's study of several expressions of the Puritan-influenced conversion narrative in various evangelical contexts. Also on the general morphology of the Puritan conversion narrative, see Edmund Morgan, *Visible Saints: The History of a Puritan Idea* (Ithaca, NY: Cornell University Press, 1963). For the preparatory stages of this process, see Norman Pettit, *The Heart Prepared: Grace and Conversion in Puritan Spiritual Life* (New Haven: Yale University Press, 1966), esp. 17-18. Patricia Caldwell's analysis of New England conversion narratives, compared with those of English Puritans, issues a helpful caution not to treat patterns as formulas, and to pay attention to local variations on the common theme; *The Puritan Conversion Narrative: The Beginnings of American Expression* (Cambridge: Cambridge University Press, 1983).

[25] Bunyan's conception of the order of salvation is charted in *A Mapp Shewing the Order and Causes of Salvation and Damnation*, in *The Miscellaneous Works of John Bunyan*, ed. W.R. Owens (Oxford: Clarendon Press, 1994), 12: 415-423. This is an interesting companion to his narrative and allegorical treatments.

assurance is tested by trials, former acquaintances, and habitual temptations, the saint experiences God's keeping and sanctifying grace. The conversion narrative could be appended by accounts of joining a local church, a call to ministry, a defense of dissenting (or Baptist) principles, or persecution for them, and, as in Fuller's narrative, the adoption of new theological convictions. Or, in broadest outline, the conversion narrative included awakening, repentance, justification through faith in Christ, assurance, assurance-testing trials, and sanctification.

The same experiential Calvinism that was inherent in the Puritan conversion narratives would, also, have been conveyed in Fuller's reading of Ralph Erskine's *Gospel Sonnets*, a collection of verse on various stages of the believer's relationship to God. Fuller recalled reading the section "The Redeemer's Work; Or Christ All in All, and our complete Redemption: A Gospel Catechism for young Christians", saying, "I read, and as I read I wept. Indeed, I was almost overcome with weeping; so interesting did the doctrine of eternal salvation appear to me."[26] Erskine's catechism tells the young reader, "that the name of *Christ* alone / Can answer every Case" (§ 2), and, then, proceeds to explore Christ's sufficiency for a great number of cases at points along the *ordo salutis*—"*Salvation-Work*" (§ 28)—not so much in strict sequence, but in the circular and repeating patterns that would be typical in much lived experience. In the preparatory stages, Christ "will of Unbelief convict, / And pave the way for Faith" (§ 22), and be the only sure defense "'Gainst legal fiery Threats of Wrath" (§ 20). At the crux of seeking justification with God, the inquirer cries, "Ah where's my Title, Right, or Claim, / To that eternal Bliss?" and the Teacher responds, "In *Christ* alone, that glorious Name, / *The Lord our Righteousness*" (§ 9). "*Jesus* did all the Debt thou owes / To divine Justice pay" (§ 15), a pardon paid by "his atoning Blood" (§ 16), received by faith which is Christ's to give (§ 21). Assurance and comfort are found only in Christ, though tested by doubts, circumstances, temptation, or acquaintances (§ 12-14, 30–31). "Heart-Holiness" is brought about by the Spirit's "gradual Change" (§ 24), and despite the tendency to stray, the believer is enabled through Christ to take "the *consecrated Way*" (§ 8). The catechism concludes by carefully and Calvinistically fencing salvation from Arminianism on the one hand ("Is nothing left to Man?" "Without *Christ* we nothing have, / Without him nothing can") and Antinomianism on the other (Why not "take carnal Ease"? "*Christ* will…come…To damn his foes that dare presume, / And thus abuse his Grace") (§ 38).

And indeed, Fuller's early familiarity with these Calvinist works of practical devotion provided the conceptual framework in which to anticipate and interpret the stages of his spiritual experience, and certainly gave him a form in

---

[26] Ralph Erskine, *Gospel Sonnets, or Spiritual Songs*, 8th ed. (London, 1762), 202-208; references to the stanzas of the catechism are noted parenthetically. Ryland, *Life of Fuller*, 13.

which to relay that experience in these more mature narrative letters.[27] Fuller, in this form, described the extent of the sins of his childhood (lying, cursing, and swearing) and youth (wrestling and other tests of daring or strength), the occasions of spiritual concern that came about because of conversation, danger, rebuke, or reflection, the passages of scripture which had particular significance to his case, doubts and temptations which dogged his early spiritual efforts, fear of damnation, and the periods of despair and hope which finally led to his conversion. His narrative, also, includes his persuasion that baptism ought to be by immersion, his joining of the Particular Baptist church at Soham, the public ignominy he experienced as a Dissenter, his call to ministry, and the shaping of his theological convictions. In all this, Fuller's conversion narrative is indebted to the general Puritan pattern. However, his narrative, also, displays some of the particularities and innovations on the received tradition that belonged to the high Calvinists, four of the most important to which we now turn. Tracing these themes—assurance, justification, spiritual ability, and preaching—demonstrates the pastoral and personal implications of high Calvinism, and provides the rationale from Fuller's own experience for the development of a renewed pastoral theology.

"Scripture impressions": Assurance in Pastoral Theology

William Perkins described the search for assurance of salvation as the greatest of all pastoral cases.[28] David Bebbington has suggested that a shift in the doctrine of assurance was the factor differentiating introspective Puritan Calvinism from active and confident evangelicalism.[29] Andrew Fuller's former experience of high Calvinism's even more exaggerated and subjective understanding of assurance eventually led him to articulate a pastoral theology which entailed an assured approach to God, sharing with evangelicalism the subsequent confidence which led to a zeal for conversion and an unhesitating activism. The function of the doctrine of assurance in high Calvinism, and its relocation in the order of salvation, is particularly evident from Fuller's narrative of receiving sudden scripture impressions, and interpreting them as a sign of assurance, rather than relying on more objective religious affections.

   Although Fuller was often spiritually affected during his adolescent years from his religious reading and from reflection on spiritual conversation or dangerous occurrences, neither his heart nor habits had altered to any great degree. Around 1767, when Fuller was thirteen or fourteen years old, he

---

[27] See Hindmarsh, *Evangelical Conversion Narrative*, 37, 309-310.

[28] William Perkins, *A Case of Conscience the Greatest that ever was; how a man may know whether he be the child of God or no*, as cited in Gordon S. Wakefield, *Puritan Devotion: Its Place in the Development of Christian Piety* (London: Epworth Press, 1957), 124-125. See also von Rohr, *The Covenant of Grace*, 122.

[29] Bebbington, *Evangelicalism in Modern Britain*, 42-50.

describes a period in which "I was, at times, the subject of such convictions and affections, that I really thought myself converted, and lived under that delusion for a long time."[30] With the benefit of hindsight, the mature Fuller identified this phase of his spiritual journey as one of false comfort or misplaced assurance of conversion. The grounds of his "delusion" rested on an experience of receiving a sudden suggestion of a verse of scripture to his mind, while walking alone and thinking seriously about "what would become of my poor soul".[31] The words that "suddenly occurred" to his mind were from Romans 6:14, "Sin shall not have dominion over you; for you are not under the law, but under grace."[32] These words may have had particular relevance for Fuller, who was keenly feeling his own powerlessness and inability to turn from sin to God. But the text's *sudden impression* on his mind had significance beyond their meaning, which Fuller describes:

> Now, the suggestion of a text of scripture to the mind, especially if it came with power, was generally considered, by the religious people with whom I occasionally associated, as a promise coming immediately from God. I, therefore, so understood it, and thought that God had thus revealed to me that I was in a state of salvation, and that, therefore, iniquity should not, as I had feared, be my ruin. The effect was, I was overcome with joy and transport. I shed, I suppose, thousands of tears as I walked along, and seemed to feel myself, as it were, in a new world. It appeared to me, that I hated my sins, and was resolved to forsake them.[33]

Fuller's experience seems to be an instance of a widespread element of eighteenth-century high Calvinist piety, in which the sudden and powerful suggestion of a text of scripture was understood to be a personal promise or revelation from God, usually respecting the precise predicament of the recipient, or perhaps the spiritual condition of another person, future events, or temporal matters. Although at times such a scripture impression closely resembled a personal application of the text of scripture, its importance was often independent of the words themselves; the fact that God had spoken directly to the anxious sinner was, itself, what made the impression such a powerful spiritual experience. Variations on this theme of sudden impressions were many. John Ryland, for example, at about the same age and also during a period of heightened spiritual anxiety, described that he "*happen'd* to see a Bible and *immediately* thought I would look at Hosea xiii.14. *I knew of no reason* why that particular number should occur to my mind, but so it was." Upon reading this verse about redemption from death, Ryland recalled, "From these words I was greatly encouraged to hope that I should partake of the

---

[30] Ryland, *Life of Fuller*, 13.
[31] Ibid.
[32] Ibid., 14.
[33] Ibid.

benefits of Redemption."[34] While Ryland claimed not to have had a reason to look up a passage of scripture, others would claim to have verses suggested to them that they had never even read. The credibility of these scripture impressions was evaluated not so much, as Ryland observed later, by the faithfulness or accuracy of their interpretation in scriptural context, as by their immediacy and unlooked-for, and, therefore, apparently more spiritual, character.[35] Although similar cases of very personal applications of scripture, or immediate spiritual impressions, have been common in a variety of historical and theological settings, the experiences of Fuller and Ryland highlight the function of such scripture impressions within the high Calvinist pattern of conversion, as an expression of that system's relocation of assurance within the *ordo salutis*, giving it an earlier place and greater priority in the conversion experience.[36] The Westminster divines had grounded assurance upon a threefold foundation, seemingly in order of importance: faith in the promises, evidences of sanctification, and the inner witness of the Spirit.[37] However, high Calvinists carefully guarded against faith being construed a duty, and mistrusted external evidences of grace as "legal". They were left with a greater reliance on the inner witness of the Holy Spirit, and the search for assurance took on a more intensely introspective and subjective character.[38] The impression of a text of scripture, therefore, functioned within high Calvinism as a sign of that assuring inner witness, and it was highly sought after in their pattern of conversion.

Fuller's later reflection, that this confidence of conversion was a false comfort or delusion, seems borne out by the immediate consequences of the experience: "Before night, all was gone and forgotten, and I returned to my former vices with as eager a gust as ever."[39] Despite there being no other grounds for an assurance of conversion in either Fuller's spiritual affections or

---

[34] John Ryland, "Autograph Reminiscences", bound ms (1807), Bristol Baptist College, 21 (emphasis added).
[35] See Hindmarsh, *Evangelical Conversion Narrative*, 311-312, for a discussion of Ryland's use of Joseph Alleine's *The Voice of God in His Promises* and *The Believer's Triumph*, two works which provide a model for personalizing the promises of God in scripture; there, however, the focus is not on isolated texts or the method of their reception, but on making a personal montage of scripture promises.
[36] Toon, *Hyper Calvinism*, 126-127.
[37] *The Westminster Confession of Faith* (Glasgow: Free Presbyterian Publications, 1985), chapter 18, section 2. Cf. Toon, *Emergence of Hyper Calvinism*, 65; and Alister E. McGrath, *Iustitia Dei: A History of the Christian Doctrine of Justification*, vol. 2, *From 1500 to the Present Day* (Cambridge: Cambridge University Press, 1986), 114-115.
[38] Daniel, "Hyper-Calvinism and John Gill", 350-352, 682-691; Daniel makes the interesting suggestion that this extremely introspective posture could be considered a kind of mysticism.
[39] Ryland, *Life of Fuller*, 14.

actions, a year later he continued to count the scripture impression as a sure promise of his salvation. He reflected:

> Yet, I still thought, that must have been a promise from God to me, and that I must have been a converted person, but in a backsliding state. And this persuasion was confirmed by another sudden impression, which dispelled my dejection, in these words: "I have blotted out as a thick cloud thy transgressions, and as a cloud thy sins." [Isaiah 44:22] This, like the former, overcame my mind with joy. I wept much at the thoughts of having backslidden so long, but yet considered myself now as restored and happy.[40]

The sudden suggestion of another text of scripture dispelled Fuller's dejection, giving him a kind of comfort, which he would later identify as false, merely assuaging a guilty conscience, rather than enabling repentance and an appeal for God's forgiveness, and, in fact, let him continue his sin unabated until his conscience was seared. His judgement was that "this also was mere transient affection. I have great reason to think, that the great deep of my heart's depravity had not yet been broken up, and that all my religion was without an abiding principle."[41]

Fuller's more mature judgement of handling sudden scripture impressions as a form of pre-conversion assurance is expressed in a letter which he wrote in 1792, twenty-five years later, to a member of his church at Kettering.[42] Similarly, John Ryland's apprehensiveness about the practice was articulated in a letter which was later published as a pamphlet, and Robert Hall, sen., included it among his stumbling blocks in the way of experimental religion in his *Help to Zion's Travellers*.[43] All of these were influenced in their mature thinking on scripture impressions by their reading of Jonathan Edwards' *A Treatise on the Religious Affections*.[44] The experiences of Fuller, Ryland, and Hall, and their need to address scripture impressions in both personal correspondence and in publication testifies that this was a widespread practice, symptomatic of a more general congregational confusion over conversion, true religious affections, prior warrant, and assurance, requiring a robust pastoral

---

[40] Ibid., 15.

[41] Ibid., 15-16.

[42] Ibid., 375-381. Fuller responded to the reliance on scripture impressions in several different places, for examples of which, see: *Works*, ii.737-762; iii.349-350 and iii.551-557.

[43] John Ryland, *Remarks upon the notion of extraordinary impulses and impressions on the imagination, indulged by many professors of religion; contained in a letter to a friend*, rev. ed. (Bristol, 1804). The volume was published under the pseudonym Agnostos. Robert Hall, *Help to Zion's Travellers: Being An Attempt to remove various Stumbling Blocks out of the Way, relating to Doctrinal, Experimental, and Practical Religion* (Bristol: William Pine, 1781).

[44] Cf. Edwards, *Religious Affections*, 142-145, 167-181, 197-239, 268-269.

response.

In his letter to the member of his Kettering congregation, Fuller addresses a question about the grounds for a cheerful sense of assurance from the Lord. He reiterates that scripture impressions had indeed been a source of his own misplaced assurance, and that "when any passage of Scripture was impressed with *weight* upon my mind, it was no other than the voice of God, speaking to me by those words", confirming that it was the suddenness of the text's suggestion that made it seem to be God's personal message.[45]

The sense of comfort and assurance derived from these scripture impressions had the appearance of being true affections because they were based on words of scripture. In reality, however, the comforting feelings were derived not from the scriptures themselves, but from the surprising quality of their impression: "though the words of Scripture were the means of the impression, yet the meaning of those words, as they stood in the Bible, was lost in the application".[46] True affections, on the contrary, resulted when the scriptures were both "opened to the mind, and impressed on the heart",[47] affections— including assurance—which were the natural response of the heart to the *understanding* of the scriptures. Both Ryland and Hall neatly distinguished between a preoccupation with the *manner* of the scripture called to mind, rather than attending to its *matter*, which should be the proper ground of affections and assurance.[48]

The real danger of affording scripture impressions such a central role in pre-conversion assurance is that they can offer only a misleading sense of comfort, or what is called by Hall "false hope", Edwards "false joy", and Fuller "ungrounded security".[49] Fuller explained further that "I have known great numbers of persons, whose conduct, gave full proof that they were unconverted men, who, nevertheless, lived in hope of being saved at last, merely because some text of Scripture had been, at some part of their lives, impressed upon their minds."[50] The scripture impressions functioned as a deterrent to real repentance, because their focus was neither the person's own sinfulness nor the mercy of God in the gospel, but on the impression as a sign of assurance in itself; thus, being (inappropriately) relieved of anxiety over their condition,

---

[45] Ryland, *Life of Fuller*, 375. Cf. Edwards, *Religious Affections*, 221-225.

[46] Ryland, *Life of Fuller*, 376.

[47] Ibid.

[48] Ryland, *Remarks on extraordinary impulses*, 4; Hall, *Help to Zion's Travellers*, 138-139, 141. Cf. Ryland, "Autograph Reminiscences", 21-22. Edwards, *Religious Affections*, 268, similarly insisted, "that affections rising from texts of Scripture coming to the mind are vain, when no instruction received in the understanding from those texts, or anything taught in those texts, is the ground of the affection, but the manner of their coming to the mind".

[49] Hall, *Help to Zion's Travellers*, 138-139; Edwards, *Religious Affections*, 172; Ryland, *Life of Fuller*, 380.

[50] Ibid., 379.

they were neither converted nor began to grow in holiness.

Fuller's concerns about seeking such a subjective basis for assurance of conversion mirrors the judgement of his theological mentor, Jonathan Edwards. Edwards contrasted the overly introspective doctrine of assurance for which these scripture impressions were the high Calvinist's elusively subjective answer with a more evangelical and affectionate spirituality. He asserted simply, "'Tis no sign that religious affections are truly holy and spiritual, or that they are not, that they come with texts of Scripture, remarkably brought to the mind."[51] At greater length, he describes their danger, and points to a more evangelical view of assurance, in which assurance accompanies conversion:

> The first comfort of many persons, and what they call their *conversion*, is after this manner: after awakening and terrors, some comfortable promise comes suddenly and wonderfully to their minds; and the manner of its coming makes them conclude it comes from God *to them*. This is the very foundation of their faith, hope, and comfort: from hence they take their first encouragement to trust in God and in Christ, because they think that God, by some scripture so brought, has now already revealed that he loves them, and has already promised them eternal life. But this is very absurd; for every one knows that it is God's manner to reveal his love to men, and their interest in his promises, *after* they have believed, and not *before*. They must first *believe*, before they have any *personal* and *possessive* interest in the promises to be revealed.[52]

Rather than clinging to the false consolation of scripture impressions as an indirect kind of assurance, then, Fuller urged his Kettering correspondent to turn directly to the promises of the gospel as the true source of comfort and assurance. In response to this promise, Fuller wrote, "My soul cleaved to Christ."[53] Edwards and Fuller insisted that faith is defined by this cleaving to the gospel, and that assurance will follow after, resting primarily on those objective promises; high Calvinists, on the other hand, regarded this subjective awareness of assurance as a necessary prerequisite to saving faith. John von Rohr's distinction between *faith of adherence* and *faith of assurance*, helpfully, describes the two positions, within the framework of Puritan thought:

> The faith of assurance may find its ground in subjective experience, but the only adequate ground for the faith of adherence, said the Puritan divines, is the objective reality of God's promises in God's Word. Without exception they claimed and proclaimed the conviction that saving faith cannot have as unstable a foundation as one's own senses or awareness....The faith that justifies, the faith

---

[51] Edwards, *Religious Affections*, 142.

[52] Ibid., 221-222. Cf. Fuller, *Works*, ii.739.

[53] Ryland, *Life of Fuller*, 376.

that adheres to God in trust, the faith that is entrance into the covenant, must rest on a firmer foundation, the covenant promises themselves.[54]

By emphasizing the soul's "cleaving" to Christ, Fuller recovers the sense of faith as adherence that was more typical of Puritan covenant theology, and the confidence that was a mark of evangelical views of the doctrine. Although the Puritan approach to assurance, certainly, involved a great degree of soul-searching, the high Calvinists' more exaggerated and idiosyncratic approach to the doctrine of assurance within the conversion experience meant that they had, as it were, even further to go than the Puritans. The resulting doctrinal shift towards evangelical confidence, then, had an even more dramatic effect upon Fuller and his peers. That shifting of assurance earlier in the experience of the *ordo salutis*, and its subjective foundation, resulted from the high Calvinist understanding of justification. And it is to Fuller's own account of the climax of his conversion and justification that we now turn.

"Presumption": Conversionism in Pastoral Theology

In his retrospective letters, Fuller described the morning in November 1769 when the fifteen year old experienced what he considered his "real conversion", in contrast to the false comforts that had resulted in no lasting transformation of life. But in this moment of climax, Fuller's narrative exemplifies the high Calvinist redefinition of the central concept of justification by faith to a faith in their (eternal) justification, and shows that their "struggle for faith was a search for confidence rather than for conversion".[55] The personal consequence of this was a preoccupying fear of spiritual presumption, and a pastoral theology that frustrated conversionism.

Fuller recalled that on that early morning as he walked alone his convictions followed him closely, becoming a load of guilt, not unlike the burden carried by Bunyan's Christian. Reflecting on his sins and broken vows, he affirmed that God would be just in his damnation, and if he were to receive "pardon and purification" it could only be by grace. To this point, Fuller's experience sounds typical of the Puritan conversion narrative. But the word that dominated Fuller's anxious thinking at that moment was "presumption".[56] He had all along been hesitating from his turn to God, despite conviction and religious sensitivity, because it would be presumptuous, as the high Calvinists taught him, to affront the glory of God and his justification of the elect from eternity without some assurance or warrant that God had indeed elected him. He writes,

---

[54] von Rohr, *Covenant of Grace*, 67.   Edwards, citing Stoddard's *Guide to Christ*, employs a similar distinction between a faith of dependence and a faith of assurance, the latter necessarily resting on the former; *Religious Affections*, 222.

[55] von Rohr, *Covenant of Grace*, 97.

[56] Ryland, *Life of Fuller*, 17.

"I was not then aware that *any* poor sinner had a warrant to believe in Christ for the salvation of his soul; but supposed there must be some kind of qualification to entitle him to do it; yet I was aware that I had no qualification."[57]

In Fuller's high Calvinist piety, the warrant, or spiritual evidence, he had in mind was not an external sign of faith or righteousness, but, rather, an assurance that he was already among the elect. The climax of the high Calvinist spiritual narrative was not, as in the Puritan narrative, a moment of faith by which the sinner would be justified, because the elect were justified in eternity. Rather than a crisis of conversion, as von Rohr asserts, the high Calvinist narrative peaked with a crisis of confidence, and justification by faith was replaced by faith as assurance of justification. Curt Daniel suggests that in this system, the individual's "faith depends on his justification, not vice-versa. Faith is but realizing that one is already perfectly justified".[58] Or, as Peter Toon observes, "justification by faith" is redefined as that subjective experience in time "through which the individual conscience of the elect person is assured that in God's sight he has always been justified".[59] Andrew Fuller describes the antinomian definition of justification by faith as "the revelation or discovery of it to the soul", and it seems that the uncertainty of subjective assurance was insufficient to allay the fear of presumption.[60]

Robert Hall identified this high Calvinist hesitation resulting from a fear of presumption as one of the great stumbling blocks to Christian experience in his generation, and describes the general condition, of which Fuller's experience is but one poignant example:

> It is common for those who are convinced of sin, and see the need of salvation to look for some good thing in them, as the ground of encouragement for their applying to, and closing with the blessed Jesus. But finding themselves altogether vile, sinful, and unworthy, they apprehend it would be daring presumption in their present condition to trust in, or apply to him for salvation. The stumbling-block in this case seems to arise from a mistaken apprehension, accounting that which supports a person's right to come to Christ is synonymous with, or equivalent to, what evidences an interest in him, or in other words, persons want to know that they are really converted before they dare apply to Jesus.[61]

---

[57] Ibid., 18.

[58] Daniel, "Hyper Calvinism and John Gill", 355. Daniel mentions one of Gill's favourite truisms borrowed from Tobias Crisp: "He is first justified before he believes, then he believes that he is justified" (320). Contrast that with Puritan Robert Bolton, *Comfortable Walking with God*: "Justifying faith is not…to be assured of pardon; but to trust wholly upon the mercy of God for pardon"—cited by von Rohr, *Covenant of Grace*, 65.

[59] Toon, *Emergence of Hyper-Calvinisn*, 60; cf. 28, 128.

[60] Fuller, *Works*, ii.759.

[61] Hall, *Help to Zion's Travellers*, 107.

The perceived need for a warrant to prove their interest in Christ is precisely what high Calvinists were seeking when they hoped for a sign such as a scripture impression, an assurance that their repentance would not be presumption.

At this moment of crisis, however, Fuller's anxiety about his eternal damnation had reached a fever pitch, and his fear of presumption gave way to desperation. Citing the examples of Job ("Though he slay me, yet will I trust in him") and Esther ("who went into the king's presence, *contrary to law*, and at the hazard of her life"), he cast his "perishing soul upon the Lord Jesus Christ for salvation", saying in great agony, "I must—I will—yes—I will trust my soul, my sinful, lost soul in his hands—If I perish, I perish!"[62]

For Fuller, Esther's and Job's examples of casting themselves on God's mercy provided needed pictures of boldness without presumption, since neither could make any claim, and, thus, God's sovereignty was guarded. These texts appear to have been common tropes in the attempt by Calvinists to mediate the individual's desire for salvation and God's sovereignty in election.[63] John Bunyan, whose influence on Fuller's conversion narrative has already been discussed, fearing God's refusal, thought of "*Esther*, who went to Petition the King contrary to the Law", phrasing adopted almost verbatim by Fuller.[64] Esther's example was also cited by high Calvinists John Gill and Anne Dutton (1692-1765).[65] From the perspective of pastoral theology, Joseph Hussey, also, drew on this episode in Esther's story, and, while not denying that the condition of a "poor sinner" is like that of Esther, he, characteristically, shifted the focus from Esther to the king, and insisted that for ministers to offer the gospel on the basis of this story is presumptuous: "For it is an Act of the *King*, not an Act of the *Ministers* to do so." It is God's place to extend mercy to whom He intends,

---

[62] Ryland, *Life of Fuller*, 18-19.

[63] Daniel, "Hyper-Calvinism and John Gill", 363.

[64] John Bunyan, *Grace Abounding to the Chief of Sinners*, ed. W.R. Owens (London: Penguin, 1987), 64 (§ 251).

[65] Gill, *Body of Divinity*, ii.397, describes that part of faith which is fleeing to Christ for refuge as "A venturing act of their souls, and of their whole salvation on him, like Esther, who ventured into the presence of King Ahasuerus, saying, If I perish, I perish! Faith at first is such a venture of the soul on Christ, not knowing as yet how it will fare with it." In pointed questions to her readers about their faith, Dutton asked, "And under a deep Sense of thy perishing Condition, hast thou been encouraged by God's Free Grace in Christ, to cast thyself at his Feet, to find Mercy: To commit thyself into the Arms of his Grace and Power, for all Life, and Salvation; with an holy Venture, saying, as Esther, 'I will go in unto the King; and if I perish, I perish. I see there is no other Way of Salvation: Here therefore I'll wait as an undone Sinner; it may be Free-Grace will save me; but if not, I can but die: And if I perish, it shall be at the Foot of God's Free Mercy in Christ.' Hast thou, I say, at any Time experienced such Resolutions wrought in thy Soul?" [Anne Dutton], *A Brief Account of the Gracious Dealings of God with a Poor, Sinful, Unworthy Creature* (London: J. Hart, 1750), 55.

whereas the "*Offer Men*" "propose what is never *Decreed* of God, and what was never *intended* to be given from above".[66] Fuller's use of these particular biblical images places him firmly within that high Calvinist tradition which was so concerned not to arrogate God's glory and to avoid any hint of presumption.

After weeping and calling for God's mercy for over an hour, Fuller found the relief and salvation that he had hesitated to seek: "I now found rest for my troubled soul; and I reckon, that I should have found it sooner, if I had not entertained the notion of my having no warrant to come to Christ without some previous qualification. This notion was a bar that kept me back for a time; though, through divine drawings, I was enabled to overleap it."[67] Andrew Fuller's eventual overleaping of the bar does show that an experience of assurance of one's conversion and justification was possible, but was greatly encumbered; he "should have found it sooner". As the last two sections have demonstrated, redefining justification by faith as an assurance of one's election, and emphasizing potentially elusive and subjective criteria for that confidence, gave an intensely introspective and hesitating character to the typical high Calvinist experience of conversion. High Calvinism frustrated the individual's assured approach to God, and it militated against an assertive conversionism. Curt Daniel succinctly summarizes the pastoral effects of this system: "Those who say they are seekers are more discouraged by warnings of presumption than encouraged by invitations of grace."[68]

---

[66] Hussey, *God's Operations of Grace*, 254. Tobias Crisp, also, deals directly with the question of presumption when assurance is lacking, drawing on the Job text quoted by Fuller. Despite Crisp's antinomianism, his ability to make a free offer of the gospel set him apart from Hussey, Gill, and Fuller's early experience. He wrote, "To come to the purpose, I say it is not only no presumption, but the blessed faith which our Saviour and the Holy Ghost every where commend, to believe in Christ, and apply the promises to themselves as their own; even then, when spiritual experiences are vanished quite out of sight or sense." Tobias Crisp, *Christ Alone Exalted*, 4th ed. (London: R. Noble, 1791), 465-466. A hymn by Edmund Jones, pastor of the Baptist church at Exon, Devon, included in John Rippon's *Selection of Hymns From the Best Authors, Intended to be an Appendix to Dr. Watts's Psalms and Hymns*, 10th ed. (London: J. Bateson, 1800), no. 355, is an extended meditation on precisely this episode of Esther's bold resolve, applied to the case of a sinner appealing to Jesus for undeserved mercy: "I'll to the gracious King approach, / Whose Sceptre Pardon gives, / Perhaps he may Command my Touch, / And then the Suppliant lives" (verse 4); "I can but perish if I go, / I am resolv'd to try: / For if I stay away, I know, / I must for ever die" (verse 6).

[67] Ryland, *Life of Fuller*, 19. Fuller's later, more evangelical perspective on presumption, *Works*, iii.556: "Is it presumption to take God at his word? Is it presumption to renounce your own righteousness, and submit to the righteousness of God? Is it presumption to believe that Christ 'is able to save to the uttermost all them that come unto God by him?'"

[68] Daniel, "Hyper Calvinism and John Gill", 358.

"An aversion to creature power": Spiritual Ability in Pastoral Theology

Fuller recalled that as a young man of about sixteen years old, then converted, he found that his mind "was now at rest in Christ", and through personal conversations he "became known among serious people", and joined the Particular Baptist church at Soham in 1770. He described that summer as "a time of great religious pleasure. I loved my pastor, and all my brethren in the church; and they expressed great affection towards me, in return."[69] With the fall of that year, however, came a series of events which produced dissension in the Soham church, the removal of Mr. Eve, the pastor, and a great deal of theological confusion for Fuller. The early crisis in the Soham church clarifies another crucial effect of high Calvinism in the Baptist congregations and on the spiritual formation of their members; the incident was, also, formative in Fuller's turn to a more evangelical Calvinism.

Fuller, already sharing the congregation's concern for strict discipline, approached a member of the church for excessive drinking, who responded by saying that he was spiritually unable to act in any other way, that he could not "keep himself" from sinning.[70] The man's case came before the church, and he was excluded, but the particular case was soon eclipsed by the larger theological issues. The abstract question was framed: whether or not it was within *"the power of sinful men to do the will of God, and to keep themselves from sin"*, or, as the matter was described in the Soham Church Book:

> Whether it is in the Power of men with the common gifts of Rationality to Will and Effect that which is morally good; and to Will, refuse, and abstain from gross Immoralities or that which is morally Evil.
> Also whether a Xn, after call'd by Grace has Power [to] choose or refuse to obey or Disobey the commands of God: as relating to ye external conduct of his Life, so as honourably to Persevere.
> …Also whether a Xn when left to himself and [sic] perform the Duties Incumbent on him, and keep himself from falling…whether their Good Works do not arise entirely from the Grace and Power of God, exclusive of their own Power and free will.[71]

A great many of the membership answered these questions in the negative, denying that persons, even when converted, have it within their own ability to keep themselves from sin, or, conversely, to do spiritual good. The defenders of this position had "an Aversion to the Notion of Creature Power, judging that it derogated from the Glory of God's keeping Grace".[72] The same concern to guard against presumption in conversion by coming to God without prior

---

[69] Ryland, *Life of Fuller*, 21-23.

[70] Ibid., 24. Fuller's account of the controversy is, also, found in the Soham Church Book, 16-29.

[71] Ryland, *Life of Fuller*, 24; Soham Church Book, 16-17.

[72] Ibid., 19. See also Ryland, *Life of Fuller*, 24.

warrant (for fear of detracting from God's glory in election) was expressed in this matter as hesitation in or denial of moral ability (for fear of detracting from God's glory in sanctification and perseverence).

The pastor, and a part of the Soham church with him, affirmed the Christian's ability, and, therefore, obligation, by distinguishing "between internal and external power". "He allowed, that men had no power of themselves to perform any thing spiritually good; but contended, that they could yield external obedience, and keep themselves from open acts of sin."[73] Their affirmation, then, was still very restricted, to encompass only external acts, such as the avoidance of sinful behaviour (for example, excessive drinking, as opposed to inwardly sinful inclinations) or attendance upon the means of grace. In fact, although the debate was deeply felt and threatened to be schismatic in the Soham church, and although it eventually led to Mr. Eve's departure, it seems that both sides of the debate were squarely within high Calvinist thought. There was disagreement only about the degree of external ability or spiritual nature. Neither side would have affirmed the ability of a sinner to repent or do anything spiritually good without the electing grace of God.

It is, also, worth noting that the man whose case initiated the lengthy doctrinal controversy at Soham was quickly and unanimously judged by the church to have been in error of making excuses, and was excluded. The fact that neither side of the debate would condone such blatant sin, even while disagreeing about the nature and extent of moral ability, helps to situate the congregation vis-à-vis practical antinomianism. It appears that the church's adherence to a strict pattern of discipline for members, and assuming all persons to have an obligation to attend to at least the external means of grace, served as a check against the excessive tendencies of antinomianism.[74] On the other hand, the popular reluctance to acknowledge spiritual ability or obligation had a dampening effect on the pursuit of holiness and spiritual maturity.

Although Fuller was deeply disturbed by the heated debate so early in his churchly life—he referred to this incident as "the wormwood and the gall of my youth"—the debates did have a formative effect in Fuller's own development as pastoral theologian. He observed, "As the disputes in the church were the occasion of turning my thoughts to most of those subjects on which I have since written, so were they the occasion of my engaging in the Christian ministry."[75] Fuller here articulates one of the main claims of this chapter, that exploring the implicit (and explicit) pastoral theology of high Calvinism provides the necessary background and foil to understand his theological project as one of evangelical pastoral theology. The seeds of discontent with high Calvinism sown by these events matured in the early years of Fuller's

---

[73] Ibid., 25.

[74] Toon, *Hyper Calvinism*, 144-145.

[75] Ryland, *Life of Fuller*, 28.

preaching ministry at Soham, as he wrestled with the "Modern Question" of free offers of the gospel.

"Free offers": Preaching in Pastoral Theology

Fuller's personal conversion narrative presents his minister's high Calvinist reticence to offer assurance, to actively encourage conversion, or to assume any degree of spiritual ability, all with profound pastoral consequences for the seeker's conversion experience and piety. In his early trials at preaching, and his subsequent call to pastoral ministry, Fuller experienced, as it were, the other side of the coin, his initial approach to preaching illustrating a fourth consequence of high Calvinist pastoral theology, its best-known, the denial of free offers of the gospel to unconverted sinners. Fuller at first carried on in the same vein, and, then, found himself, biblically and experientially, compelled to question it.

Fuller was set apart by the Soham church as their pastor in 1774, then twenty years old. Recalling that period, he wrote that "being now devoted to the ministry, I took a review of the doctrine I should preach".[76] What was Fuller's early preaching like, at the time of this review of his pastoral theology? He had earlier described Mr. Eve, the preacher of his Soham youth, as having "little or nothing to say to the unconverted".[77] Now a preacher himself, he had not fallen very far from the tree; Fuller's own high Calvinist tenets admitted "nothing spiritually good to be the duty of the unregenerate, and nothing to be addressed to them, in a way of exhortation, excepting what related to external obedience". Although he had begun to question these restrictions, he "durst not, for some years, address an invitation to the unconverted to come to Jesus".[78]

The denial of invitations to the unconverted can be traced back to Joseph Hussey's *God's Operations of Grace, but No Offers of His Grace* (1707), then was vigorously debated during the 1730s in a volley of pamphlets on the "Modern Question", after which it became a kind of shibboleth of high Calvinist orthodoxy, taken as a matter of logical consistency by its ablest eighteenth-century proponent, John Gill.[79] The denial of free offers of the

---

[76] Ibid., 31.

[77] Ibid., 11.

[78] Ibid., 31, 32.

[79] The use of the language of "free offers" seems to have taken on this demarcating function, even among those with an, otherwise, evangelistic ministry. Gill's prefatory comments in Richard Davis' *Hymns Composed on Several Subjects*, v, are indicative of this, as well as of his own clear position on the question of offers: "I have only one thing more to observe, that whereas the phrase of offering Christ and Grace, is sometimes used in these Hymns, which may be offensive to some persons; and which the worthy Author was led to the use of, partly thru' custom, it not having been at the writing of them objected to, and partly thro' his affectionate concern and zeal for gaining upon souls, and encouraging them to come to Christ; I can affirm upon good and sufficient

gospel was, he said, "of a piece with the rest of our tenets". In a tract defending the doctrine of election and reprobation, Gill asserted that in making invitations of salvation to the unconverted, the minister derogates God's glory and electing initiative, making the cruel presumption that any of his hearers could respond, when, in fact, there were some who were not elect and eternally justified, and therefore not granted the gift of saving faith: "...how irrational it is, for ministers to stand offering Christ, and salvation by him to man, when, on the one hand, they have neither power nor right to give; and on the other hand, the persons they offer to, have neither power nor will to receive?"[80] To make an offer of salvation was to rely on the individual's faith as necessary to salvation, an Arminian "condition" against which Gill was careful to fence off both the finished work of Christ and the justification of the elect from eternity:

> ...the gospel is a declaration of salvation already wrought out by Christ, and not an offer of it on conditions to be performed by man. The ministers of the gospel are sent to *preach the gospel to every creature* [Mark 16:15]; that is, not to offer, but to preach Christ, and salvation by him; to publish peace and pardon as things already obtained by him. The ministers are...*criers or heralds*; their business is...to *proclaim* aloud, to publish facts, to declare things that are done, and not to offer them to be done on conditions...[81]

It remained for Gill, and other high Calvinists, to define the role of preaching apart from such a conversionist approach, which they did by carefully distinguishing between *preaching* or publishing the gospel and *offering* it.[82] To preach with offers excluded led to an emphasis on doctrinal clarity and orthodoxy as an end in itself. Gill's friend and colleague, John Brine, described the twofold duty of preaching ministry as "the defense of the principles of revelation" and convincing hearers of their "lukewarmness, indifferency and sad declension" but not offering hope that the biblical revelation could apply to their spiritual condition.[83] In a sense, offering the gospel is the missing middle term between these two duties; the invitation is what personalizes the gospel for the individual. As Fuller's early experience

---

Testimony, that Mr. Davis, before his death, changed his mind in this matter, and disused the phrase, as being improper, and as being too bold and free, for a minister of Christ to make use of." So, Morden, *Offering Christ to the World*, 13-14. See, also, Robert Hall, jun., *The Works of Robert Hall*, ed. Olinthus Gregory (London: Holdsworth and Ball, 1832), 4:444-47; and Hayden, "Evangelical Calvinism", 330. Cf. Fuller's discussion of the positions of Hussey, Brine, and Gill on "free offers"; *Works* ii.422 (footnote).

[80] John Gill, *A Collection of Sermons and Tracts* (London: George Keith, 1773), ii.146-147.

[81] Ibid. See also Daniel, "Hyper Calvinism and John Gill", 430.

[82] Toon, *Hyper Calvinism*, 80.

[83] Ibid., 101.

witnesses, defining preaching without this middle term could leave the unconverted person indifferent or caught up in introspective uncertainty of whether or not they have any "interest" in the gospel described in their hearing.

During his reading and reflection on doctrinal and practical divinity, Fuller came across a pair of pamphlets that related to the "Modern Question", which, he said, in their presentation of scriptural examples of gospel invitations, "revived all my doubts on what was called the High Calvinistic system, or the system of Dr. Gill, Mr. Brine, and others, as to the duty of sinners, and of ministers in addressing them".[84] But he perceived that a modification in his inherited theology would be as radical for pastoral practice as it would be difficult to overcome: "But, as I perceived this reasoning would affect the whole tenor of my preaching, I moved on with slow and trembling steps; and, having to feel my way out of a labyrinth, I was a long time ere I felt satisfied."[85]

Indeed, the whole tenor of Fuller's preaching was to change as his questions and reading led him further into the scriptures, and, eventually, he was introduced to the writings of Jonathan Edwards. The result was his embrace of a more evangelical and experiential Calvinism, bearing the marks of Puritan affective piety and evangelical confidence. He was to reintegrate offers of the gospel into preaching and, in fact, he made such a conversionist approach to ministry the defining criterion of preaching, the duty of preachers matched to the obligation of hearers. The formulation of his understanding of Calvinism and its implications for pastoral theology, painstakingly arrived at in Soham, is found in his *The Gospel Worthy of All Acceptation*, written by 1781, though not published until 1785.

The Gospel Worthy of All Acceptation: An Evangelical Pastoral Theology

The roots and aim of *The Gospel Worthy of All Acceptation* are pastoral: its roots found in Andrew Fuller's pastoral experience of high Calvinism, its aim the renewal of the pastoral theology of his generation of Particular Baptists. Fuller's evangelicalism is articulated at precisely this pastoral juncture, in addressing the pastoral cases of individuals and the definition of pastoral responsibility. Each of the preceding instances of the pastoral function of Fuller's early high Calvinism finds its evangelical response in his seminal work.

The main claims of *The Gospel Worthy of All Acceptation* can be summarized in relationship to the unconverted: "Unconverted sinners are commanded, exhorted, and invited to believe in Christ for salvation", and have both capacity and duty to respond to God's revelation, which entails their

---

[84] Ryland, *Life of Fuller*, 34, 37. These were pamphlets by Abraham Taylor and John Martin.

[85] Ibid., 32.

THE

GOSPEL *of* CHRIST

WORTHY OF ALL

ACCEPTATION:

OR THE

OBLIGATIONS of MEN

FULLY to CREDIT, and CORDIALLY to APPROVE,

WHATEVER

GOD MAKES KNOWN.

WHEREIN IS CONSIDERED

The NATURE of FAITH in CHRIST,

AND THE

DUTY OF THOSE WHERE THE GOSPEL

COMES IN THAT MATTER.

BY ANDREW FULLER.

Go—PREACH THE GOSPEL TO EVERY CREATURE;—HE
THAT BELIEVETH, AND IS BAPTIZED, SHALL BE
SAVED,—BUT HE THAT BELIEVETH NOT SHALL BE
DAMNED! Mark xvi. 15, 16.

NORTHAMPTON: Printed by T. DICEY & Co.
And fold by J. BUCKLAND, MATTHEWS, and T. SOCKETT,
in London; A. BROWN & SON, on the Tolzey, Bristol;
and SMITH, at Sheffield.
[Price ONE SHILLING and SIX-PENCE.]

Figure 5: Title page of first edition of *The Gospel Worthy of All Acceptation*

ability and obligation to have a converting faith in Jesus Christ.[86] An assured approach of the individual to God is not only possible, it is required; whereas high Calvinism made subjective assurance of election the basis of an approach to God (e.g., scripture impressions), Fuller defines faith as the confident approach to God on the basis of the objective promises of the gospel and their implicit imperative. He wrote, "[T]he proper object of saving faith is not our being interested in Christ, but the glorious gospel of the ever-blessed God, (which is true, whether we believe it or not)."[87] Fuller demonstrated how this more assured and objective view of faith was related to conversionism and spiritual ability (as seen in his personal experience), by answering anticipated objections from high Calvinists who considered such a conception of faith to presume upon God's electing prerogative on the one hand, and overstate the sinner's spiritual ability on the other.

Fear of presumption in high Calvinism frustrated conversionism from the perspective of both awakened individual and preacher. Fuller noted that the emphasis of the representative, John Brine, on the eternal decrees and justification meant "that a sinner may know himself to be regenerate before he believes", prompting a crisis of pre-conversion assurance, or "that the first exercise of faith is an act of presumption", resulting in fearful hesitation.[88] Rather, Fuller argued, the seeking individual does not need to be conscious or assured of his regeneration in advance of turning to Christ, but has all the warrant needed in the gospel itself.

Addressing the same reluctance to arrogate the glory of God's eternal decrees evident in preaching, Fuller drew on the authority of strict Calvinist, John Owen. Discussing "the duty of ministers of the gospel; in the dispensing of the word, in exhortations, invitations, precepts, and threatenings committed unto them", Owen refers to the important distinction "between man's duty and God's purposes", to combat such a fear of presumption:

> A minister is not to make inquiry after, nor to trouble himself about, those secrets of the eternal mind of God, viz. Whom he purposeth to save, and whom he hath sent Christ to die for in particular; it is enough for them to search his revealed will, and thence take their *directions*, from whence they have their *commissions*. Wherefore there is no conclusion from the universal precepts of the word, concerning the things, unto God's purpose in himself concerning persons: they command and invite all to *repent* and *believe*; but they know not in particular on whom God will bestow repentance unto salvation, nor in whom he will effect the work of faith with power.[89]

Whereas high Calvinists insisted that uncertainty about which of their hearers

---

[86] Fuller, *Works*, ii.343. The *Works* contain the revised edition of 1801.
[87] Ibid., ii.333.
[88] Ibid., ii.383.
[89] Ibid., ii.373, citing John Owen, *Death of Death*, book 4, chapter 1.

were among the elect was reason for hesitation and restrictions of offers of the gospel, Owen, and Fuller following him, turned this logic around, insisting that not knowing who is elect is reason for the most urgent of invitations in preaching and mission; they insisted that God's glory was best served in the faithful offering of the gospel, which is revealed, rather than guarding the secret decrees of God, which are not.

To keep from falling into the ditches of Arminianism on the one side, and antinomianism on the other, high Calvinists described spiritual ability as either internal and external, or spiritual and natural abilities, only the latter for which the unconverted were counted responsible. The result was a pastoral care that could not expect sinners to respond to the gospel, and indeed, in the popular context, also, frustrated sanctification. Not wanting to presume spiritual ability among those who did not possess it, high Calvinist preachers did not urge repentance or belief in the gospel (requiring an internal ability), not going further than urging hearers to external obedience and attendance on the means of grace (requiring only, they said, external ability). Fuller describes the situation: "Having done their duty, the minister has nothing more to say to them; unless, indeed, it be to tell them occasionally that something more is *necessary* to salvation. But as this implies no guilt on their part, they sit unconcerned."[90] Fuller rejected the distinction altogether, saying that *all* response to God is spiritual in nature. He dealt with the issues of ability and duty together in his discussion of moral and natural ability, which he borrowed from Jonathan Edwards.[91] Sinners are often "unable" to respond to the gospel, he argued, not because such an invitation is inappropriate, but because they have set their will against such obedience; this willful disobedience, however, is chosen rather than necessary, and so does not remove the duty or obligation of faith in the gospel.[92] As Fuller expressed this distinction in a later sermon, "The first concern of a sinner is to receive the Saviour. It ought not to be a question whether he *may* receive him, since the gospel is addressed to every creature....The only question is whether he be *willing* to receive him."[93]

If Fuller stressed the duty *of* unconverted sinners, it was, also, part of his pastoral intentions to delineate the duty of ministers *toward* unconverted sinners. Indeed, the whole of the work had pastoral implications, as the obligation of ministers could be mapped onto the obligations of hearers. His

---

[90] Ibid., ii.387.

[91] Cf. Jonathan Edwards, *Freedom of the Will*, in *The Works of Jonathan Edwards*, ed. Paul Ramsey (New Haven and London: Yale University Press, 1957), 1: 159, 305, 309. For the use of the same distinction for the same evangelical ends, see Fuller's Independent counterpart, Edward Williams, *An Essay on the Equity of Divine Government and the Sovereignty of Divine Grace*, in *The Works of the Rev. Edward Williams, D.D.*, ed. Evan Davies (London: James Nisbet and Co., 1862), iii.124-133.

[92] Fuller, *Works*, ii.332, 376-379.

[93] Ibid., i.275.

conclusions, also, drew out the specific application of his assertions for preaching, observing that "The work of the Christian ministry, it has been said, is to *preach the gospel*, or to hold up the free grace of God through Jesus Christ, as the only way of a sinner's salvation." And, in case there was any confusion about whether or not "preach" ought to include offering the gospel, he insisted that "it is the duty of ministers not only to exhort their carnal auditors to believe in Jesus Christ for the salvation of their souls; but IT IS AT OUR PERIL TO EXHORT THEM TO ANY THING SHORT OF IT, OR WHICH DOES NOT INVOLVE OR IMPLY IT".[94] Rather than drawing distinctions between preaching and offering, Fuller reintegrated offers of the gospel into preaching, making it a defining necessity of pastoral practice.

Summary

Fuller's narration of his early religious experience and conversion elucidates the pastoral function of high Calvinism at the level of individual experience, particularly in its elusive understanding of assurance, its frustrated conversionism, its restricted assessment of spiritual ability, and its careful guarding against free offers of the gospel in preaching. His narrative, also, witnesses his sense of discomfiting tensions: in the dissonance between high Calvinist reticence from the pulpit and Puritan conversionism in his devotional reading; in the Soham church's dispute over spiritual ability; in the seeming contradictions between the writings of John Bunyan and John Gill; and supremely, between his own hesitation to address the unconverted in preaching and the invitations and imperatives of the New Testament. These tensions provoked further study and exploration, and, eventually, the drafting of *The Gospel Worthy of All Acceptation*, which was at once pastoral and evangelical. Fuller properly identified the extent of the renewal of his pastoral theology early in its formation: "I perceived this reasoning would affect the whole tenor of my preaching."[95]

The evangelical nature of Fuller's renewed pastoral theology is evidenced by its affirmation of the unconverted person's assured approach to God and the more assertively conversionist approach of the preacher to the unconverted. Fuller's most important book addresses the pastoral circumstances of individual seekers *and* the pastoral aims of preachers. The claim is not, of course, that high Calvinists did not allow conversion, but rather, as the difficulties and obstacles of Andrew Fuller's own experience illustrate, both seeker and minister were encumbered rather than urged in its pursuit, as Fuller remarked upon finding rest for his own troubled soul: "I reckon, that I should have found it sooner."[96] By contrast, Fuller's renewed pastoral theology used the language

---

[94] Ibid., ii.386.
[95] Ryland, *Life of Fuller*, 32.
[96] Ibid., 19.

of "obligation" and "duty": urgent, affectionate, conversionist, and evangelical.

Figure 6: Portrait of Andrew Fuller from Morris, *Memoirs*

CHAPTER 2

"There are no bonds to bring them together, or to keep them together, but love."

Ecclesiology: The *Context* of an Evangelical and Affectionate Pastoral Theology

In a periodical essay on the state of dissenting discipline, Fuller queried whether a "lively and evangelical ministry" and dissenting "discipline and government" were necessarily mutually exclusive.[1] Might it not be possible to have a view of ministry that was *both* energetically *conversionist* and solidly *congregational*? He lamented, "Such, alas! is the contractedness of the human mind, that, while attending to one thing, it is ever in danger of neglecting others of equal if not superior importance."[2] Nor did the religious landscape of the mid-eighteenth century seem to promise much by way of a synthesis of evangelical aims and congregational ecclesiology. Describing the early evangelical leaders and their Methodist followers, Fuller asserted, "It is a fact which cannot be denied, that many, who have exhibited the common salvation with great success to the unconverted have at the same time been sadly negligent in enforcing the legislative authority of Christ upon their hearers." However, of his own Particular Baptist heritage, especially under high Calvinism, he admitted, "Nor is it less manifest that others, who have been the most tenacious of the forms of church government and discipline, have at the same time been woefully deficient in preaching the gospel to the unconverted."[3]

As a way of bridging this gulf between evangelical aims and orderly ministry and discipline, the Evangelical Revival saw the use or emergence of alternative ecclesiological constructions which particularly emphasized voluntarism. The Methodist construction, a "new form of religious polity", which Fuller described as "half Dissenting", consisted of voluntary societies

---

[1] Fuller, *Works*, iii.477.

[2] Ibid., iii.478.

[3] Ibid.

under the leadership of regularly-rotated itinerant evangelists, and existed more or less alongside church or chapel; over the whole "connexion", Wesley exercised an authority that he considered voluntary in nature.[4] The construction employed by evangelical Anglican clergy and laity was the "religious society", in which a small fellowship within the local church voluntarily embraced a more rigorous rule of piety and discipline than could be found in typical parish worship and life.[5] These were both creative and practical evangelical responses to problems in ecclesiology, voluntary and conversionist in their tone.

The pastoral theology of Andrew Fuller demonstrates that there was another evangelical response: the renewal of congregational ecclesiology, neither alongside nor within, but the disciplined local church itself and its ordained ministry. Fuller was representative of an ecclesiological "third way", combining a "lively and evangelical ministry" with congregational order and discipline. He asserted the conversionist aims of settled pastors, the essence of ordained ministry as voluntary, and the voluntaristic nature of congregational discipline under pastoral leadership for the purpose of the pursuit of holiness. Or, in other words, Fuller's evangelical pastoral theology expressed a congregational ecclesiology and theology of ordained pastoral ministry characterized by voluntarism, conversionist aims, and affectionate bonds. While the primary focus of this chapter is to establish the nature of Fuller's congregationalism as the context of his pastoral theology by tracing the ecclesiological themes which arose from the call to ministry and from the ordination service, even here there emerges evidence of Fuller's more evangelical and affectionate accent.

Called to an Evangelical and Affectionate Ministry

Andrew Fuller described the essential qualifications for gospel ministry in terms that were at once congregational and affectionate. He suggested that, besides questions of character, a candidate for pastoral ministry should be recognized to have, first, "*a true desire after it*" and, second, "*an ability for it*".[6] As will be demonstrated, Fuller defined "desire" in terms of affectionate concern, and "ability" in the context of congregational recognition and nurture, maintaining a balance between interior and exterior, subjective and objective, personal and corporate, and mystical and mediated aspects of divine vocation, themes which are illustrated by Fuller's own call to ministry. Crucial to Fuller's description of both affectionate desire and the orderly recognition of ability was their evangelical intention.

---

[4] Walsh, "Religious Societies", 284-295, esp. 287; Fuller, *Works*, iii.477; Frederick Dreyer, *Genesis of Methodism* (Bethlehem: Lehigh University Press, 1999), 93-109.

[5] Walsh, "Religious Societies", esp. 280-284, 295-302; Hindmarsh, *John Newton*, 199-202.

[6] Fuller, *Works*, iii.793-794.

Fuller's pastoral desire emerged and his ministerial ability was first tested during 1771-1773, while the Soham Baptist church was relying on the preaching of their own lay members after the departure of their minister. He recalled that before his first opportunity to preach, he had been riding on business and meditating on a Psalm, formulating and preaching a sermon to himself.[7] The next day he discovered that his friend, Joseph Driver, would be prevented by illness from expounding as he had been doing, and Fuller was asked to read a passage of scripture and, if he felt liberty, to "drop any remarks, which might occur". Expounding for half an hour, Fuller did experience "considerable freedom". Although his next attempt was less successful and prevented him from accepting such requests for most of the year, he did, eventually, resume preaching with greater confidence and appreciative response. Describing the confluence of emerging desire and recognized ability, Fuller wrote, "From this time, the brethren seemed to entertain an idea of my engaging in the ministry, nor was I without serious thoughts of it myself. Sometimes, I felt a desire after it; at other times, I was much discouraged, especially through a consciousness of my want of spirituality of mind, which I considered as a qualification of the first importance."[8]

The language of affectionate desire and an inner call to ministry was certainly not unique to Fuller's experience or pastoral theology. Self-examination of motives was expressed, to cite a well-known example, in the Church of England's form for ordaining priests, in its question, "Do you think in your heart, that you be truly called, according to the Will of our Lord Jesus Christ, and the Order of this Church of England, to the Order and Ministry of Priesthood?"[9] The emphasis on such inner desire was intended as a guard

---

[7] Ryland, *Life of Fuller*, 28-31.

[8] Ibid., 30.

[9] Edmund Gibson, *Codex juris ecclesiastici Anglicani: or, the statutes, constitutions, canons, rubricks and articles, of the Church of England* (London, 1713), 1:160. Note that there, too, desire is set in the context of order. Gilbert Burnet, *A Discourse of the Pastoral Care*, 4th ed. (Dublin: J. Hyde and R. Gunne, 1726), 92-93, offered this commentary on this point in the ordination rubric: "The true meaning of it must be resolved thus: The motives that ought to determine a man to dedicate himself to the ministering in the church, are a zeal for promoting the glory of God, for raising the honour of the christian religion .... And when to this he has added a concern for the souls of men, a tenderness for them, a zeal to rescue them from endless misery, and a desire to put them in the way to everlasting happiness; and from these motives, feels in himself a desire to dedicate his life and labours to those ends .... This man, and only this man, so moved and so qualified, can in truth, and with a good conscience, answer, That he trusts he is inwardly moved by the holy ghost." For other eighteenth-century Baptist perspectives, see Gill, *Body of Divinity*, ii.579; and Isaac Backus, *A Discourse Showing the Nature and Necessity of an Internal Call to Preach the Everlasting Gospel* [1754], 65-128, in William G. McLoughlin, ed., *Isaac Backus on Church, State, and Calvinism:*

against those who sought ordination for more worldly reasons—"ease, affluence, or applause"—but at the same time avoided the language of unchecked autonomy which would invite the charge of "enthusiasm".[10]

Fuller vibrantly described the "special desire" or "thirst" for pastoral ministry as "a kind of fire kindled in the bosom, that it would be painful to extinguish".[11] This deeply felt and affectionate desire, however, also had evangelical substance; the potential minister's desire should be an evangelical and conversionist "concern to glorify God and promote the salvation of men".[12] As elsewhere in Fuller's thought, "evangelical" and "affectionate" help define each other: a deeply felt concern for the salvation of others.

This affectionate and evangelical inner desire was balanced by an orderly congregational testing of evangelical ability. For about a year after his initial attempts at preaching, Fuller shared the responsibility for weekly preaching, of which he wrote, "to our unexpected, unlooked for comfort, the Lord was pleased to make use of such weak means for the conversion of some Souls".[13] In January 1774, occasioned by a request for him to preach a member's funeral sermon, the Soham church gave formal recognition of Fuller's gifts. The Church Book records that when Fuller was twenty years old, "the church met for Solemn fasting and Prayer and having judged Bro. Fuller's gifts to be ministerial, after his having likewise given in before them his Internal call to the Work; gave him a call publickly to preach the Gospel &c".[14]

The congregational setting of a ministerial call is nicely expressed by the Soham church's two kinds of engagement with Fuller: examining his ability for ministry by the objective results of his preaching, and, also, scrutinizing the narrative of his subjective inner call. Fuller's fitness for ministry was discerned first, then, by the church's examination of his abilities in preaching, whether or not he was "apt to teach". Affirming this orderly, corporate context, he contended, "Whether we be 'apt to teach' is a question on which we ought not

---

Pamphlets, 1754-1789 (Cambridge, Mass.: Harvard University Press, 1968). James Puglisi, *The Process of Admission to Ordained Ministry: A Comparative Study*, trans. Michael S. Driscoll and Mary Misrahi (Collegeville: Pueblo, 1996), ii.107, suggests that the distinction between internal and external call is decidedly modern; in the patristic tradition of pastoral theology, exemplified by Gregory Nazianzan and Gregory the Great, the bishop was often ordained against their desire, rather than according to it. The narrative accounts of resisting ordination may have functioned, as a literary form, in much the same way as later narratives of an internal call, as evidence of self-examination and pure, rather than self-aggrandizing, motives. See Purves, *Pastoral Theology in the Classical Tradition*, 36.
[10] Fuller, *Works*, iii.793.
[11] Ibid.
[12] Ibid.
[13] Soham Church Book, 30.
[14] Ibid., 35.

to decide ourselves: those are the best judges who have heard us, and have been taught by us", "those with whom we stand connected".[15] The criteria by which the church would evaluate a candidate's gifts included, in addition to doctrine, an "inventive mind", and "a kind of natural readiness in communicating his ideas".[16] Perhaps the most determinative criterion, however, was the fruit of a candidate's trial ministry, which in Fuller's case was of an evangelical nature: "the conversion of some Souls".[17]

The church, also, provided a public context for discerning Fuller's call to ministry in a second way which intentionally balanced the affective and congregational elements of that call. At some point over the previous year of preaching, he had "given in before them his Internal call to the Work"; that is, it appears that Fuller had to narrate his ministerial vocation in a way not dissimilar to the narration of conversion prior to church membership. Just as the fruit of Fuller's ministry was evaluated on its ability to encourage conversion, so, he narrated his internal call as he had narrated his own conversion. Bruce Hindmarsh's observations about the narratives of early Methodist preachers, also, apply to Fuller's context: "Conversion first led these autobiographers to preach, and then their call to preach was experienced like a conversion, and then finally their preaching resulted in new conversions."[18] But the public narrating of an internal call to ministry is similar to the church's reception of conversion narratives in another way. In congregational churches, the sharing of conversion narratives in a church meeting was prerequisite to membership, the reception and examination of these narratives being an expression of active congregational ecclesiology and discipline.[19] Similarly, hearing the narrative of an internal call allowed the church to be active in the identification and election of its ministry. In both cases the public narration made objective an experience that was subjective, made public that which was personal, and balanced the affectionate with the orderly in a congregational context. Within this congregational context, pastoral vocation was recognized, then, when a candidate's trial ministry was evangelical in content as well as intent, when conversionist affections were matched by evangelical ability and fruit.

Fuller's public call to preach typifies the process by which churches with congregational discipline tested ministerial gifts and call. The public call was not yet an invitation for Fuller to become their settled pastor, nor was it his

---

[15] Fuller, *Works*, iii.794.

[16] Ibid., iii.793.

[17] Soham Church Book, 30.

[18] Hindmarsh, *Evangelical Conversion Narrative*, 250; see 247-252.

[19] Ibid., esp. chapters 1 and 9. For Fuller's description of the use of oral and written "experiences", or as he preferred, a "profession of repentance toward God and faith in Jesus Christ", see his letter to Mr.___, 7 February 1814, in Andrew Fuller, Bound autograph volumes of transcribed correspondence, Compiled by A. G. Fuller, volume one, Fuller Baptist Church, Kettering, Northamptonshire.

ordination (both of which occurred in the following year), but was, rather, a strong affirmation of teaching gifts, an encouragement to practice them in their midst, and a statement that to do so was in good order.[20] In some cases such a call would be prefatory to sending candidates to an academy or to apprentice with a minister, and for others, the church's action was a way to place lay itinerant preaching under the authority and order of the local church.[21] This practice accords with the Soham church's statement, in their 1774 "Principles of Church Order and Discipline", that "As the Church of Christ is his nursery in which he trains up and sends forth ministers, we think every measure tending to discover and encourage such gifts ought to be taken", locating ministerial call and ministerial formation within congregational life and discipline.[22]

Congregational discipline and its orderly ministry found a balance, in Andrew Fuller's experience and pastoral theology, with affectionate desire and evangelical concern. While the inner call was put in corporate context by its public narration and the testing of ministerial ability, true desire for pastoral ministry consisted of a passion for the salvation of souls, and whether a person was "apt to teach" was judged by its confirmation through conversions. The congregational ecclesiology to which Fuller gave an evangelical and affectionate accent was given particular shape in the act of ordination.

The Shape of Ordinations and Aspects of Congregational Ecclesiology

The leading elements of a tradition's pastoral theology and ecclesiology are embodied in an ordination, the service being a careful delineation of the relationship between a church and its ministers. A study of what James Puglisi has described as the "morphology of ordinations" will "reveal the structuring of

---

[20] See the statement of such a balance between inner desire and outer order by Hercules Collins (d. 1702), *The Temple Repair'd: Or, an Essay to Revive the Long-Neglected Ordinances, of Exercising the Spiritual Gift of Prophecy for the Edification of the Churches; and of Ordaining Ministers Duly Qualified* (London: William and Joseph Marshal, 1702), 58: "The inward Call doth enable him to act in that Station, the outward Call doth enable him to act regularly."

[21] For instances of such occasions during Fuller's Kettering ministry, see Kettering Church Book, 102-103, 138; and for samples of the ordination-like rubric, see Ken R. Manley, *"Redeeming Love Proclaim": John Rippon and the Baptists*, Studies in Baptist History and Thought (Carlisle: Paternoster Press, 2004), 73; and Hayden, "Evangelical Calvinism among Eighteenth-Century British Baptists", 189-191.

[22] Soham Church Book, 40. The Soham church's recognition of itself as a "nursery" for the training of ministers echoes one of the main concerns of the earlier Baptist, Hercules Collins, *The Temple Repaired*, 3-5 and 13: "That the Churches which are the Schools of Christ may be stir'd up to see what Spiritual Gifts God hath given them, and put them into their proper Exercise" and that churches intentionally adopt the practice of regularly testing and instructing ministerial gifts.

the Church" and "determine the relationships which are established in the actions of the liturgical institution".[23] The shape of Particular Baptist ordinations suggests many of the themes of their congregational ecclesiology, several of which will be taken up in this chapter. The ordination service reveals the ecclesiological frame in which the evangelical and affectionate pastor of Fuller's theology was portrayed.

When the Soham congregation invited Andrew Fuller to become their pastor, they set aside a day for prayer and fasting "to plead the Lord's blessing on their future proceedings", and a week later, on 3 May 1775, he was ordained. The Soham Church Book describes the ordination in these words:

> The Church met together with the Pastors and members of other Churches whom they had invited to come and behold their order and having introduced the work of the day by singing and prayer the Church recognized their choice of Brother Fuller to the pastoral office, having previously thereto publicly signified by an elder as a mouth for the rest of the [church] the dealings of the Lord with them since their being destitute of a Pastor, and the steps they had taken relative to their present Pastor, and he gave likewise the same relative to his acceptance of the office. He then gave a short account of his faith in the Doctrines of the Gospel. Then Brother [Robert] Hall [sen.], Pastor of the Baptist Church at Arnsby, Leicestershire, being requested, delivered an address to the Pastor from Acts 20/29–and Brother Emery, Pastor of the Church at Little Staughton, Bedfordshire, delivered an address to the Church from Gal. 5/13 last clause. The whole was then concluded with singing and prayer.[24]

The shape of Andrew Fuller's ordination service at Soham is illustrative of a pattern that was used consistently among Baptist and Independent churches for the whole of the eighteenth century, giving expression to their congregational eccelsiology. Thomas Crosby's first-hand account of the ordination of Joseph Burroughs at Barbican, London, in 1717, for example, shared the same elements with the mid-century settlement of John Collett Ryland at Northampton and the description of dissenting ordinations by Philip Doddridge, all of which would be familiar to the congregation gathered for Fuller's ordination at Soham.[25] That this pattern of ordination service prevailed until the

---

[23] Puglisi, *Process of Admission to Ordained Ministry*, i.27.

[24] Soham Church Book, 45.

[25] Thomas Crosby, *The History of the English Baptists, from the Reformation to the Beginning of the Reign of King George I* (London, 1740), 4.183-189; John Ryland, "History of the Baptist Church at Northampton", autograph notebook, Northamptonshire Record Office, College Street Baptist Church Records, c. 1793; Philip Doddridge, *An Appendix relating to the usual methods of Ordination among the Protest Dissenters*, in *The Miscellaneous Works of Philip Doddridge* (London: Joseph Ogle Robinson, 1830), 883-885. See, also, Horton Davies, *Worship of the English Puritans* (Westminister: Dacre Press, 1948), chap. 13; Robison, "The Particular Baptists in England", 295-324;

end of the century, and beyond, is evident from a survey of the descriptions of mainly Particular Baptist ordinations in John Rippon's periodical, *The Baptist Annual Register*. Over ninety ordinations are described in that final decade of the eighteenth century, the summaries usually a paragraph in length, but occasionally occupying several pages.[26] The morphology of ordination exemplified by Andrew Fuller's ordination service at Soham, which was consistently maintained during eighteenth-century dissenting ordinations, can be outlined as follows:

i.   *Introduction*: The reading of passages of scripture relevant to the ministry of churches and pastors, the most common including Ezekiel 3 and 33, Psalm 132 and 133, Ephesians 4, 1 Timothy 3, and Titus 1.

ii.   *Apologetic*: An introductory discourse on the nature of ordination and pastoral ministry, and an apologetic for dissenting principles and ecclesiology.

iii.   *Examination*: Questions addressed to the church and the minister. The "usual questions" to the church included whether the candidate was in full membership with the church, the process of their discernment and their willingness to voluntarily call this minister as their pastor. A senior deacon usually spoke on behalf of the church, who would signify their assent by raising their right hands. The minister was similarly asked about the steps leading him to this church, and to confirm "his acceptance of the office".

iv.   *Confession*: The minister delivered, as did Fuller, "a short account of his faith in the Doctrines of the Gospel".

v.   *Prayer of ordination*: Delivered extemporaneously by one of the participating ministers.

vi.   *Imposition of hands*: The prayer was almost always accompanied by

---

and Nigel Wheeler, "Eminent Spirituality and Eminent Usefulness: Andrew Fuller's (1754-1815) Pastoral Theology in his Ordination Sermons" (Ph.D., University of Pretoria, 2009), chap. 4. Examples of printed ordination services, introductory discourses, confessions of faith, charges, and sermons can be found in the bibliography.

[26] John Rippon, *The Baptist Annual Register*, 4 vols. (London, 1790-1802). A survey of ordination summaries in the *Evangelical Magazine*, covering roughly the same time period, suggests the same pattern. See, also, the editors' description, *Evangelical Magazine*, 3 (June 1795), 244, of "the mode of ordaining dissenting ministers", which they said was "generally the same".

the laying on of hands by the ministers present.[27]

vii.   *Charge*: Delivered to the minister on some aspect of the ministry, often a more senior pastor, who, as in the case of Robert Hall to Fuller, was a formative influence, or perhaps the ordinand's former pastor or tutor. The most regularly repeated texts for the charge included Acts 20:28, Colossians 4:7, and 1 Timothy 4:16, passages which indicate the duties and character of a minister.

viii.   *Sermon*: Preached to the church on aspects of their relationship to their minister, or their own responsibilities as a church. Regular texts included Deuteronomy 1:38, Ephesians 5:2, and 1 Thessalonians 5:12-13.

ix.   *Prayers and hymns*: Prayers and congregational songs, generally "lined out", were usually interspersed throughout the service, and led by participating ministers.

Such a service would, generally, last three to four hours, occasionally split between morning and afternoon services; in many cases there was, also, an evening service. The ordination of deacons was a frequent addition to the day. This practice of Baptist ordination was stable throughout the eighteenth century, deriving its justification and its ecclesiology from the example of the "Primitive Church".[28]

---

[27] See Ernest Payne, "Baptists and the Laying on of Hands", *Baptist Quarterly* 15 (1954): 203-215. On the imposition of hands as usual but not essential, see Davies, *Worship of the English Puritans*, 224-227. In some cases the imposition of hands seems to have been replaced by "the right hand of fellowship", offered by the other ministers present.

[28] The commissioning services for missionaries to India, under the auspices of the Baptist Missionary Society, were an interesting variation on the pattern of ordination services. The scripture readings and addresses, while overlapping with those chosen for ordinations, had more directly missionary and evangelistic themes; the apologetic was for the missionary enterprise itself (rather than dissenting ecclesiology and order), along the lines of Carey's *An Enquiry into the Obligations of Christians to Use Means for the Conversion of the Heathens* (1792). See Andrew Fuller's addresses on two such occasions in *Works* i.510-515, and descriptions of two missionary commissionings in Haykin, *One Heart and One Soul*, 258-261 and 277-278. More generally, the Indian mission could be considered a kind of experiment in ecclesiology, often raising important questions and testing the limits of congregationalism. As the unofficial theological mentor for the mission, and a frequent correspondent with the missionaries, Fuller often articulated his positions on the nature of apostolic authority, strict versus open communion, and other matters of practical ecclesiology. See, for example,

As Puglisi has suggested from his comparative study, the ordination service gives expression to a church's ecclesiology and its pastoral theology. The elements are often the same, this one or that one receiving more or less emphasis, the words or symbolic actions changing with the tradition. The central and basic liturgical acts of the service are the ordination prayer and the imposition of hands. Beyond these, ordination has usually been comprised of these elements: *electio* (vocational discernment), *iudicum* (the judging of abilities, doctrine, and character), *suffragium* (the free choice and vote of the church), and *testimonium* and *consensus* (the concurrence of neighbouring pastors and churches).[29] The continuity of these elements in varying traditions speaks to an essential continuity in pastoral theology, but of course, it is the discontinuities which characterize particular ecclesiologies. The shape of these Baptist ordinations embodied various aspects of congregationalism: in the apologetic discourse, there was an emphasis on order and discipline which found its roots in both scriptural conviction and social circumstances; in the examination of the candidate and church, there was a strong emphasis on the voluntary election of the people, and the voluntary nature of the pastoral relationship; and in the prayer of ordination and accompanying imposition of hands, there was an embodiment of the tension between independence and association. Adapting the insightful distinctions of Geoffrey Nuttall's study of congregationalism, we might suggest that each of these themes in the ordination service corresponds with an aspect of Baptist ecclesiology and its pastoral theology: *dissenting* in relation to society and establishment, *independent* in relation to other churches, and *congregational* in the relation between pastor and people.[30] The following survey of Andrew Fuller's convictions about these aspects provides a more precise view of the congregational ecclesiology in which he expressed his evangelical and affectionate pastoral theology.

A *Dissenting* Ecclesiology: Ordination and order in scripture and society

The congregational ecclesiology embodied in the Baptist ordination services had an emphasis upon *order* and *regularity* in the organizing and exercise of its

---

"Thoughts on the principles which the Apostles proceeded, in forming and organizing Christian churches, and regulating various religious duties" (1804, *Works* iii.451-459).

[29] Puglisi, *Process of Admission to Ordained Ministry*, i.24-26.

[30] Geoffrey Nuttall, *Visible Saints: The Congregational Way, 1640-1660* (Oxford: Basil Blackwell, 1957), viii. Nuttall actually discusses the churches as Separatist, Congregational, Independent, and Saints. I have, more or less, collapsed the congregational and saintly aspects for the purposes of this discussion, and have referred to separatism as dissent, recognizing that the terms do not always overlap. And by way of clarifying usage, "Independent" will denote the denomination, and "independent" the approach to ecclesiology.

pastoral ministry. This has already been encountered in the way an individual's call to ministry was set firmly within the boundaries of corporate scrutiny. Dissenting concern with an orderly practice of ordained ministry arose from scriptural precedent *and* social conditions, both of which were evident in the opening apologetic discourses of their ordination services.

Andrew Fuller was typical of his peers, grounding the concern for order on the words of Paul: "Let all things be done to edifying.—Let all things be done decently, and in order" (1 Cor. xiv.26, 40)."[31] Michael Walker has observed, "The one underlying concern that held together Baptist churches until the end of the eighteenth century, despite a limited diversity of practice, was that of church order. Their understanding of the ministry has to be related to that concern."[32] Pastoral theology and specific practices were based on biblical injunction, the edification of the church, the use of reason, and the protection of the flock. Dangerous "enthusiasm" or "popish practices" were checked by this emphasis on biblical order and discipline.[33]

If the congregational concern for order in pastoral theology and ordination had scriptural example, it was, also, born of social necessity. It is an indication of the social context of Dissenters that ordination services in the eighteenth century began with an apologetic discourse, in which they offered a defense of the nature of their ordinations, and usually a more general "vindication of the principles of Dissent".[34] These introductory discourses provided a careful delineation of the orderliness and regularity of Baptist and dissenting ordinations and discipline, against the Anglican polemic that such practices were at best an "enthusiastic" denigration of regular preaching, and at worst the creation of alternative authority structures that threatened the order and peace of the nation. While an Established Church was widely seen to be an integral part of the nation's social fabric and constitution, Dissent and radical politics were, often unfairly, paired together.[35] Although there was not the threat of persecution that there had been before the Act of Toleration, the fears of social disorder and radicalism ignited by the revolutions in America and France further threatened to marginalize Dissent in public life.

Contention over orderliness and authority was particularly pointed when

---

[31] Fuller, *Works*, iii.453.

[32] Michael Walker, *Baptists at the Table: The Theology of the Lord's Supper Amongst English Baptists in the Nineteenth Century* (Didcot: Baptist Historical Society, 1992), 137.

[33] Stephen Brachlow, *The Communion of Saints: Radical Puritan and Separatist Ecclesiology, 1570-1625* (Oxford: Oxford University Press, 1988), 182-183.

[34] See an essay by Fuller on this theme in *Works*, iii.463-473.

[35] James Bradley, *Religion, Revolution, and English Radicalism: Nonconformity in Eighteenth-Century Politics and Society* (Cambridge: Cambridge University Press, 1990), 388, 417-419; Robert Hole, *Pulpits, Politics and Public Order in England, 1760-1832* (Cambridge: Cambridge University Press, 1989), 36, 85, 108, 125.

discussing ordination, and it seems that congregational ordinations were often considered, from an Establishment perspective, along the same dangerous continuum as the more "enthusiastic" practices of popular ordinations and lay itinerant preaching, a concern evident at both ends of the century. Richard Greaves has argued that the earlier lay ordination controversy of the seventeenth century was an instance of emerging individualism challenging established institutional and ecclesial authority, as individuals claimed the ability to confirm and act upon the Spirit's internal call to preach.[36] Deryck Lovegrove, exploring itinerant and lay preaching at the end of the "long" eighteenth century, contends that although these activities were often charged as being disorderly or sowing republican ideals, they were, in fact, largely apolitical responses to the conversionist impulse of renewed orthodox Dissent and to the pastoral lapses in the Church of England's parochial system.[37] Establishment fears of enthusiasm or radicalism resulting from typical dissenting lay or itinerant preaching seem to have been exaggerated at both ends of the eighteenth century, since the churches and associations were, generally, careful to insist on oversight and accountability for their preachers.[38] However, the concern remained, and it was left to Dissenters to explain repeatedly that their alternative ordinations were orderly in their own way.

Andrew Fuller's dissenting contemporaries emphasized the necessity of an internal call, insisted on congregational, rather than episcopal, ordination, and were increasingly supportive of itinerant preaching, but they were careful to distance themselves from the spectre of "enthusiasm" by defending the reason and regularity of their practices for ordaining ministers, their benign contributions to public life, and perhaps most importantly, the scriptural warrant for their ordinations.[39] Far from allowing non-episcopal ordinations from degenerating into a subjective and unaccountable ministry, Fuller in fact emphasized that perhaps the key reason for the participation of other ministers and churches in an ordination was to ensure the ordaining church's order and the minister's suitability.[40] Order in congregational ordination was an emphasis

---

[36] Richard L. Greaves, "The Ordination Controversy and the Spirit of Reform in Puritan England" *Journal of Ecclesiastical History* 21, no. 3 (July 1970): 225-241. Comments by Collins, *The Temple Repair'd*, 8-9, suggest that the controversy was still current in 1702.

[37] Lovegrove, *Established Church, Sectarian People*, 132-133.

[38] Greaves, "Ordination Controversy", 227; Lovegrove, *Established Church, Sectarian People*, 162.

[39] See Fuller, *Works*, iii.640-641; Watts, *Dissenters*, ii.357.

[40] Fuller, *Works*, i.524-525; see also *Works*, iii.494, in which he describes the concurrence of ministers in keeping "bad characters" out of pastoral ministry. Daniel Turner, *A Compendium of Social Religion; or the Nature and Constitution of Christian Churches, with the Respective Qualifications and Duties of Their Officers and Members*, 2nd ed. (Bristol: W. Pine, 1778), 67-68, expressed similar sentiments: "I speak thus

mandated by scripture and necessitated by the social position of Dissenters.

An *Independent* Ecclesiology:
Ordination and order between church and association

The large ecclesiological frame of Andrew Fuller's pastoral theology can, also, be studied in its independent aspect, in relation to other churches. This is concisely expressed in a note appended to the end of the staunchly independent Soham church's record of Fuller's ordination: "Note—The Pastors of the other Churches disclaimed all authority or superintendency over or amongst us in any act whatever wherein they assisted or made requests, we maintaining that form of Church government called Independency."[41] Their forthright claim notwithstanding, the shape of that very ordination service, and others of which it was typical, actually presents a more complicated picture, suggesting a tension between independence and association. Ordination was considered an act of the local church, yet the service, itself, was presided over, almost exclusively, by neighbouring ministers. Ordination services began with an apologetic for congregational government, usually delivered by a minister from outside the congregation. Most poignantly, during the prayer of ordination the hands laid on the ordinand were those of other ministers, and not those of the church that had chosen him. Deryck Lovegrove has noted this same incongruity in early nineteenth-century association literature as congregationalists became more active and cooperative in evangelism: "In spite of this contemporary emphasis upon the resilience and vitality of the congregational principle, it is impossible to ignore the real movement towards association, interdependence and the growth of external authority: a process not capable of reversal, arising as it did from the confluent pressures of permanent social change and the practicalities of concerted evangelism."[42] Within this tension between independency and association, how did Andrew Fuller describe the source and scope of ordained ministry, and what were the emphases of his congregational ecclesiology as viewed from this angle?

The act of ordaining, and the pastoral ministry and authority that derived from it, was conceived to belong to the local church by its voluntary choice,

---

cautiously and with so many restrictions in favour of mere popular ordinations, because I apprehend too great an indulgence here would open the way for bold and forward men, to thrust themselves unqualify'd into the christian ministry; the consequence of which, must be the destruction of all public order in the church, and the bringing the public worship of God into contempt, as we see amongst the fanatics of the present day."

[41] Soham Church Book, 45.

[42] Lovegrove, *Established Church, Sectarian People*, 29. See also Deryck Lovegrove, "Idealism and Association in Early Nineteenth Century Dissent", in *Voluntary Religion*, ed. W. J. Sheils and Diana Wood, Studies in Church History (Oxford: Basil Blackwell, 1986), esp. 304-305.

rather than finding its authority from without. Fuller wrote to a Glasgow church seeking advice, "Every church, I conceive, is competent to appoint and ordain its own officers."[43] His Independent contemporary Edward Williams (1750–1813) asserted, "We profess .... that as the right of ordaining is primarily and chiefly vested in the *society itself*, so it must be considered as *their act*."[44] In an ordination sermon exploring the nature of a church's obedience to its pastor, Fuller insisted on the free and independent election of their minister as the essence of ordination, writing, "It is necessary that your pastor be *freely chosen by you* to his sacred office."[45] He continued:

> If your pastor, I say again, had been imposed upon you by any human authority, against or without your own consent, I should not be able to prove, from the Scriptures, that you were bound to obey, or submit to him. But it is not so. You have heard him and known him; and from an observation of his spirit and conduct, and an experience of the advantages of his ministry, you have chosen him to watch over you in the Lord.[46]

The examination of an ordinand's conversion narrative, confession of faith, and understanding of pastoral vocation, and the corresponding questions to the church to confirm their voluntary choice of this minister, were the public culmination of what was actually a much longer process of congregational examination. The questions were anything but perfunctory, following as they did at least a year of probationary ministry, a process which reflects a seriousness in sharp contrast, it has been suggested, to the laxity and informality of ordination examinations in the Church of England and, indeed, the lack of standards in many of the professions.[47] Fuller's defense of this independency in election was an echo of the remarks of John Sutcliff in his introductory discourse earlier in the same ordination service:

> Now, the power of chusing [*sic*], such as we approve; such as we have first tried and proved; such as appear to possess the qualifications necessary for such stations in the church: together with the power of rejecting them when they act unworthy of their character, is a privilege so evidently our native right, and so

---

[43] Andrew Fuller, letter to a church in Glasgow, February 25, 1804, Typewritten transcription, Angus Library, Regent's Park College, Oxford.

[44] Edward Williams, "An Introductory Discourse on the Nature of an Ordination", in *Three Discourses Delivered at the Ordination of the Rev. Daniel Fleming; at Nuneaton, in Warwickshire* (Coventry: M. Luckman, 1793), 7. See Fuller, *Works*, iii.459-63; and Ward, "Pastoral Office", 317.

[45] Fuller, *Works*, i.197.

[46] Ibid.

[47] Peter Virgin, *The Church in an Age of Negligence: Ecclesiastical Structure and Problems of Church Reform 1700-1840* (Cambridge: James Clark & Co., 1989), 137-138.

plainly consonant to the practice of the primitive church, as recorded in the New Testament, that we stand astonished at the manner in which it is surrendered by multitudes.[48]

One could argue from this emphasis on "chusing" and election that the climax of the ordination service was actually the dual affirmation of voluntary consent, or the declaration of a contract, rather than the ordination prayer itself. Or, in other words, the ordination was enacted by the declaration of mutual consent, and was commissioned in an orderly way in the prayer and the participation of other ministers; the essence, though, was in the voluntary election of the congregation.[49]

The impulse of voluntarism was a crucial aspect of Fuller's congregational and independent ecclesiology, and was the foundation for the ongoing pastoral relationship with a particular congregation; "The connexion of pastor and people, in dissenting churches, is altogether voluntary. There are no bonds to bring them together, or to keep them together, but love."[50] Voluntarism was not only a principle of initial election, but, as Fuller's language of loving,

---

[48] John Sutcliff, "Introductory Discourse", in John Ryland, Andrew Fuller, John Sutcliff, and Thomas Morgan, *The Difficulties of the Christian Ministry, and the Means of Surmounting Them; with the Obedience of Churches to Their Pastors Explained and Enforced ... Delivered ... At the Ordination of Thomas Morgan, to the Pastoral Office* (Birmingham: J. Belcher, 1802), 5.

[49] Note the comment by Puritan Thomas Hooker, quoted in Nuttall, *Visible Saints*, 88: "Election of the people rightly ordered by the rule of Christ, gives the essentials to an Officer. ... [Ordination] doth not give essentials to the outward call of a Minister. [It] presupposeth an Officer constituted, does not constitute; therefore it's not an act of Power, but Order." See, also, on the strong tradition of independency within congregational ecclesiology: Brachlow, *The Communion of Saints*, 162; B.R. White, *The English Separatist Tradition: From the Marian Martyrs to the Pilgrim Fathers* (Oxford: Oxford University Press, 1971), 63, 152-153; Benjamin Keach, *The Glory of a True Church, and Its Discipline Display'd* (London, 1697), 16; Gill, *Body of Divinity*, ii.579-580; Watts, *Dissenters*, i.317.

[50] Fuller, *Works*, i.529; cf. i.478, 497. The voluntary nature of ordination and pastoral authority was grounded, in congregational ecclesiology, in the voluntary constitution of the local church. John Locke's (1632-1704) assertion that churches are "onely voluntary societyes which men by their owne consent enter into for the ends of Religion", was echoed by eighteenth-century congregationalists. John Locke, "Critical Notes upon Edward Stillingfleet's *Mischief* and *Unreasonableness of Separation*", in *John Locke: Writings on Religion*, ed. Victor Nuovo (Oxford: Clarendon Press, 2002), 75. On Locke's influence on ecclesiology, see Alan P.F. Sell, *John Locke and the Eighteenth-Century Divines* (Cardiff: University of Wales Press, 1997), chap. 5. See, also, Fuller, *Works*, iii.348; Gill, *Body of Divinity*, ii.566; Turner, *Compendium of Social Religion*, 21.

affectionate bonds indicates, was, also, crucial to the ongoing practice of pastoral care. At the heart of this statement of congregational order and discipline, we find evidence of Fuller's evangelical and affectionate pastoral theology. It has been noted that an emphasis on voluntarism within Anglican Latitudinarian pastoral theology was a crucial element of its renewal and encouragement of diligent pastoral care, still within the parochial system, exhibited most distinctly by Gilbert Burnet's *Discourse of the Pastoral Care*.[51] This association between voluntarism and renewed pastoral practice was one reason why Fuller and his contemporaries found their congregational ecclesiology as conducive to evangelical transformation as the ecclesiological innovations of John Wesley's Methodist societies. Frederick Dreyer has argued, for example, that Wesley conceived his authority to direct the connexion of societies in consensual and voluntary terms: "I cannot guide any soul unless he consent to be guided by me. Neither can any soul force me to guide him, if I consent not".[52] Interestingly, Dreyer also observes Wesley's explicit differentiation between voluntary authority and ordination; his authority in the connexion derived not from his ordination as a minister, but rather, from voluntary consent. As an independent and congregationalist, by contrast, Fuller asserted that *the church itself* was constituted as a voluntary society, and not only societies within or outside it. And in terms of pastoral theology, he emphasized the voluntary essence of *ordination and the pastoral relationship itself*, rather than circumventing ordination to validate voluntary pastoral authority.

Evangelical Anglicans who scrupled the perceived irregularity of Methodist societies but wanted the advantages of the "gathered church", revived the use of voluntary religious societies within the parish to encourage serious evangelical piety.[53] John Newton (1725-1807) planted a number of such *ecclesiolae in ecclesia* at Olney, and to one correspondent offered this enthusiastic evaluation: "I think nothing has been more visibly useful to strengthen my heart, and to unite the people closely together in bonds of love."[54] Fuller, also, perceived that a voluntary and affectionate relationship between pastor and people was the most suitable bond for the promotion of evangelical religion: "Christian love is

---

[51] Burnet, *Discourse of the Pastoral Care*, 96, 99; and Goldie, "John Locke, Jonas Proast and Religious Toleration", 165-166; Walsh and Taylor, "Introduction", 17-18; Jeremy Gregory, "The Eighteenth-Century Reformation: The Pastoral Task of Anglican Clergy after 1689", in Walsh et al., *The Church of England, c.1689-c.1833: From Toleration to Tractarianism* (Cambridge: Cambridge University Press, 1993), 69-70; Walsh, "Religious Societies", 279, 282. For a concise statement of voluntarism and individual commitment as a background to the emergence of evangelicalism, see Noll, *The Rise of Evangelicalism*, 147-148.

[52] Dreyer, *Genesis of Methodism*, 104; see also 93, 100-101.

[53] Walsh, "Religious Societies", 297.

[54] As cited in Hindmarsh, *John Newton*, 200.

love for Christ's sake. ... Personal religion is now to be the bond of union."[55]
"Personal religion" is a phrase nicely expressing evangelicalism's concern for a
sincere and voluntary faith, and it is *this* which is to be, Fuller asserted, the
"bond of union". Fuller's voluntary description of the pastor's relationship with
those in his church was heightened, or further defined, by employing the
language of affectionate religion. "An affectionate concern after their
salvation", Fuller wrote, is "one of the most important qualifications for the
ministry."[56] Isabel Rivers suggests that in the evangelical dissenting tradition,
the essence of revived personal religion "lay in the relationship between
minister and congregation, a relationship based on close knowledge of the heart
and close application by the minister of evangelical doctrine to the special
circumstances of the individual member of the congregation".[57] So, while
Newton and Fuller shared this common concern for the voluntary nature of the
bonds which promoted evangelical piety, they differed on the *location* of such a
pastoral relationship, with Fuller insisting that the voluntarily-gathered
congregation, itself, could be the place of personal renewal.[58]

How, then, did Fuller reconcile this emphasis on voluntary election and
congregational independence with the prominent leadership of other ministers
and the significantly associational cast of the ordination service? What did
Fuller believe was being symbolized in the imposition of hands? The laying on
of hands was a flashpoint for debating the independent nature of ordination, due
in large part to sacerdotal associations the practice obtained by its use in
Anglican and Roman Catholic rubrics.[59] Although the congregational churches

---

[55] Fuller, *Works*, i.523.

[56] Ibid., i.508.

[57] Rivers, *Reason, Grace and Sentiment*, i.171.

[58] Independent Edward Williams, "An Introductory Discourse", similarly, argued that
the congregational form of ordination is "better calculated to answer the great ends of
the pastoral relation" (8). He suggested that a people who are "awakened to a true sense
of spiritual and eternal things, are anxiously desirous of the ministration of the word of
God and his ordinances" can choose a minister "whose views and feelings are similar to
their own" (8). .... "Our mode of establishing a relation between a pastor and his flock,
is in itself, we think, better calculated to promote Christian discipline and social
affection. ... A union founded in love, and hopes of usefulness in promoting the cause of
God, however attended with imperfection, has advantages not a few. Social affection
takes place of a distant reserve; counsel and advice are sought without embarrassment
..." (10).

[59] Nutall, *Visible Saints*, 91. On the Anglican rubric, see Paul Bradshaw, *The Anglican
Ordinal: Its History and Development from the Reformation to the Present Day*, Alcuin
Club Collections (London: SPCK, 1971), especially his comments, pages 105-112, on
attempts to revise the ordinal during the eighteenth century, and the growing adherence
to Apostolic Succession. See, also, Walker, *Baptists at the Table*, chaps. 3 and 4, for the
Baptist response to the nineteenth-century Catholic renewal; and Puglisi, *Process of
Admission to Ordained Ministry*, vol. 2. Although it was probably the "establishment" of

usually incorporated the act because of New Testament precedent, it was singled out for ecclesiological clarification. The denial of presbyterian authority or episcopal succession was vividly expressed by the image of the "empty hands": John Sutcliff denied that the laying of ministerial hands upon an ordinand "convey[ed] any extraordinary gifts, or additional qualifications to the person ordained, fitting him for the work upon which he is entering. No; Our hands are empty".[60] John Gill thought the matter quite straightforward: "The hands of ministers being now empty, and they having no gifts to convey through the use of this rite, of course it ought to cease, and should."[61] And, Charles Spurgeon (1834-1892), later, posed the logical question of independent eccesiology, "Since there is no special gift to bestow, why in any case the laying on of empty hands?" and answered it by forgoing such an ordination.[62]

Having fenced the imposition of hands against possible episcopal misinterpretation, Fuller went on to explain the grounds upon which he justified his frequent participation in the practice:

> The only end for which I join in an ordination, is to unite with the elders of that and other churches in expressing *my brotherly concurrence in the election, which, if it fell on what I accounted an unsound or unworthy character, I should withhold.* Though churches are so far independent of each other as that no one has a right to interfere in the concerns of another without their consent, unless it be as we all have a right to exhort and admonish one another, yet there is a common

---

the Church of England, rather than a more voluntary constitution, that was Fuller's principle source of contention (see *Works*, iii.459-473), in discussions of ordination it was not uncommon to invoke this language of succession and sacerdotalism, since the Church's rubrics, if not always its actual practice, invited this ecclesiological distinction. Typical of Fuller and his peers was this disavowal: "In doing this [i.e., imposition of hands], I claim not to be a successor of the apostles, any otherwise than as every faithful pastor is such ... nor to impart power or 'authority to administer the gospel ordinances'"; Fuller, *Works*, iii.494.

[60] Sutcliff, "Introductory Discourse", 7.

[61] Gill, *Body of Divinity*, ii.583. See pages 581-584 for Gill's very congregational exegetical argument that in the book of Acts the action signified the people's extension of hands in voting rather than imposition on the head of the ordinand. Walker, *Baptists at the Table*, 122, misreads Gill as encouraging the practice of laying on of hands.

[62] Charles Spurgeon, *The Autobiography of Charles H. Spurgeon*, ed. Susannah Spurgeon and W.J. Harrald (Philadelphia: American Baptist Publication Company, c. 1897-1900), i.355; see the whole of chap. 31, "Divine and Human Ordination", and his comment, i.357, "It seems to me that other ministers have no more to do with me as your minister, than the crown of France has to do with the crown of Britain". See also Doddridge, *Appendix*, 885; and Timothy George, "The Ecclesiology of John Gill", in *The Life and Thought of John Gill (1697-1771): A Tricentennial Appreciation*, ed. Michael A.G. Haykin (Leiden: Brill, 1997), 232.

union required to subsist between them, for the good of the whole; and so far as the ordination of a pastor affects this common or general interest, it is fit that there should be a general concurrence in it.[63]

Fuller mediated the tension between congregational independence and cooperative common interest with voluntary "consent" on the part of the church and orderly "concurrence" on the part of the other ministers. The wider association of churches affirmed what the local church had already enacted by their election. As reasons for the involvement of other ministers in the ordination and its imposition of hands, Fuller suggested that it encouraged good order and discipline, that such "common union" promoted evangelical "common interest", and that it enabled a vigilant self-scrutiny among ministers.[64]

A vignette provides a case study to clarify Fuller's independent views on congregational ordination and pastoral ministry. During one of his trips to Scotland, Fuller was approached by a deputation from a Baptist church recently formed at Old Deer, north of Aberdeen.[65] Their minister had been elected from among their membership, and was "set apart" by the church alone, there being no other Baptist minister within reasonable proximity. Since "they could not ordain him by the laying on of hands of the presbytery" they were in some doubt as to whether the ordination was valid, and inquired whether Fuller would come to ordain him. Fuller replied that the test of orderliness was satisfied in their circumstances, and that the ordination by the church was indeed valid: "I told them, if I had been present when Bro. Leslie was set apart to his office, I would have joined in the laying on of hands with all my heart: but considering that act is valid, I could not conscientiously do it now. Such a conduct would seem as if I had something to impart to him, which I had not. They seemed pretty well satisfied."[66] Faced with this "desert island" scenario, Fuller clarified that he considered the imposition of hands by neighbouring ministers as keeping with New Testament order and example, but that the nature of ordination was founded in the free choice of the church itself; the imposition of hands was proper and orderly, but not essential. In fact, in a letter to a church in Glasgow on another occasion, he suggested that since the local

---

[63] Fuller, *Works*, iii.494.

[64] See, also, ibid., i.523; iii.495. It may be that such self-conscious monitoring of doctrine and character among dissenting ministers represented a step towards professionalization. Anthony Russell, *The Clerical Profession* (London: SPCK, 1980).

[65] Andrew Fuller, letter to W. Ward, 12 Sept. 1805, Baptist Missionary Society–Home Officers: Letters and Papers, Angus Library, Regent's Park College, Oxford. There is another account of this experience in Fuller, *Works*, iii.495. Also, see Fuller's to a church in Glasgow, April 24, 1804 (Typewritten transcription, Angus Library, Regent's Park College, Oxford), where he addressed many of the same issues.

[66] Fuller, letter to Ward, 12 Sept. 1805.

church is competent to ordain, in the absence of other ministers, "let the members of the Church lay hands on him, while one of their most aged brethren prays over him and lays his hands upon him".[67] While Fuller was an advocate of associational cooperation, he denied that pastoral authority was imposed by other churches or imparted by other ministers, but was bestowed and maintained by the independent local church's voluntary and affectionate election.

A *Congregational* Ecclesiology:
Ordination and order between pastor and people

Considering the inner life of the local church—the *congregational* aspect of ecclesiology—one discovers an almost necessary tension between the ordained ministry and the priesthood of all believers. W.R. Ward has observed that rather than "abolishing the Pastoral Office" as the Quakers did, the earliest congregationalists "reshaped the Office in the context of the spiritual life of the congregation".[68] This reshaped pastoral ministry was defined entirely with reference to the congregation: its election voluntary, its authority derivative, its compass the local church, and the acts of ministry and discipline shared (to a greater or lesser extent). Within that context, where did Andrew Fuller locate the common ground and the boundaries between pastor and people?

Whereas the tension between voluntary election and association was expressed in the act of laying on of hands in the ordination, the issue of presidency at the ordinances of baptism and Lord's Supper provides a useful lens through which the relationship between pastor and people can be viewed. While maintaining a concern for order, Fuller asserted that both ordinances and ordained ministry were derived from the presence of Christ in the local church; ordained ministry was not essentially defined by the ordinances, since these were actions of the local church.[69] Since "the ministry was not of the essence of the Church" its authority "was both derived from and circumscribed by the authority of the congregation".[70] Fuller demonstrated a surprising willingness to understate the uniqueness of ordained ministry in order to foster a more active and evangelistic congregationalism.

That the authority to preside over the exercise of the ordinances was not given to ministers by other ministers is typical of Fuller's congregational heritage; more unexpected was his claim that it was not even limited to ordained ministers:

---

[67] Fuller, letter to a church in Glasgow, February 25, 1804.

[68] Ward, "Pastoral Office", 317; the whole essay is a study of this theme in Protestantism.

[69] Fuller, *Works*, i.522.

[70] White, *English Separatist Tradition*, 63.

It appears to me that every approved teacher of God's word, whether ordained the pastor of a particular church or not, is authorized to *baptize*; and with respect to the *Lord's supper*, though I should think it disorderly for a young man who is only a probationer, and not an ordained pastor, to administer that ordinance, yet I see nothing objectionable, if, when a church is destitute of a pastor, it were administered by a deacon or an aged brother; I know of no scriptural authority for confining it to ministers. Nay, I do not recollect any mention in the Scriptures of a minister being employed in it, unless we reckon our Lord one. I do not question but that the primitive pastors, whose office it was to preside in all spiritual affairs, *did* administer that ordinance as well as receive and exclude members; but as a church when destitute of a pastor is competent to appoint a deacon or aged brother to officiate in these cases, I know of no reason to be gathered from the Scriptures why they should not be the same in the other.[71]

Fuller makes three important points about the relationship between ordination and the ordinances, or pastor and people. First, he contended that ordinances are a function of general congregational teaching rather than ordination, a comment, it may be taken, on the priority of pulpit over table among the heirs of the Puritans. Second, leading in the ordinances need not be confined to ministers, but order dictates that it be a responsibility carried out only by someone with the express recognition and trust of the church, which qualified a respected deacon, but not an uncalled probationer.[72] Third, he appealed to a comparison between ordinances and decisions about church membership; while on the surface simply pragmatic, Fuller drew attention to the basic nature of congregational discipline: a congregation that is competent to decide those who will communicate with them at the table is competent to appoint those who will serve at the table. Ordained ministry and the ordinances are both primarily *of* and *by* the church, rather than the ordinances being *of* the ordained ministry and done *for* the church.

When asked by a Baptist church in Edinburgh whether, in the absence of a pastor, they were right to have "communicated at the Lord's table without the assistance of a minister", Fuller replied, "I told them that probably there were

---

[71] Fuller, *Works*, iii.494.

[72] Cf. ibid., iii.495. Walker, *Baptists at the Table*, 124 and 131, overstates Fuller's restrictions on this point. While Fuller considered it disorderly for a probationer or otherwise unordained person *with ministerial aspirations* to preside at the table, he more liberally affirmed the orderly right of the church to appoint others among the congregation, typically "aged brethren", to so preside. Walker's observation, 131-132, from George Wallis' diary, that the Kettering church did not, in fact, observe "ordinance day" during Fuller's final illness is more apropos, and does query how much of an activist Fuller was for this position in his own church. On the other hand, the period in question was one of mourning for their long-time pastor, and the ministry of Fuller's unordained assistant, John Keen Hall, did not have unanimous approval. See Wallis "Memoirs", May - November 1815.

few of my brethren who might be of my mind; but I had long been of opinion that there was no scriptural authority for confining the administration of the Lord's supper to a minister."[73] Fuller's willingness to limit the exclusive province of ordained ministry, or more accurately, to recognize the full ministry of the congregation, distinguished him from the received tradition. Benjamin Keach (1640-1704), for example, responded to the question of whether a deacon or teacher could lead in the ordinances by writing, "You may as well ask, May a Church act disorderly? Why were Ministers to be ordained, if others unordained might warrantably do all their Work?"[74] Fuller even suggested to the Edinburgh church that the common practice, which he, himself, had performed, of neighbouring ministers serving at the Lord's Supper in the absence of their own, was an unnecessary concession to propriety: "I could wish, however that it were otherwise, and that every church, when destitute of a pastor, would attend to the Lord's supper *among themselves*."[75] It would be a more consistent expression of congregational ecclesiology to affirm the local church had the right to exercise the whole of their discipline and ministry.

Here, too, there might be a useful comparison with other evangelical ecclesiological innovations. John Wesley's connexional ecclesiology intentionally operated alongside or outside the church and its ordained ministry, and for that reason, as John Walsh observed, "the societies were deliberately stinted at the administration of the Sacraments, which Wesley saw as the crucial line dividing a voluntary society from the Church itself".[76] Fuller's vigorous congregationalism suggested that the local church, itself, was a voluntary society, and that both its ordinances and ordained ministry were rooted there. Anglican evangelicals within the church made good use of voluntary religious societies as a way to encourage robust spiritual growth and active ministry, but Fuller's concern was, to an extent beyond even other congregationalists, to recover a lively and evangelical ministry of the church itself. He insisted, "It is not for ministers only to take an interest in the salvation of men; the army of the Lamb is composed of the whole body of Christians. Every disciple of Jesus should consider himself a missionary"; and to that end, Fuller advocated for the local church to recover its own priestly ministry, and that the renewal of such vital and evangelical congregational ministry was as much a sign of its evangelicalism as the sending of missionaries.[77]

---

[73] Fuller, *Works*, iii.496.

[74] Keach, *Glory of a True Church*, 16-17. See Gill, *Body of Divinity*, ii.592 for a similar opinion.

[75] Fuller, *Works*, iii.496.

[76] Walsh, "Religious Societies", 293.

[77] Fuller, *Works*, i.315. Cf. ibid., i.171, 434.

Summary: An *Affectionate* and *Evangelical* Ecclesiology

This exploration of the ecclesiological context of Andrew Fuller's pastoral theology has developed his claim that a "lively and evangelical ministry" and congregational "discipline and government" could coexist. Fuller was attempting to demonstrate that congregational order and discipline were not the unique property of high Calvinists, nor were voluntarism and evangelicalism only expressed in the ecclesiological experiments of Anglican and Methodist religious societies. Rather, evangelical faith was not only compatible with, but in fact could thrive in, a robust congregational discipline supported by an orderly ordained ministry. This is a key reason why Fuller turned his attention to the evangelical renewal of pastoral theology, as well as advocating other expressions of that renewal alongside and beyond the local church.

Considering the personal and corporate contexts of a call to pastoral ministry, Fuller balanced congregational discipline and its orderly ministry with affectionate desire and evangelical concern. The typical morphology of an ordination service embodied the kind of congregational ecclesiology which Fuller advocated, expressing its various tensions and aspects: dissenting (in relation to scripture and society), independent (in relation to other churches), and congregational (the relation between pastor and people), a survey of which defines Fuller's particular expression of congregational ecclesiology and pastoral theology. We noted that the dissenting concern with an orderly practice of ordained ministry arose from scriptural precedent *and* social conditions. Fuller's expression of the independent aspect of congregationalism laid particular stress upon the voluntary nature of ordination and how such affectionate bonds between pastor and people were particularly conducive to evangelical ends. And, in his discussion of ordination and the ordinances of baptism and the Lord's Supper, Fuller demonstrated a surprising willingness to understate the uniqueness of ordained ministry in order to foster a more active and evangelistic congregationalism. Fuller combined what might be described as "low clericalism" and "high congregationalism". Fuller's evangelical pastoral theology expressed a congregational ecclesiology and theology of ordained pastoral ministry characterized by voluntarism, conversionist aims, and affectionate bonds.

Fuller's congregationalism was the arena in which he expressed his evangelicalism, as the Methodist connexion or Anglican religious societies were the arenas where others expressed their evangelical commitment to voluntary religion and conversionism. It was not in spite of his evangelicalism that Fuller was vigorously congregational, but because of it; his evangelical and affectionate emphasis was the motivation for promoting active congregationalism and renewed pastoral ministry.

Figure 7: Portrait of Andrew Fuller from *The Baptist Magazine*
(October 1815)

CHAPTER 3

"Beware that you do not preach an unfelt gospel."

Preaching:
The *Application* of an Evangelical and Affectionate
Pastoral Theology

The Northamptonshire pastor and educator, Philip Doddridge, exemplified the dissenting expression of evangelicalism early in the eighteenth century, and its usually eager reception of the Evangelical Revival. Sketching the elements of an evangelical pastoral theology, he observed, "He who would be generally agreeable to dissenters, must be an evangelical, an experimental, a plain and an affectionate preacher."[1] Andrew Fuller, that Northamptonshire pastor of the later eighteenth century, exemplified the renewal of such an evangelical pastoral theology in the transformed dissenting churches, a renewal that was particularly evident in his preaching: *plain* in composition and delivery, *evangelical* in content and concern, and *affectionate* in feeling and application.

The transformation of dissenting churches, Deryck Lovegrove has convincingly demonstrated, was expressed and effected in part by the rapid growth and wide promotion of itinerant preaching by settled pastors, lay preachers, and full-time evangelists.[2] Questions of order and education, the relationship between ministers and laity, and competing priorities for settled pastors were all raised as a result of this new practice and its evangelistic concern. Andrew Fuller was himself an advocate of village and itinerant preaching, had a circuit of village preaching stations surrounding Kettering, and encouraged several lay preachers from his church (some of whom were later ordained) in the practice.[3] But, the weekly congregational preaching of Fuller

---

[1] Philip Doddridge, *Free Thoughts on the Most Probable Means of Reviving the Dissenting Interest* (1730), quoted in Rivers, *Reason, Grace, and Sentiment*, i.164

[2] Lovegrove, *Established Church, Sectarian People*, esp. 14-40.

[3] See Fuller, *Diary*, entries for 1784, for a sense of this village preaching; Fuller, *Works*, i.221-228, for a sermon specifically noted as preached in a village setting; Ibid., i.148, iii.484, on his advocacy of the practice; Fuller, *Remains*, 24-46, for the sermon "The

or his contemporaries did not remain static while evangelical concern produced change elsewhere; as the first chapter demonstrated, the wholesale renovation of preaching and pastoral care was one of the inciting motivations of *The Gospel Worthy of All Acceptation*. It is the task of this chapter to explore what that transformed preaching looked like, and to see how Fuller's evangelicalism was defined and practiced in this, the "principal work [of] a Christian minister", the aspect of pastoral ministry most directly affected by his evangelical renewal.[4]

Diarist George Wallis recorded that the Baptist meeting house during Fuller's preaching ministry was home to a "profusion of truly Evangelical, melting and affectionate discourses".[5] Fuller's evangelically-renewed pastoral theology was manifest in his concern that preaching be plain, evangelical, and affectionate.

"The Simplicity of the Gospel": Fuller's Plain Style of Preaching

Andrew Fuller embraced a "plain style" of address that was particularly well suited for his evangelical aims: vernacular in language, simple in composition, intentionally perspicuous, and more affecting than affected in its rhetoric. He, also, used common sermon forms which had a tendency toward application, and an extemporaneous delivery which made his sermons more affectionate and direct.

This plain style was not uniquely the product of evangelicalism, representative as it was of a more general move toward plain prose in literature and correspondence, as well as homiletics. If it did not originate with them, still it was widely and effectively employed by evangelicals, who recognized that the increasingly voluntaristic relationship between preacher and hearers required an address more understandable and persuasive. Fuller not only employed the plain style for evangelical aims, he, also, defined simplicity in preaching in terms of the affections (a direct and heartfelt address to the experience of the hearer) and evangelical intentions (not removing very far from the basic Christian gospel).

Fuller observed that "the form or manner in which a sermon is composed and delivered is of some importance, inasmuch as it influences the attention, and renders the matter delivered more or less easy of being comprehended and retained".[6] Examining the mode of composition and delivery of sermons, then,

---

Conversion of Sinners" (1802), preached before the Baptist Itinerant Society; and Fuller, *Works*, i.717-723, for a letter on sermon composition written expressly for the use of lay preachers from his own congregation.

[5] Fuller, *Works*, i.712.

Wallis, "Memoir", 28 April 1805; cf. 14 July 1811; 23 Feb. 1812; 15 March 1812; 23 April 1815.

[6] Fuller, *Works*, i.717.

will be an aid to understanding how Fuller intended to communicate with his own hearers, with whom he held in common some basic rhetorical expectations. Some study of the art of Fuller's sermon composition and that common rhetorical context, also, aids modern readers, as Wilson Kimnach noted in his study of the preaching of Jonathan Edwards: "A modern reader must respect the formal requirements of the sermon in much the same way as he might those of the ballad or even the sonnet if he is to appreciate what is going on in it."[7] Familiarity with the development of the plain style, Fuller's use of common sermon forms, and his extempore delivery, will help the reader of his sermons distinguish innovation from convention, and appreciate how Fuller employed this style for his evangelical purposes.

Fuller's application of the "plain style"

Fuller confessed himself to be an inheritor, rather than an innovator, in his approach to sermon composition. His friend and biographer, J.W. Morris rightly observed one of the most important sources for Fuller and his contemporaries: "One of the first books that Mr. Fuller read, after entering on the ministry, and which he frequently recommended to others, was CLAUDE's ESSAY on the composition of a Sermon; and to that work he acknowledged himself indebted, for any just ideas which he entertained upon the subject."[8] When Fuller wrote his own essay on the composition of a sermon to provide some instruction for lay preachers from his congregation who were engaged in village evangelism, he concluded by noting that "Those, however, who wish to pursue this inquiry, and to become acquainted with the different methods of constructing a discourse, will meet with ample information in 'Claude's Essay on the Composition of a Sermon,' as well as from other publications of subordinate merit."[9]

---

[7] Wilson Kimnach, "General Introduction to the Sermons: Jonathan Edwards' Art of Prophesying", in *Jonathan Edwards, Sermons and Discourses 1720-1723*, ed. Wilson H. Kimnach, vol. 10, *The Works of Jonathan Edwards*, ed. Harry Stout (New Haven: Yale University Press, 1992), 32. On the common fund of rhetorical theory among sermon hearers and readers in the seventeenth century, see Fraser Mitchell, *English Pulpit Oratory from Andrewes to Tillotson: A Study of Its Literary Aspects* (London: SPCK, 1932), 43.

[8] Morris, *Memoirs*, 69.

[9] Andrew Fuller, "Essay on the Composition of a Sermon: or, Plain and Familiar Thoughts, Addressed to a Young Minister from his Pastor", in *The Preacher; or Sketches of Original Sermons, Chiefly Selected from the Manuscripts of Two Eminent Divines of the Last Century, For the Use of Lay Preachers and Young Ministers*, ed. anon. (Philadelphia: J. Whetham & Son, 1842), 21. This essay is the same as that included in *Works* i.717-723, although the reference to Claude has been left out of that version. Rolf P. Lessenich, *Elements of Pulpit Oratory in Eighteenth-Century England*

Fuller's reliance on Claude's *Essay on the Composition of a Sermon* was not unique, representing, as it did, something of a consensus in eighteenth-century protestant homiletics. Jean Claude's (1616-1687) *Essay* was translated and annotated at great length by Baptist Robert Robinson (1735-1790) in 1779, and was, also, made available in more abridged editions by Anglican Charles Simeon (1759–1836) in 1796, and Independent Edward Williams in 1800. The ready reception of this French Huguenot work demonstrates its accord with the trajectory of English sermon composition, away from the "metaphysical" style of Lancelot Andrewes (1555-1626) and John Donne (1572-1631), toward a less ornamental "plain style".

The impetus toward simplicity and plainness in art and rhetoric, Peter Auksi has argued, is a significant stream within the Christian tradition.[10] By removing or reducing excess, artifice, and needless complexity, the "plain style" makes possible at least three aims: "Plainness in expression enables audiences to measure without distraction the spiritual, moral quality of the agent; to attend to the substance as opposed to the mere covering of expression; and to concentrate on their relationship to the prime giver of the gifts being enjoyed, God."[11] It is perhaps unsurprising, then, that it was the Puritans who reaffirmed plainness and simplicity in the history of English sermon composition, in response to the "metaphysical preachers".[12] Influential in this Puritan turn toward plainness was the thought of Peter Ramus (1515-1572), who subjected rhetoric to logic, making style a servant to the subject of an oration. Ramist thought, also, paired doctrine with application, providing the organizing structure (doctrine and use) and movement (toward application to individual cases) of Puritan sermons.[13] This was eminently the case for William Perkins, who asserted in his *Art of Prophesying* that two things are essential in preaching: "(i) the hiding of human wisdom, and (ii) the demonstration or manifestation of the Spirit".[14] Of the

---

(1660-1800) (Köln: Böhlau-Verlag, 1972), 84 n. 6, cites Fuller's recommendation of Claude to lay preachers as a statement of Claude's general usefulness, and as representative of his wide acceptance. Cf. the mention of Claude by Samuel Pearce in correspondence included in Fuller, *Works*, iii.443. Jean Claude, *Essay on the Composition of a Sermon*, 3rd ed., trans. Robert Robinson, 2 vols. (London: Scollick and Wilson & Spence, 1788).

[10] Peter Auksi, *Christian Plain Style: The Evolution of a Spiritual Ideal* (Montreal and Kingston: McGill-Queen's University Press, 1995).

[11] Ibid., 7-8.

[12] See Perry Miller, *The New England Mind: The Seventeenth Century* (New York: Macmillan, 1939), chap. 12; David Hall, *The Faithful Shepherd: A History of the New England Ministry in the Seventeenth Century* (Chapel Hill: University of North Carolina Press, 1972), 52-55.

[13] Miller, *New England Mind*, 326; Donald K. McKim, "The Functions of Ramism in William Perkins' Theology", *The Sixteenth Century Journal* 26, no. 4 (1985): 503-517.

[14] William Perkins, *The Art of Prophesying, with the Calling of the Ministry* (1606;

former, Perkins elaborated that in public exposition, a minister's private use of "the general arts and of philosophy" "should be hidden from the congregation, not ostentatiously paraded before them. As the Latin proverb says, *Artis etiam celare artem*—it is also a point of art to conceal art."[15] This same Ramist influence and "calculated carelessness of finish" has been noted by Wilson Kimnach in the preaching of Jonathan Edwards, whose sermons Andrew Fuller held up as exemplary.[16] In outlining general rules for sermons, Claude emphasized clarity and comprehension, warning that obscurity is "the most disagreeable thing in the world in a gospel-pulpit". Rather, "a preacher must be *simple* and *grave*. *Simple*, speaking things full of good natural sense without metaphysical speculations; for none are more impertinent than they, who deliver in the pulpit abstract speculations, definitions in form, and scholastic questions, which they pretend to derive from their texts."[17] By the time Fuller read Robinson's English edition of Claude's *Essay*, there had been almost a century of the development of a plain style in English prose more generally, a departure from the proliferation of sub-headings which had characterized some Puritan preaching, and a fairly broad consensus as to simplicity in Protestant preaching across the theological spectrum, allowing, of course, for individual personality and theological content.[18]

The emphasis on plainness and simplicity in preaching was an important element of Fuller's instructions about preaching, and his own sermons were characterized by clarity, applicability, and biblical language. One of the editors of his collected *Works*, Joseph Belcher, wrote of Fuller's preaching, "You are struck with the clearness of his statements; every text is held up before your view so as to become transparent."[19] Joseph Ivimey's appraisal was that Fuller "greatly excelled in the simplicity of his compositions".[20] Fuller employed the language of simplicity to encompass the whole of the preaching experience, taking in content, composition, and delivery. He emphasized that plainness of pulpit speech best reflected the perspicuity of the scriptures, and was most conducive to usefulness and personal application for a wide range of hearers. He and many of his peers were in hearty agreement with the sentiment nicely expressed by Robert Robinson in an essay included in his edition of Claude's *Essay*: "Plainness in religion is elegance, and popular perspicuity true

[15] reprint, Edinburgh: Banner of Truth Trust, 2002), 71.

[16] Ibid.

[17] Kimnach, "General Introduction", 17, 32; Fuller, *Works*, i.719-720.

[18] Claude, *Essay*, i.11, 21.

Mitchell, *English Pulpit Oratory*, 275, 304, 371; Lessenich, *Elements of Pulpit Oratory*, 1-2.

[19]
[20] Fuller, *Works*, i.197, editor's note.

Quoted by Thomas Nettles, *By His Grace and for His Glory: A Historical, Theological, and Practical Study of the Doctrines of Grace in Baptist Life* (Grand Rapids: Baker Book House, 1986), 109.

magnificence".[21]

Preaching, insisted Fuller, should be plain and simple so that its central content—the gospel of Jesus Christ—could be clearly communicated. This gospel, he said, is a message of deep wisdom, "and therefore we ought to possess a deep insight into it, and to cultivate great plainness of speech".[22] Not only should preaching be as perspicuous as the gospel it reveals, but simplicity should, also, be the standard by which its subject matter should be selected. In an ordination sermon entitled, "The Satisfaction Derived from Godly Simplicity", on 2 Corinthians 1:12, Fuller contrasted "fleshly wisdom" with "the grace of God" and noted that preaching that is characterized by the latter will be simple and sincere. Of the matter of preaching, godly simplicity means that "the doctrine we preach will not be selected to please the tastes of our hearers, but drawn from the Holy Scriptures".[23]

Fuller was, likewise, concerned that the language, as well as the doctrines, of sermons be drawn from the language of scripture. "There are many sermons, that cannot fairly be charged with untruth, which yet have a tendency to lead off the mind from the simplicity of the gospel."[24] Convinced of the perspicuity and inspiration of the scriptures, he emphasized the Spirit's witness to the *simplicitas evangelica*, rather than the use of language and terminology which instead highlighted the cleverness of the speaker: "To be sure, there is a way of handling Divine subjects after this sort that is very clever and very ingenious; and a minister of such a stamp may commend himself, by his ingenuity, to many hearers: but, after all, God's truths are never so acceptable and savoury to a *gracious* heart as when clothed in their own native phraseology."[25] Plainness, as a standard for the subject matter of sermons, meant for Fuller that they focus on the gospel of Jesus Christ, that their language be scriptural, and that their aim be the salvation of their hearers: "characterized by simplicity; not thinking of ourselves, but of Christ and the salvation of souls".[26]

Plainness of style and composition, also, meant that preaching would be more than "merely an art", and that it would be focused in its construction, and understandable and useful to the least-educated of hearers.[27] A sermon, insisted Fuller, should not be a "mob of ideas", multiplying headings and themes, but should instead have "unity of design".[28] "A preacher, then, if he would interest a judicious hearer, must have an object at which he aims, and must never lose

---

[21] Robert Robinson, "A Brief Dissertation on the Ministration of the Divine Word by Publick Preaching", in Claude, *Essay*, ii.iv.

[22] Fuller, *Works*, i.495-496.

[23] Ibid., i.540.

[24] Ibid., i.140; see also Fuller, *Diary*, 10 January 1780.

[25] Fuller, *Works*, i.140.

[26] Ibid., i.540.

[27] Ibid.

[28] Ibid., i.719.

sight of it throughout his discourse", something which Fuller wrote was "of far greater importance than studying well-turned periods, or forming pretty expressions". He wrote that it is this unity and simplicity which "nails the attention of an audience".[29] A sermon that is composed of a central theme (and, as we shall see, one that is constructed with a familiar rhetorical structure) is an aid to the judicious and attentive hearer, but Fuller was, also, concerned that the less educated in the congregation can, also, comprehend and apply the message:

> In general, I do not think a minister of Jesus Christ should aim at fine composition for the pulpit. We ought to use sound speech, and good sense; but if we aspire after great elegance of expression, or become very exact in the formation of our periods, though we may amuse and please the ears of a few, we shall not profit the many, and consequently shall not answer the great end of our ministry. Illiterate hearers may be very poor *judges* of preaching; yet the effect which it produces upon them is the best criterion of its real excellence.[30]

The concern for the simple vernacular in pulpit language, as a reflection of their congregations, was characteristic of evangelical preaching in New Dissent, Methodism, and among the evangelical Anglican clergy, in contrast to the learned discourses prepared (or read) by many ministers in the church. Anthony Russell notes the frequent observation that "a large part of the appeal of nonconformity lay in the more energetic and colloquial preaching of ministers whose social and educational situations more closely approximated that of their congregations".[31] These evangelicals were less concerned about the sermon as literature *per se*, and preached with comprehension and application in mind, so that their sermons could be "read", rather, on the pages of hearers' lives, as they applied the gospel (see 2 Corinthians 3:1-3).

Fuller's desire for simplicity in preaching, also, included studied reticence in

---

[29] Ibid.

[30] Ibid., i.717.

[31] Russell, *Clerical Profession*, 88-89. Fuller's modest parentage, theological self-education, and provincial manners corresponded with a great proportion of his hearers. J.W. Morris' generally positive assessment of Fuller's ministry and preaching included this candid observation, *Memoirs*, 68-69: "He had none of that eloquence which consists in a felicitous selection of terms, or in the harmonious construction of periods; he had a boldness in his manner, a masculine delivery, and great force of expression. His style was often deformed by colloquialisms and coarse provincials." It may, also, be instructive to compare the "plain style" of preaching, and Fuller's intentional accounting for the capacities of illiterate hearers, with the principles of hymnody espoused by Isaac Watts, in his *Hymns and Spiritual Songs*: "The Metaphors are generally sunk to the Level of vulgar Capacities, I have aim'd at Ease of Numbers and Smoothness of Sound, and endeavoured to make the Sense plain and obvious"; quoted by Hindmarsh, *John Newton*, 267.

delivery, as well as composition. He eschewed performance as much as scholasticism: "Avoid all affectation in your manner—Do not affect the man of *learning* by useless criticisms: many do this, only to display their knowledge. Nor yet the *orator*, by high-sounding words, or airs, or gestures. Useful learning and an impressive delivery should by no means be slighted; but they must not be affected ...."[32] As we will see below, rather than affected gestures or emotions, Fuller urged preachers to enter into their ministry with true godly feelings and affection, which would be communicated more authentically than those which were contrived. He echoes John the Baptist's "I must decrease, he must increase", by writing, "In preaching the gospel, we must not imitate the ORATOR, whose attention is taken up with his performance, but rather the HERALD, whose object is to publish, or proclaim, good tidings."[33]

Finally, preaching that is plain and perspicuous to the hearer must be grounded, wrote Fuller, in the straightforward, diligent, and spiritual study of the preacher: "To preach the gospel as we ought to preach it requires, not the subtlety of the metaphysician, but the simplicity of the Christian."[34] Preacher and hearer, alike, come to the gospel in its simplicity, so that, spiritually discerned, it can be practically applied.

The genres of Fuller's sermons

Not only did Fuller adhere to Claude's emphasis on the plain style, but he, also, followed his guidance in the genres and structures of sermons. The structures of composition were usually very near the surface of eighteenth-century sermons, which to modern sensibilities may seem wooden. We are reminded again, however, that in a period in which sermons had a more prominent place in public discourse, hearers and preachers had common rhetorical expectations, whose familiar logic was an aid to listening, understanding, and memory.[35] Attending to the distinctions between sermon types similarly assists later readers to feel the appropriate force of statements, and to appreciate nuance.

Following the general categories used by Claude and others, Fuller distinguished between *expositions*, characterized by "expounding the Scriptures", and *sermons*, described as "discoursing on Divine subjects", the latter including both doctrinal and practical discourses.[36] Or in other phrasing, he referred to them as "textual" and "topical" approaches to preaching.[37] In what follows, we will survey the nature of expositions, and then the two kinds

---

[32]
[33] Fuller, *Works*, i.489.
[34] Ibid., i.716.
[35] Ibid., i.496.
[36] See Kimnach, "General Introduction", 33-35, 167; and Fuller, *Works*, i.717.
[37] Fuller, *Works*, i.712.

Ibid., i.721, 724-725. Lessenich, *Elements of Pulpit Oratory*, 84, refers to Claude's division in this manner as "analytic" (textual) and "synthetic" (topical).

of sermons, doctrinal discourse and practical exhortations.

i. Expositions

In 1805, Fuller wrote a dedicatory preface in his *Expository Discourses on the Book of Genesis* to the church at Kettering, having ministered there for 22 years. Among his remarks are these observations about his practice of preaching in the expository mode, and its effect on himself and his people:

> During the last fifteen years it has, as you know, been my practice to expound among you, on a Lord's day morning, some part of the Holy Scriptures, commonly a chapter. From all that I have felt in my own mind, and heard from you, I have reason to hope these exercises have not been in vain. They have enabled us to take a more connected view of the Scriptures than could be obtained merely by sermons on particular passages; and I acknowledge that, as I have proceeded, the work of exposition has become more and more interesting to my heart.[38]

Fuller notes here that an expository discourse might consider a chapter, or other large section of scripture, as with his published sermons on Genesis and Revelation. Another approach, often used by Fuller, was what he sometimes called "expository remarks", organizing his exegetical and doctrinal observations according to the phrasing of a shorter verse of scripture. In both cases, doctrinal observations and practical exhortations are introduced as they arise in the text.

Fuller's practice of weekly, continuous exposition of the books of the Bible was a particularly pastoral, settled practice, depending on the weekly interaction of preacher and people. While each sermon would offer insight and relevance by itself, it was, as Fuller noted, the "connected view of the Scriptures" which was its chief value. Recommending the practice, he wrote, "It is also advantageous to a people that what they hear should come directly from the word of God, and that they should be led to see the scope and connexion of the sacred writers. For want of this, a great number of Scripture passages are misunderstood and misapplied."[39]

ii. Doctrinal sermons

The expository sermons provided, particularly in their weekly context, a wide and connected view of the scriptures. Some texts required more sustained elaboration, and some themes necessitated a more systematic or synthetic form of discourse: "There is a great variety of *subjects*, both in doctrinal and practical religion, which require to be illustrated, established, and improved;

---

[38]   Fuller, *Works*, iii.1. For a sense of the scope of Fuller's expositional preaching, see Ryland, *Life of Fuller*, 382.
[39]   Fuller, *Works*, i.712.

which cannot be done in an exposition. Discourses of this kind are properly called *sermons*."[40]

Concurrent with the evolution of the "plain style" of English preaching, there developed a tripartite structure for doctrinal sermons, the movement of which was from text to application. Fuller delineated this outline by saying that doctrines were to be "illustrated, established, and improved", or, as he described it in other places, the truth of a text was to be "matured, proved, and improved" in a discourse.[41] Whereas, in his expository sermons Fuller would consider a chapter of scripture, in the doctrinal discourses he typically meditated upon a single verse or phrase, and drew out its central truth or doctrine.

This general outline of "the plain and profitable way of doctrine, reasons, and uses" was urged by the English Puritans, and by, among others, John Wilkins (1614-1672) in *Ecclesiastes, Or, A Discourse Concerning the Gift of Preaching as it falls under the Rules of Art*, which was a formative influence on Jonathan Edwards.[42] The influence of Ramist logic and Puritan affective piety ensured that the doctrine explained and proved would then receive personal application to a variety of cases and circumstances.

Fuller's employment of this pattern is evident in a sermon he preached to the church at an ordination, an outline of which clarifies its use. "The Reward of a Faithful Minister" is a discourse on 1 Thessalonians 2:19: "For what is our hope, or joy, or crown of rejoicing? Are not even ye in the presence of our Lord Jesus Christ at his coming?"[43] By way of exordium and introduction are two brief paragraphs relating the text to both ministers and Christians, generally. The doctrine and the divisions of the sermon are expressed simply and directly: "The import of this passage is, that *the salvation of his hearers is the reward of a faithful minister*. In discoursing on this interesting subject, I shall endeavour to explain it—account for it—and apply it."[44] Fuller's *explanation*, first, clarifies that such a reward means that a minister disclaims any other kind of rewards or mercenary motives, and, second, that the text's language signifies the necessity and perseverance of true religion. He accounts for, or "*proves*", the text's doctrine, by drawing the logical inferences that 1) faithful ministers will have the same mind as Christ, 2) that they will rejoice in what brings honour to Christ (namely, people believing and remaining in Him), and 3) that they will love and value the souls of people as Christ does. In "*applying the subject*", he urges the church to see their "deep interest", urging them to respond to the salvation offered them, to see that the reward of the minister in this case coincides with their own interests, and poignantly reminds them that at

[40] Ibid., i.714.
[41] Ibid., i.714, 724-725.
[42] Miller, *New England Mind*, 339-340, Kimnach, "General Introduction", 28-33.
[43] Fuller, *Works*, i.542-543.
[44] Ibid., i.542.

Judgement they will have to be presented in some way, and how much better it would be if it were in rejoicing over their salvation.

iii. Practical exhortations

The doctrinal sermons had, by virtue of their structure, a logical momentum toward application, but scriptural texts which were essentially practical or exhortative required a different mode of discourse. Fuller recommended his own practice:

> I have generally found that exhortations include matter for a twofold division, and have very commonly proposed, first to inquire into the meaning and extent of the exhortation; secondly, to enforce it. Under the former there is room to expiate upon every idea or branch of the duty. In the latter, to introduce any motive that serves either for that or other texts.[45]

The twofold structure of these exhortations is manifestly expressed in sermon titles which contain the recurring phrases: "The ___ Explained and Enforced", "The Qualifications and Encouragements of ___", and most ubiquitously, "The Nature and Importance of ____". In each of these, the meaning and extent of the exhortation was explored, and, then, various motives and benefits for its duty (or negative consequences for its neglect) were given. The great majority of Fuller's ordination charges were preached in this exhortatory mode. The common genres which he employed were embodiments of the plain style, and had a momentum toward application which suited Fuller's evangelical aims.

Fuller's extempore delivery

Fuller's plain style of composition was complemented by his practice of extempore delivery, which allowed him to address his hearers more directly and affectionately. It is, certainly, the case that Fuller's habits of study and delivery were, in some measure, dictated by his demanding schedule, but his delivery, nevertheless, was conducive to his evangelical preaching.

In the wake of the Evangelical Revival, James Downey has observed, "The carefully prepared manuscript (the Tillotsonian ideal) and statuesque delivery gave way to a mode of address more extemporaneous and gesticulary."[46] As we will discuss below, Fuller was not among the most 'enthusiastic' of evangelical preachers, but he was known for being affectionate, direct, and riveting. His

---

[45] Ibid., i.725.

[46] James Downey, *The Eighteenth Century Pulpit* (Oxford: Clarendon Press, 1969), 20. See also, Watts, *Dissenters*, ii.177-178; and Manley, *Redeeming Love Proclaim*, 253. By contrast, Russell, *Clerical Profession*, 87, notes that handbooks produced for Anglican clergy in the late eighteenth century almost universally condemned extempore preaching.

son suggested that "Sleepy hearers were not often found in Mr. Fuller's congregation", (although the custom of afternoon services occasionally tested their alertness).[47] Fuller recommended that preachers not "overload [their] memory with words", but work from a simple organizing and mnemonic outline. "Never", he urged, "carry what you write into the pulpit."[48] This practice encouraged simplicity of argument, and as Perry Miller suggested of Puritan extempore preaching, working from memory was an aid to stirring up "inward emotion" in preaching, making it both more engaging and more affectionately "interesting" to the hearers.[49]

The comments of Fuller's biographer and publisher, J.W. Morris, about Fuller's preparation of sermons, seems an accurate representation:

> The composition of a sermon seldom cost Mr. Fuller much trouble; owing to his constant habits of thinking, it was generally the easiest part of all his labours. And though it would be highly improper to propose such an example for imitation, especially to young ministers, and those less competent to the undertaking, yet an hour or two at the close of the week would commonly be sufficient for his purpose; and when much pressed for time, as he often was, his preparations would be made on the Sabbath, during the intervals of preaching; yet it required more than common strength of mind to digest such discourses as he was in the habit of delivering. It should also be observed that Mr. Fuller's sketches for the pulpit consisted only of a few brief outlines, committed to memory, and enlarged at the time of preaching. He never filled up any written discourse, except when it was intended for the press, and after it had been delivered.[50]

If such a method of composition had been Fuller's habit for most of his preaching ministry, it seems certain that it became a necessity after the formation of the Baptist Missionary Society in 1792, when heavy responsibilities of travel and correspondence were added to his pastoral duties, all of which were complicated by an increasing number of health problems. One of Fuller's letters, written from Kettering in 1793 to John Fawcett, provides his own perspective:

> Thanks for your kind inquiry after my health. I am still incapable of mental application, without suffering from the head-ache, and probably I shall never be much better. I am just able to preach twice on a Lord's day. As to composing sermons, I have reason to be thankful that, in twenty years' labour, my mind has been, in some measure, furnished with knowledge, otherwise I should now find it difficult to go on. However, my heart is as much in my work as ever; and my

---

[47] A.G. Fuller, *Andrew Fuller*, 80.
[48] Fuller, *Works*, i.724.
[49] Miller, *New England Mind*, 301.
[50] Morris, *Memoir*, 70.

anxiety for the salvation of souls has increased. Under these impressions, I find but little difficulty in preaching without much premeditation.[51]

Fuller's extempore preaching was, then, rooted in the overall pattern of his ministry, but these comments to Fawcett, also, point to his affectionate ("my heart is as much in my work as ever") and evangelical ("my anxiety for the salvation of souls has increased") aims in preaching, both of which were aided by his extempore delivery.

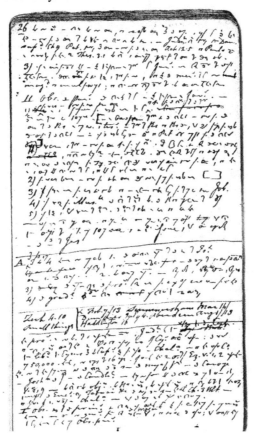

Figure 8: A page from Fuller's sermon notebook

---

[51] Andrew Fuller to John Fawcett, transcribed letter, 1793, Angus Library, Regent's Park College, Oxford.

There is, also, an interesting documentary witness to Fuller's practice of extemporaneous preaching. He remarked in one of his essays on preaching: "I have found it not a little useful to keep a book in which I write down all my expository notes, which, though illegible to others, yet answer two purposes to myself: first by looking them over before I go into the pulpit, I have a clear understanding of every sentence; and, secondly, I can have recourse to them on future occasions."[52] There remains at the Baptist church in Kettering a manuscript notebook of Fuller's sermon outlines and expositions, which may be one of those books so helpful to him, if illegible to others. It is numbered "XXX", and so apparently one of a series, and dated from 26 August to 19 December 1813. The book's pages measure 4 by 7 inches, each full of notes in a form of shorthand, and even this in small handwriting. The expository notes and / or sermon outlines occupy about a page each, and seem to be entered as occasion dictated. In many cases, it is noted where and when the sermons were preached, whether at his own congregation at "Kettg Ch.", village preaching at, for instance, Haddington, or abroad for the Baptist Missionary Society, at places like Aberdeen. The book has a "table of texts" at the front, with the passages listed in canonical order with page numbers. Even with the small, shorthand writing, the notes seem to furnish only the barest outline, and would scarcely be appropriate for reading in a dimly-lit meeting house for an evening sermon. The notebook is an eloquent witness to Fuller's commitment to simple outlines in the plain style, the use of familiar, application-oriented preaching genres, and his habit of extempore preaching, a practice that would be as suited to his evangelical and affectionate aims at home in Kettering as it would while village preaching.[53]

---

[52] Fuller, *Works*, i.714.

[53] Fuller's practice of outlined manuscripts and extempore delivery makes it difficult to get a sense of the actual experience of a preached sermon as an oral event, particularly in his own church setting. The sermons that were published during his lifetime would have been transcribed and, then, expanded, often with the addition of notes. Those additional sermons which were collected posthumously are more likely to have been abbreviated versions of the preached sermon, relying on the outlined notes. In addition, a great many of Fuller's printed sermons were preached at extra-congregational events, such as ordinations, association meetings, funerals, or London fund-raising meetings, possibly because Fuller's notes for these were of greater length, or possibly as an editorial decision about the significance of the events. Perhaps most representative of his *congregational* preaching, at least in the expository manner, are his discourses on Genesis (Fuller, *Works*, iii.1-200). Interestingly, contained in the collected editions of his works are also a few sermons which were transcribed by W.B. Gurney (1777-1855) (Fuller, *Works*, i.379-384; and sermons in Fuller, *Remains*). Gurney's grandfather was the inventor of Brachygraphy shorthand, and himself published further editions of his grandfather's shorthand manual, and was appointed shorthand writer to Parliament, which is all to say that his transcription of these sermons can be taken as reliable

"Preaching Christ": The *evangelical* nature of Fuller's preaching

To say that Fuller preached the gospel, or that he was an evangelical preacher, is not to say enough. Fuller, himself, felt the need to define and defend the gospel and the evangelical nature of preaching ministry in his own day, and delineating Fuller's convictions about preaching helps us to appreciate what made him an evangelical, as well as a Baptist and a Calvinist. Fuller was concerned with just this further definition of evangelical preaching when he said, in an ordination charge, "I have heard complaints of some of our young ministers, that though they are not heterodox, yet they are not evangelical; that though they do not propagate error, yet the grand, essential, distinguishing truths of the gospel do not form the prevailing theme of their discourses."[54] Those essential truths which by their prevalence distinguished evangelical from generally orthodox preaching focused on the person and work of Jesus Christ. As Fuller told ministerial students, "the person and work of Christ must be the leading theme of our ministry".[55] Similarly, in an ordination charge Fuller declared "preaching Christ" to be "the grand theme of the Christian ministry". He continued unequivocally, "Preach Christ, or you had better be any thing than a preacher. The necessity laid on Paul was not barely to preach, but to preach Christ."[56]

Fuller's insistence on Christ as the criterion for preaching was representative of evangelical preaching, but it could, of course, have been otherwise. While the movement toward a plain style of composition was more or less common across the theological boundaries of the eighteenth century, the perceived purposes of preaching in the religious lives of hearers were more varied. High Calvinists, evangelical Calvinists, and evangelical Arminians had distinct, if overlapping, understandings of the agency of God, preacher, and hearers in the preaching event, and these were markedly different again from those of Unitarians, Deists, and Universalists. The goal and content of preaching might be perceived as a reformation of morals, the cultivating of civil society, the encouragement of good works, or perhaps an exercise in classical rhetoric, and it is partly over against these competing visions of the preaching task that Fuller wanted to define its evangelical nature.

> I have also heard many an ingenious discourse, in which I could not but admire the talents of the preacher; but his only object appeared to be to correct the grosser

---

specimens of Fuller's sermons *as preached*.

[54] Fuller, *Works*, i.509. Cf. also Fuller, *Remains*, 359: "It is possible for a minister not to go into any remarkable errors, and yet all his lifetime be aside from the doctrine of the cross. We may deliver sermons, and deliver them well; and yet they may have very little of the savor of Christ in them. The leading theme should be the doctrine of the cross .... Let all our preaching have some relation to the cross."

[55] Fuller, *Works*, i.516.

[56] Ibid., i.503.

vices, and to form the manners of his audience, so as to render them useful members of civil society. Such ministers have an errand; but not of such importance as to save those who receive it, which sufficiently proves that it is not *the gospel.*[57]

Evangelical preaching's emphasis upon the gospel of Jesus Christ can be further delineated by examining, in turn, the central prominence of the atoning death of Christ on the cross, and the zeal for conversion effected by the preaching of that doctrine.

The centrality of the cross of Christ

The specific doctrinal content of Andrew Fuller's preaching of the gospel was the atoning death of Jesus on the cross, an emphasis described as "crucicentrism" by David Bebbington in his delineation of the marks of evangelicalism.[58] Emphasizing the cross, Fuller wrote, "*Every sermon should contain a portion of the doctrine of salvation by the death of Christ. ... A sermon, therefore, in which this doctrine has not a place, and I might add, a prominent place, cannot be a gospel sermon. It may be ingenious, it may be eloquent; but a want of the doctrine of the cross is a defect which no pulpit excellence can supply.*"[59] Elsewhere, Fuller insisted: "The death of Christ is a subject of so much importance in Christianity as to be essential to it. ... It is not so much a member of the body of Christian doctrine as the life-blood that runs through the whole of it. The doctrine of the cross is the Christian doctrine."[60] This doctrine entailed the urgent need of sinful humanity and the salvation exclusively made available through the atoning death of Christ. In his sermon, "The Nature of the Gospel and the Manner in Which It Ought to be Preached", Fuller relayed his conviction that "Salvation by Jesus Christ is God's last remedy—his ultimatum with a lost world."[61] In another charge, he urged the preacher to "Hold up [Christ's] atonement and mediation as the only ground of a sinner's hope.—It is the work of a Christian minister to beat off self-righteous hope, which is natural to depraved man, and to direct his hearers to the only hope set before them in the gospel."[62] Understanding the atoning death of Jesus to be the unique source of salvation, Fuller urged that evangelical preaching give it repeated emphasis and great prominence.

Not only did Fuller give the doctrine of the cross prominence above all other

---

[57]
    Ibid., i.715; cf. i.503, iii.487. See Russell, *Clerical Profession,* 88; Lessenich, *Elements of Pulpit Oratory,* chap. 7.
[58]
[59] Bebbington, *Evangelicalism in Modern Britain,* 3, 14-17.
    Fuller, *Works,* i.716.
[60] Ibid., i.310.
[61]
[62] Ibid., i.495.
    Ibid., i.503.

themes in preaching, but his evangelical crucicentrism was, also, expressed by emphasizing the cross's connection and interrelation with other themes in doctrine, practice, and, therefore, preaching. Early in his Kettering ministry, reading in John Owen prompted him to write in his diary, "'Christ, and his cross be all my theme.' Surely I love his name, and wish to make it the centre in which all the lines of my ministry might meet!"[63] Later, to his father-in-law, Rev. William Coles, Fuller wrote from Ireland, "The doctrine of the cross is more dear to me than when I went. I wish I may never preach another sermon but what shall bear some relation to it."[64] The relation was found in his treatment of both scriptures and doctrine, the cross of Christ being, for Fuller, something of an exegetical touchstone, and to mix metaphors, the centre of gravity for his theological system.

Fuller believed that the whole of scripture bears witness to Jesus, and that, therefore, expositions of any part of the Bible inevitably manifest something of his person or work. The necessary centrality of Christ did not impose a restriction upon the preacher's themes, but rather, supplied a central thread through the canon: "If you preach Christ, you need not fear for want of matter. His person and work are rich in fulness. Every Divine attribute is seen in him. All the types prefigure him. The prophecies point to him. Every truth bears relation to him. The law itself must be so explained and enforced as to lead to him."[65] He was careful to note, however, that this did not lead to allegorical, ahistorical, or speculative readings of the scriptures (particularly the Old Testament), but, rather, took a more nuanced view that these connections were typical, prophetic, trinitarian, and theological in nature.

Considering a plan of systematic divinity, begun at the request of John Ryland (though never completed), Fuller intended to "begin with the centre of Christianity—*the doctrine of the cross*". He asserted that "The whole of the Christian system appears to be *presupposed by* it, *included in* it, or to *arise from* it."[66] Fuller believed that this doctrine functioned as the "heart" to which all doctrinal and practical subjects were organically connected. By holding to a christological gravitational centre for systematic divinity, Fuller was able to maintain the priority of God's gracious initiative in a way consistent with his Calvinist beliefs, but in a less specious way than by making the decrees of God that centre. It was on this basis that Fuller was able to insist on human agency in conversion, and on obedience in sanctification, without venturing into either Arminianism or high Calvinism. Fuller did not wish to neglect other themes in doctrine or duties in practice, but did contend, "that as there is a *relation* between these subjects and the doctrine of the cross, if we would introduce

---

[63] Fuller, *Diary*, 21 August 1784.

[64] Fuller, *Works*, i.83.

[65] Ibid., i.503. Cf. "The Uniform Bearing of the Scriptures on the Person and Work of Christ", ibid., i.702-704.

[66] Ibid., i.690.

them in a truly evangelical manner, it requires to be *in that relation*".[67]

Zeal for conversion

The centrality of Christ and the exclusivity of his atoning death as the means of salvation leads to and is combined with an urgency, in evangelical preaching, for sinners to respond to that gospel in conversion. Just as evangelicalism is marked by giving proportionally more attention to the cross of Christ than, say, the incarnation, so, also, does evangelicalism afford to conversion more urgent concern within the *ordo salutis* than to, for example, election or assurance. Such an evangelical "conversionism" or "zeal for conversion" was expressed by Fuller in a sermon on "The Conversion of Sinners", in which he urged both settled and itinerant preachers to consider "the importance of a zealous perseverance in the use of all possible means for the conversion of sinners".[68]

The emergence of such urgency in conversion was the most significant development in Andrew Fuller's theology and pastoral practice, the story of which was told in Chapter One. Central to that account was Fuller's rediscovery of preaching as a central means by which conversion was effected, and seeing the "unconverted" as the proper recipient of gospel preaching. From being reticent to include invitations to his hearers to respond to the gospel, he went on to write *The Gospel Worthy of All Acceptation* to insist that such conversionist means were the very essence of preaching. From saying, during his first years of preaching at Soham, that he "durst not ... address an invitation to the unconverted to come to Jesus", he came to say in his confession of faith, on settling at Kettering:

> I believe, it is the duty of every minister of Christ plainly and faithfully to preach the gospel to all who will hear it; and, as I believe the inability of men to be spiritual things to be wholly of the *moral*, and, therefore, of the *criminal* kind, - and that it is their duty to love the Lord Jesus Christ, and trust in him for salvation, though they do not; I, therefore, believe free and solemn addresses, invitations, calls, and warnings to them, to be not only *consistent*, but directly *adapted*, as means, in the hand of the Spirit of God, to bring them to Christ. I consider it as a part of my duty, which I could not omit without being guilty of the blood of souls.[69]

As David Bebbington has observed, Fuller's articulation of "duty faith", or the obligation of all people to respond to the gospel, was the essential difference between evangelical and high Calvinists, who otherwise shared a great fund of orthodox and Calvinist theology, a difference with great practical, or we might

---

[67] Ibid., i.716.

[68] Bebbington, *Evangelicalism in Modern Britain*, 3, 5-10, and as cited by Morden, *Offering Christ to the World*, 19; Fuller, *Remains*, 34.

[69] Ryland, *Life of Fuller*, 32, 68.

say pastoral, implications: "If believing was an obligation, preachers could press it on whole congregations. If it was not, they could merely describe it in the hope that God would rouse certain predetermined hearers to faith."[70] In a discussion of what it meant for preaching to be "truly evangelical", Fuller, echoing his argument in *The Gospel Worthy of All Acceptation*, insisted that preaching must be both crucicentric and urgently conversionist to be evangelical:

> Though the doctrine of reconciliation by the blood of Christ forms the ground-work of the gospel embassy, yet it belongs to the work of the ministry, not merely to declare that truth, but to accompany it with earnest calls, and pressing invitations, to sinners to receive it, together with the most solemn warnings and threatenings to unbelievers who shall continue to reject it.[71]

Fuller's evangelical preaching was defined by the prominence of the atoning death of Jesus as the unique hope of salvation, a theme that was central to and connected to all others. This gospel gave him a "rationale for urgent evangelism" leading him to preach in a way that was searchingly personal and inviting in its concern for conversion.[72] As this sense of urgency suggests, Fuller's evangelicalism was not only defined by its content, but, also, its accent, or, in eighteen-century parlance, both its matter and its manner. If its evangelical matter of Fuller's preaching was decidedly Christ-centred and conversionist, the manner of its expression was affectionate.

"Affecting the hearts of the people": The *affectionate* nature of Fuller's preaching

In a letter to William Carey, Fuller wrote from Kettering, "My ♡ has been more drawn out of late than formerly to preach the doctrine of the cross", and that "testifying the way of salvation by Christ" had made an impression on him again, while engaging in evangelistic village preaching.[73] These comments neatly synthesize the crucicentrism and conversionism which we have explored as defining elements of Fuller's evangelical preaching, and, also, make it clear that there was a crucial role to be played by the heart in his preaching: there must be an impression on the affections of both preacher and hearer. Indeed, Fuller insisted that the Christ-centred *matter* of preaching must be accompanied by an affectionate *manner* of delivery, arising from *motives* in the minister's

---

[70] Bebbington, *Evangelicalism in Modern Britain*, 64-65.
[71] Fuller, *Works*, i.717.
[72] Bebbington, *Evangelicalism in Modern Britain*, 64-65.
[73] Andrew Fuller, to William Carey, autograph letter, 25 Aug 1806, Baptist Missionary Society Home Missionary Society papers, Officers: Letters and Papers, Angus Library, Regent's Park College, Oxford.

own evangelical affections. And, so, he could state not only, "Preach Christ, or you had better be any thing than a preacher", but, also, "You had better do any thing than be a minister, if your heart is not engaged in it".[74] Neither the cross nor the heart were negotiable, if pastoral theology and practice were to be evangelical. Or, as Fuller often enjoined, "Beware that you do not preach an unfelt gospel".[75] Fuller's regular use of the vocabulary of the affections— "heart", "feeling", "love", "zeal", "affectionate"—as a defining feature of his preaching, is as much a mark of its evangelical nature as his emphasis on conversion and the cross. So, how did Fuller use the language of the affections to express his evangelicalism? With regard to preaching his affectionate vocabulary generally incorporated three main elements: i) the gospel must be felt and experienced by the preacher in his own life to communicate it to others; ii) a spiritual concern for the conversion of his hearers; and iii) the integration of head and heart, or doctrine and affectionate experience. Each of these elements will be explored briefly.

"If you would affect others, you must feel": Affections and evangelical experience

Fuller employed the language of the affections to denote faith that was practical and experimental, personal and sincere. Affectionate preaching had the deeply felt faith of two subjects in view—both preacher and hearer—and the heart to heart manner of the sermon's delivery. Isabel Rivers has noted that evangelicalism was characterized by orthodox doctrine and personal, "experimental" faith, which meant, she writes, "both the believer's own experience of religion, and acquaintance with the variety of experience of others".[76] It was an affectionate faith which joined doctrine and experience, and

---

[74] Fuller, *Works*, i.503, Fuller, *Remains*, 361.

[75] Fuller, *Works*, i.489. On the particular phrase "unfelt gospel", cf. i.496: "To preach these things with an unfeeling heart is not to preach 'as we ought' to preach"; iii.733: "the heavenly messengers ... did not preach an unfelt gospel". Michael Haykin, *One Heart, One Soul*, 60, notes the use of this phrase in a letter from Bristol student John Geard to John Sutcliff ("never preach an unfelt gospel but continually feel the power and influence of the truths we deliver unto others upon our own hearts"), which Haykin takes as indicative of the "evangelistic spirit which was prevalent at the academy during the principalship of Hugh Evans". Cf., also, its use by John Leland (1754-1841) in America, urging that "it is of the primary importance that the preacher should be clothed with the garment of salvation ... without this robe, he will preach a distant Jesus, by an unfelt gospel, and with an unhallowed tongue"; cited in Iain Murray, *Revival and Revivalism: The Making and Marring of American Evangelicalism, 1750-1858* (Edinburgh: Banner of Truth, 1994), 303.

[76] Rivers, *Reason, Grace, and Sentiment*, i.167. See Kimnach, "General Introduction", 17, summarizing Jonathan Edwards on this theme: "The preacher must believe and feel

which allowed one person to communicate that experience to another, particularly in preaching. Fuller poignantly summarized: "If you would affect others, you must feel."[77] First, then, the preacher's own spirituality or experience of godly affections, and then his expression of that experience through preaching to affect his hearers.

The personal experience of faith, and not merely a disinterested knowledge, is a distinctive marker of evangelicalism and Fuller considered such sincere piety no less essential for evangelical ministers themselves: "We had better be any thing than preachers of the gospel, unless we be personally in it."[78] He recognized, though, that a disjunction between profession and experience was something of a vocational hazard for preachers, and a particularly insidious one at that. Fuller very often distinguished reading, studying, or praying *as a Christian* from doing so *as a minister*. After some conversation at a ministers' meeting at Northampton fairly early in his own pastoral ministry, Fuller wrote in his diary that they agreed that a lack of success in pastoral ministry was not infrequently because of "the want of reading and studying the Scriptures more as Christians, for the edification of our own souls. We are too apt to study them merely to find out something to say to others, without living upon the truth ourselves."[79] This oft-repeated distinction emphasized that the calling of pastors to live as Christians first was prior to, even foundational to, their pastoral vocation. While personal and regular Christian practice tends to enliven the pastor's own affections, engaging in the religious activities that are so much of pastoral work without the heart is apt to make one desensitized, as another of Fuller's comparisons illustrates:

> If we study the Scriptures as Christians, the more familiar we are with them, the more we shall feel their importance; but, if otherwise, our familiarity with the word will be like that of soldiers and doctors with death—it will wear away all sense of its importance from our minds.[80]

While a spiritual sense of divine truth engages both heart and mind, and impresses the beauty and reason of the gospel, handling religion at a professional distance has just the opposite effect, making truth more speculative and impersonal. The ability to have the heart respond to truth, as well as the mind, is the basis of both personal faith, and, also, of an evangelical ministry.

---

[77] intensely what he preaches; he must then communicate his personal feelings with the message so that he preaches experience, as it were".

[78] Fuller, *Works*, i.479.

Ibid., i. 507; see iii.319, where Fuller admonished the members of the Northamptonshire Baptist Association, "Do not float upon the surface of Christianity, but enter into the spirit of it."

Fuller, *Diary*, 30 September 1785. On the distinction between living as a Christian and a Minister, see, also: Fuller, *Works*, i.142, 482, 484, 498, 501, 505, 507, and 517.

[80] Ibid.; on the comparison with surgeons and soldiers, see, also, i.142, , 482, and 501.

Since what is being sought in evangelical preaching is not only intellectual assent, but, also, a personal, affectionate interest, Fuller considered it crucial for the preacher to communicate both doctrine and delight, both the cognitive and the affective, speaking from his own experience. He wrote, "Indeed, without feeling, we shall be incapable of preaching any truth or of inculcating any duty aright. How can we display the evil of sin, the love of Christ, or any other important truth, unless we feel it?"[81] Or, again, "we must preach from the heart, or we shall seldom, if ever, produce any good in the hearts of our hearers."[82] Such an assertion echoes seventeenth-century Baptist Hercules Collins ("that which comes from the Heart is generally carried to the Heart"), and Fuller's older colleague, John Collet Ryland ("To move the Audience, he *first moved himself*; propagated his own Heat to kindle their Passions, and TRANSFUSED HIS VERY SOUL INTO THEIR BOSOMS").[83] Fuller typified that evangelical insistence on both orthodox doctrine and affectionate response, scriptural truth applied to the personal experience of his hearers. He said to one church, "You may as well have no minister, as one that never makes you feel"; the preacher could, Fuller believed, communicate the truth, beauty, or urgency of the scriptures only if such feelings were part of his own spiritual experience. [84]

Questions may be asked, however, about the emphasis on "feeling" in evangelical preaching. The preaching of the early evangelicals has been characterized by James Downey for its "latent emotionalism" and "scriptural idiom", and, more strongly, by Michael Watts as "extempore, emotional, passionate, dramatic, designed to bring the hearer to a pitch of excitement at which he would respond to the call to confess that he was a sinner and that he was in need of salvation".[85] They describe a preaching experience in which the preacher, himself, was highly affected, with an emotional style intended to create a strong sense of attention and connection with his audience, the goal of which was to elicit a highly emotional response to the message. It seems to be implied in these characterizations, though, that there was something of the irrational, if not actually contrived or manipulative, in such preaching, a faith more deeply felt than carefully considered. How does Andrew Fuller's preaching (which was, to be sure, of a different evangelical variety than, say, early Methodist itinerants), and particularly this emphasis on affectionate religion, align with this description of the preaching of evangelical Dissenters?

On the one hand, it is accurate, as far as it depicts Fuller's emphasis on

---

[81]
[82] Fuller, *Works*, i.480.
[83] Ibid., i.546.

Collins, *The Temple Repair'd*, 34, John Collet Ryland, *The Christian Preacher Delineated* (London: D. Nottage, 1757), 8. See, also, Lessenich, *Elements of Pulpit Oratory*, 154-155.
[84]
[85] Fuller, *Works*, i.198.

Downey, *Eighteenth Century Pulpit*, 99; Watts, *Dissenters*, ii.177-178; Manley, *Redeeming Love Proclaim*, 253.

conversion, the importance of direct offers of the gospel to the unconverted, his emphasis on feeling and the heart in both preacher and hearer, and the more emotionally intense and variegated delivery that was enabled by his practice of extempore delivery. On the other hand, such a characterization sets at odds qualities which Fuller laboured to keep in careful balance: Fuller employed the language of the affections precisely because it married deep feelings and considered doctrine. The more recent category of emotions, as Thomas Dixon has argued, tends to be less voluntary and is often defined over against the rational and cognitive, whereas the more nuanced eighteenth century psychology of the affections intentionally avoided that polarization.[86] To clarify that it was not an emotional style of delivery that he was advocating, Fuller contrasted true evangelical affections with affectation: "Affected zeal will not do."[87] He warned preachers against

> an *assumed earnestness*, or *forced zeal*, in the pulpit, which many weak hearers may mistake for the enjoyment of God. But though we may put on violent emotions–may smite with the hand, and stamp with the foot–if we are destitute of a genuine feeling sense of what we deliver, it will be discerned by judicious hearers, as well as by the Searcher of hearts, and will not fail to create disgust.[88]

Just as Fuller's emphasis on a simple and plain style meant adopting an unadorned rhetoric, so the manner of delivery was to be unaffected by contrived emotional expressions or gestures. He continued by explaining that true affections—expressions of love, sorrow, wonder, or gratitude—were the heart's honest response to spiritual and rational understanding of the scriptural message:

> If, on the contrary, we feel and realize the sentiments we deliver, emotions and actions will be the natural expressions of the heart; and this will give weight to the doctrines, exhortations, or reproofs which we inculcate; what we say will come with a kind of Divine authority to the consciences, if not the hearts of the hearers.[89]

Fuller recognized the important place of feelings, the heart, and emotional responses to the gospel, but this emphasis upon the affections did not displace, but rather arose from, thoughtful preaching and reasoned hearing.

Fuller's comments on expressing affections to give weight to a preacher's addresses, also, begin to explain just how an authentically affectionate manner of preaching does more effectively communicate evangelical experience; he noted that natural expressions of the heart give a kind of Divine weight or

---

[86] Dixon, *From Passions to Emotions*, especially 3, 64-65.

[87] Fuller, *Works*, i.480.

[88] Ibid., i.137; cf. i.480.

[89] Ibid., i.137.

authority, a personal testimony to God's message that strikes the hearer with more poignancy than a more disinterested address could do. Richard Baxter, also, suggested some explanation for why the evangelical affections of the preacher himself should make such a difference, noting that "[when] hearts are savingly affected with the doctrine which they study and preach, they will study it more heartily, and preach it more heartily: their own experience will direct them to the fittest subjects, and will furnish them with matter, and quicken them to set it home to the conscience of their hearers".[90] And Isaac Watts noted that "the Affections being once engaged, will keep the Soul fixed to divine Things", and "the Sense of them is imprest [sic.] deeper on the Mind".[91] These observations suggest that the affections, far from being irrational emotions, actually engage the mind to a greater degree, giving the preacher a better sense of proportion and importance within Christian doctrine, and similarly assist the hearer with greater attention and understanding.

Fuller's use of the language of feeling, the heart, and the affections—and his disavowal of feigned affection—signaled the importance of a sincere personal experience of faith, first in the experience of the minister, and, then, by its affectionate communication, in the lives of his hearers.

"An affectionate concern after their salvation":
 Affections and evangelical concern

Fuller used the language of the affections to give warmth and feeling to his particularly evangelical zeal for conversion, the concern for which was discussed above. In his ordination charge, "The Affectionate Concern of a Minister for the Salvation of His Hearers", the use of affectionate language to communicate conversionist concern is, particularly, clear. Fuller wrote that he considered "the feeling of a true minister of Christ towards the people of his charge" and "an affectionate concern after their salvation" to be the kind of important qualifications for the ministry "without which the greatest gifts, natural and acquired, are nothing as to real usefulness". He concluded the charge by exhorting the ordinand: "O my brother, enter into these feelings. Realize them. Let them inspire you with holy, affectionate zeal."[92] The source of such evangelical and salvation-oriented affections? Love. "A Christian minister must love his people, and in proportion as he loves them he will feel

---

[90] Richard Baxter, *The Reformed Pastor*, ed. William Brown (1656; reprint, Edinburgh: Banner of Truth Trust, 2001), 61. Baxter, 150, more generally, observed that "In preaching, there is a communion of souls, and a communication of somewhat from ours to theirs. ... so must the bent of our endeavours be ... to warm their hearts, by kindling in them holy affections as by a communication from our own."
[91] Watts, *Discourses of the Love of God*, 164.
[92] Fuller, *Works*, i.508, 510.

concerned for their eternal happiness."[93]

It was this sense of the urgent necessity of the salvation of his hearers which would compel the preacher to give proportionally greater weight to the doctrine of the cross, and to preach in a way that encourages conversion. So, Fuller observed, "The gospel is a message of love, and therefore it ought to be preached with great affection. ... Cultivate the affectionate. Christ wept over sinners, and so must we. If we trifle with men, or be careless about their salvation, or deal forth damnation with an unfeeling heart, we do not preach 'as we ought'."[94] Fuller said that it is contrary to the nature of the gospel to preach in a way that does not sufficiently concern itself with the conversion of sinners in pursuit of other aims, or conversely, to point out the judgement of sin without identifying with the hearers' spiritual plight and holding out the hope of the gospel.

"Enlightening the minds and affecting the hearts": *Affections and evangelical* doctrine

The language of the affections was employed by Fuller to describe preaching which communicated personal experience, and which expressed an urgency for salvation. Discourse about the affections, also, drew upon some fairly well-developed views about psychology (the nature of the human person) and epistemology (the nature of knowing), and based on these assumptions, Fuller made practical applications to the work of preaching. Among these assumptions about psychology and epistemology was the belief that it was in the very nature of religious truth to require and elicit a response of the whole person. To apprehend the beauty or excellency of God, or to appreciate the message of the cross, for example, certainly required reason and consideration, but to fully know such a doctrine was to have a sense and inclination of the heart: to love, relish, and feel truth in a personal way. Without such a holistic response of both head and heart, the doctrine in question was only partially known. Jonathan Edwards simply summarized this nature of religious knowledge thus: "If the great things of religion are rightly understood, they will affect the heart."[95] Or, as Fuller put it, "the doctrines of the Scriptures, Scripturally stated, are calculated to interest the heart".[96] Fuller, therefore, insisted on the careful balance of heart and mind in the practice of preaching. In order for evangelical teaching to be truly communicated and applied, the heart must be inclined and moved, as well as the mind instructed, which meant that preaching must address itself to both intellect and passions: *"enlightening the minds* and

---

[93] Ibid., i.546.
[94] Ibid., i.496.
[95] Edwards, *Religious Affections*, 120.
[96] Fuller, *Works*, i.509.

affecting the hearts of the people".[97]

Fuller's concern for this balance between doctrine and delight, the rational and the affective, is well-expressed in a 1796 Association sermon entitled "The Nature and Importance of an Intimate Knowledge of Divine Truth".[98] The phrase "intimate knowledge", itself, nicely conveys the integration of both personal, experiential knowledge and close, reasoned study, which is signified by the language of the affections. Fuller notes that it was common enough among their Particular Baptist churches to have some hearers developing a preference for doctrinal preaching, while others liked to hear chiefly experimental, experiential sermons. The former wanted nothing to do with mere feelings, the latter found doctrinal preaching "dry and uninteresting". Fuller, however, insisted that "knowledge and affection have a mutual influence on each other". "Affection is fed by knowledge" and "by the expansion of the mind the heart is supplied with objects which fill it with delight".[99] With a vivid image, Fuller portrayed how affections arise from truth (and therefore doctrinal preaching): "doctrinal and experimental preaching are not so remote from each other as some persons have imagined; and that to extol the latter, at the expense of the former, is to act like him who wishes the fountain to be destroyed, because he prefers the stream".[100] Having established the integration of doctrine and affectionate experience, he spelled out the implications for preaching doctrine so that it would indeed engage the whole person. If a sermon expressed "the pure gospel of Jesus, well understood by the preacher, and communicated from the fullness of his heart", then both mind and feelings would indeed be interested.[101]

Fuller's application of this religious psychology to homiletics was markedly less formal and methodical than in that of previous generations. John Collet Ryland's sermon, *The Wise Student and Christian Preacher*, for example, ended with a section entitled, "Address to the Passions", in which his text was applied in turn to fear, hope, gratitude, ambition, justice, interest, compassion for souls, pleasure, honour, glory, and shame.[102] The language, tone, and intensity of each of these addresses changes in accordance with the affection, passion or even type of hearer being addressed. Such a formal address seems to have been rarely used by Fuller, perhaps because the rhetorical expectations of a typical congregation had shifted, and certainly Fuller's education was less classical than Ryland's. Fuller was more likely to address the affections of his hearers *throughout* a sermon, depending on the response elicited by the text or

---

[97]
[98] Ibid., i.479.
[99] Ibid., i.160-174.
[100] Ibid., i.169.
[101] Ibid., i.170.
[102] Ibid.
John Collet Ryland, *The Wise Student and Christian Preacher: A Sermon Preached at BroadMead* (Bristol: W. Pine, 1780), 33-41.

doctrine, and by the heightening of his own feelings while preaching. The less formulaic address to the affections may well have been influenced by the simplifying tendency within Claude's directions on affecting the heart:

> The understanding must be informed, but in a manner, however, which *affects the heart*; either to comfort the hearers, or to excite them to acts of piety, repentance or holiness. There are two ways of doing this, one formal, in turning the subject to moral uses, and so applying it to the hearers; the other in the simple choice of the things spoken; for if they be good, solid, evangelic, and edifying of themselves, should no application be formally made, the auditors would make it themselves; because subjects of this kind are of such a nature, that they cannot enter the understanding without penetrating the heart.[103]

While some of this difference in sermon composition may, indeed, be accounted for in terms of homiletic training or generational differences, it seems likely that Fuller's more simplified, less formal approach expressed his conviction that all doctrine is to be preached affectionately and that all true affections arise from striking truths.

The language of the affections was one of the most characteristic aspects of Fuller's pastoral theology. His creative use of that vocabulary was broad, encompassing the preacher's inner life (himself experiencing the gospel) and motivations (a concern for conversion and maturity in his hearers), the manner of delivery (sincerely and feelingly communicated, but not affected), and a nuanced set of views on how truth is holistically known and therefore preached.

Summary

Fuller's sympathetic editor and contemporary, Joseph Belcher, described the experience of hearing the Kettering minister preach: "You are melted by his pathos, and seem to have found a man in whom are united the clearness of Barrow, the scriptural theology of Owen, and the subduing tenderness of Baxter or Flavel."[104] The references are intriguing, setting Fuller within a larger context of English theology and preaching, and at the same time, personalizing the essentially evangelical elements of Fuller's preaching. The comparison with Barrow's clarity is a witness to Fuller's commitment to the "plain style" of preaching, the mention of Owen invokes his evangelicalism in the Calvinist vein, and the reference to Baxter and Flavel suggesting the affectionate and direct nature of his address. Fuller's pastoral theology applied to preaching, we have demonstrated, was *plain* in composition and delivery, *evangelical* in content and concern, and *affectionate* in feeling and application. Each of these three aspects of Fuller's preaching complemented and helped to define the

---

[103] Claude, *Essay*, i.22-23.

[104] Fuller, *Works*, i.197, editor's note.

others, the plain style and affectionate manner arising from and supporting his evangelical emphases.

These expressions of Fuller's renewed pastoral theology could, also, be explored in other aspects of his ministry. Reflecting on an early experience of pastoral visiting, he recorded his commitment to simplicity in all aspects of ministry: "Convinced that no art was necessary in religion, resolved to proceed with all plainness and openness."[105] Crucicentrism was communicated in Fuller's leadership at the Lord's Supper, as well as in his preaching, as George Wallis, the Kettering diarist recorded on "ordinance days" that "Christ crucified has this day been preach'd to my senses."[106] And advising a colleague on the exercise of discipline, he expressed his affectionate concern: "The grand secret, I think, to render this part of our work as easy as possible, is to love the souls of the people."[107] But, particularly, in the principle work of weekly congregational preaching, Fuller demonstrated that here, too, as well as in itinerant ministry, was the evangelical renewal of pastoral theology, an "affectionate, experimental, evangelical ministry".[108]

---

[105] Fuller, *Diary*, 14 June 1780.

[106] Wallis, "Memoir", 31 March 1805; 29 Sept. 1805

[107] Fuller, *Works*, i.492-493.

[108] Rivers, *Reason, Grace, and Sentiment*, i.171.

Figure 9: Silhouette portrait of Andrew Fuller from Ryland,
Life of Fuller

Conclusion

The evangelical transformation of the Particular Baptist churches of the late eighteenth century included, in addition to the more frequently noted aspects of outward expansion and activism, the renewal of their pastoral theology. Evangelical theology and piety certainly issued in international missions, voluntary societies, and itinerant preaching, but was also expressed in Andrew Fuller's recovery of a conversionist pastoral theology, his emphasis on the voluntary nature of the local congregation, and his weekly preaching, which was plain, evangelical, and affectionate. Preaching, pastoral care, and the shepherding of congregational order continued to be givens, but the character of those duties underwent an evangelical renewal.

Andrew Fuller's pastoral theology is one instance of a distinctly evangelical contribution to pastoralia, a renewed approach to Christian ministry. This study has examined Fuller's evangelical pastoral theology in three of its aspects. In Chapter One, we explored the pastoral implications of his general theological system, and, specifically, his first and most prominent work, *The Gospel Worthy of All Acceptation*. Set against the background of high Calvinism, Fuller's work was essentially pastoral: demonstrating the ability—even the obligation—of sinners to respond in faith to the gospel, and concluding with the commensurate obligation and urgency for preachers to freely offer that gospel to their hearers. The evangelical Calvinism which was an important impetus for William Carey's call to use means, through international missions, for the conversion of those in India and elsewhere, had an equally important and widespread effect upon preachers at home, freeing them to have a more directly confident and conversionist stance in offering the gospel. Chapter Two examined Fuller's pastoral theology within the context of ecclesiology, defining the relationship between pastor and congregation. Fuller urged a vigorous and lively form of congregationalism as a means of evangelical ministry, and his pastoral theology emphasized the voluntary and affectionate bonds which constitute the local church itself, as well as the relationship with their pastor. While Anglicans made use of voluntary societies within the church, and Methodists created the "connexion" alongside it, as expressions of evangelical renewal, Fuller was among those who believed that the local congregation, itself, could be the vehicle of evangelical piety and activism. The application of Fuller's pastoral theology, in his primary work of preaching, was the theme of Chapter Three. While Fuller was himself an eager participant in the spread of itinerant and village preaching, the evangelical renewal of his pastoral theology was just as importantly expressed in his weekly congregational preaching. His preaching was characterized by a plain style and extempore delivery, evangelical concern and cross-centred content, and affectionate motivations and communication. Andrew Fuller's thought and practice demonstrates that the evangelical transformation of the church included the renewal of its pastoral theology. Within the broader corpus of pastoralia, Fuller offers one instance of the shape that a pastoral theology can take when guided by the concerns of evangelical theology and piety.

"Very affecting and evangelical"

Kettering deacon and diarist George Wallis described Fuller's preaching as "truly Evangelical, melting and affectionate" and as "very affecting and evangelical",[1] using language and emphases that are arguably the most characteristic of Fuller's pastoral theology. Fuller employed the language of the affections to express his evangelicalism, and that vocabulary was most concentrated and prominent in his pastoral theology. Drawing on this affectionate discourse was a way for Fuller and his contemporaries to balance orthodox doctrine and personal, heart-felt experience, rather than the polarizing tendencies to either rationalism or enthusiasm. Affections described the heart's response to the mind's reasoning—an integrated, holistic knowledge.

Fuller's use of affectionate language is evident throughout the various aspects of his pastoral theology: as he insisted on the obligation of ministers to offer the gospel, as he expressed the importance of voluntary and affectionate bonds between pastor and people as the basis for congregational ministry, and in his instructions for pastors in their tasks of visiting, evangelism, and presiding over the church's discipline. But it was, particularly, in his discussion of preaching that affectionate discourse was so central and creatively developed in Fuller's pastoral theology. He used the language of the heart to prescribe the evangelical experience of the preacher ("If you would affect others, you must feel"), the manner of its delivery (affectionate but not affected), the evangelical motivations for conversionist preaching ("an affectionate concern after their salvation"), and at a foundational level, the balance between doctrine and experience ("enlightening the minds and affecting the hearts"). The affectionate and the evangelical helped define each other in Fuller's pastoral theology.

The language of the affections was uniquely appropriate to give voice to evangelicalism—the religion of the heart. Affectionate discourse, with its vocabulary of the heart, experience, and feeling, expressed evangelicalism's emphasis on faith as personal and sincere, rather than merely nominal or rational assent. Compared with the demonstrative expressions of the earlier Evangelical Revival, the congregational culture of Calvinist dissent tended to be more restrained. However, the nuanced psychology of the affections allowed evangelicals such as Watts, Edwards, and Fuller to emphasize the heart in a way that did not marginalize reason or doctrine. To the extent that Andrew Fuller's pastoral theology was "very affecting", it was "truly evangelical".

---

[1] Wallis, "Memoir", 28 April 1805 and 14 July 1811.

Fuller as a particular kind of evangelical

Exploring the contours of Fuller's pastoral theology has offered some further definition of "evangelical" in his generation, noting how he appropriated and expressed the characteristics, beliefs, language, emphases and activities which he shared in common with other evangelicals. Fuller's pastoral theology, certainly, bears the marks of David Bebbington's quadrilateral of essential evangelical characteristics: activism, conversionism, biblicism, and crucicentrism. The activist, expansionist impulse of evangelicals was fully embraced by Fuller in his considerable role in supporting the Baptist Missionary Society and, also, in his practice of evangelistic village preaching, but, also, in the more intentionally evangelistic cast of his weekly preaching and pastoral care. The hallmark of his moderate Calvinism was a recovery of a sense of moral ability and personal agency, urging hearers to be converted through faith, and obligating preachers to offer the gospel as the means of that conversion. Fuller's biblicism figured most prominently, in this study, when noting his experience of tension between high Calvinist scruples and New Testament invitations, when deferring to scriptural example for a relatively low clericalism and vigorous view of congregationalism, and in his insistence on a simple mode of address because of the perspicuity of the Bible's central message. And his pastoral theology was crucicentric in the prominence he gave to the work of Christ in preaching, and the affectionate concern for the salvation of his hearers.

Fuller's pastoral theology, also, shares other features of evangelical thought and language. The recovery of the objective grounds of assurance, and the realignment of the *ordo salutis* to emphasize justification by faith, identifies Fuller as an evangelical in comparison with high Calvinists and (in the matter of assurance) with Puritans. Voluntarism, though not unique to evangelicals, was, also, essential to the emergence of evangelicalism as a distinctive strain of piety, and Fuller emphasized the personal nature of conversion, the voluntary nature of congregational life and pastoral bonds, and the corresponding need to preach in an accessible, affective, and engaging mode. The language of the affections, finally, which was one of the defining aspects of Fuller's pastoral theology, was characteristic of evangelical discourse in a way that set it apart from unorthodox rationalism, but at the same time was expressive of the particularly eighteenth-century concern for sentiment and moral psychology. The emphasis on the affections was an important way of emphasizing what Ernst Stoeffler called the "experiential strain" of evangelical piety, giving priority to personal and to sincere religious experience.[2] One could add to this catalogue Fuller's dependence on the Puritans and a wide swath of evangelical writers—always with Jonathan Edwards in prominence—as main sources in the formation of his evangelicalism, as well as the transdenominational character of

---

[2] Stoeffler, *The Rise of Evangelical Pietism*, 13-15.

his friendships and correspondence, particularly in matters of mission and activism. Andrew Fuller considered himself, his theology, and his ministry as evangelical, and he provides a valuable instance in defining those essential features of evangelical thought and practice.

But Fuller was, also, a certain kind of evangelical. That is, he not only provides another exhibit of generic evangelicalism, but an expression of evangelicalism in particular contexts, with important nuances: a hyphenated evangelicalism. We might speak, for example, of Fuller as a Calvinist evangelical, more directly indebted to the Edwardsean than the Wesleyan strain of the Evangelical Revival. Or, we could mention the accent of Fuller's evangelicalism as influenced by the culture of orthodox Dissent, or by his, specifically, Baptist convictions. But, it is Fuller's congregational ecclesiology that this study has particularly noted as definitive for his expression of evangelicalism.

It is, perhaps, because of his ecclesiology that Fuller emphasized the evangelical renewal of the congregation and its pastoral theology. What evangelical Anglicans did within the *ecclesiolae in ecclesia* of religious societies, and what Methodists did in their connexions, and arising from the same basic concerns for evangelical piety and voluntarism, Fuller sought to do within the reinvigorated life of congregations themselves. While it is certainly true that in terms of fellowship, cooperation, and a self-consciousness of themselves as part of a movement, evangelicals subordinated church order to evangelical piety,[3] Fuller saw a vigorous congregationalism as entirely compatible with—even a means of promoting—evangelical piety and mission. Perhaps Fuller's expression of a congregational evangelicalism gives support to Roger Olson's claim that "free church ecclesiology, properly understood, is more compatible with the evangelical Protestant ethos and spirituality, properly understood, than its alternatives".[4] At the very least, however, the renewal of Andrew Fuller's pastoral theology and his commitment to congregationalism *because* of his evangelicalism highlights the variety of forms through which the same basic evangelical emphases were expressed.

The evangelical experience and affections of the pastor

In a heartfelt revelation of his personal formation as a pastor, Fuller recorded in his diary his concern to have a sense of the heart to understand and fully enter into his pastoral vocation:

---

[3] Bruce Hindmarsh, "Is Evangelical Ecclesiology an Oxymoron? A Historical Perspective", in *Evangelical Ecclesiology: Reality or Illusion?* ed. John G. Stackhouse, Jr. (Grand Rapids: Baker Academic, 2003), 15-37.

[4] Roger Olson, "Free Church Ecclesiology and Evangelical Spirituality: A Unique Compatibility", in Stackhouse, ed., *Evangelical Ecclesiology*, 162; cf. 175.

> I think I have never yet entered into the true idea of the work of the ministry. ... I
> think I am by the ministry, as I was by my life as a Christian before I read
> *Edwards on the Affections*. I had never entered into the spirit of a great many
> important things. Oh for some such penetrating, edifying writer on this subject!
> Or, rather, oh that the Holy Spirit would open my eyes, and let me into the things
> that I have never yet seen![5]

A few days later, he similarly prayed, "O would the Lord the Spirit lead me into
the nature and importance of the work of the ministry! Reading a wise and
spiritual author might be of use: yet, could I, by Divine assistance, but penetrate
the work myself, it would sink deeper, and be more durable."[6]

The diary entries, of course, bear testimony to the profound influence of
Jonathan Edwards—particularly the *Religious Affections*—upon Fuller's
spiritual and theological development. These words, written while still in his
formative years in Soham, also, place Fuller in the role of one seeking wisdom
among the writers of pastoral theology, a literature to which he later made his
own evangelical contribution. Primarily, however, Fuller expressed his
conviction that only a spiritual and very personal understanding of the nature
and importance of pastoral theology would be sustaining and effective. He was
applying the affectionate and evangelical piety he had learned from the
Religious Affections to his pastoral work.

Indeed, one of the themes that emerges throughout the study of Fuller's
pastoral theology is the spiritual experience of the pastor. The emphasis was,
certainly, not unique to Fuller, but it is a prominent characteristic of his pastoral
theology, and one which expressed his evangelical convictions. The interior life
of the pastor was not incidental to pastoral work, but, rather, was quite
necessary for its evangelical aims. The pastor must, himself, be converted, as
well as seeking the conversion of his hearers. The voluntary bonds between a
minister and a congregation require the affectionate, loving disposition of
pastor for church. And for spiritual truth to be communicated in preaching, it
must be personally experienced and affectionately delivered. The sincere and
affectionate experience of the individual was an emphasis of evangelism, and
was a particular concern for Fuller as a pastor and a Christian. The evangelical
and affectionate renewal of the pastor was a significant emphasis within
Andrew Fuller's renewed pastoral theology, itself, an evangelical contribution
to pastoralia, and an aspect of the evangelical transformation of the church.

---

[5] Fuller, *Diary*, 3 February 1781.
[6] Ibid., 8 February 1781.

he Qualifications and Encouragement of a faithful Minister, illustrated by the Character and Success of Barnabas. And, *Paul's Charge to the Corinthians respecting their Treatment of Timothy, applied to the Conduct of Churches toward their Pastors.*

Being the SUBSTANCE of

TWO DISCOURSES,

DELIVERED AT

The SETTLEMENT of

The Rev. Mr. *Robert Fawkner*,

In the PASTORAL OFFICE,

OVER

The BAPTIST CHURCH

AT THORN, in BEDFORDSHIRE,

October 31, 1787.

The former by ANDREW FULLER.
The latter by JOHN RYLAND, jun.

PUBLISHED AT THE REQUEST OF THE CHURCH.

Sold by J. BUCKLAND, Pater-noster-Row, London
[Price SIX-PENCE.]

Figure 10: Title page of published ordination sermons (see Appendix 1)

APPENDIX 1

The qualifications and encouragement
of a faithful minister
illustrated by the character and success of Barnabas.[1]

"He was a good man, and full of the Holy Spirit, and of faith; and much people was added to the Lord".—Acts xi.24.

MY DEAR BROTHER,

It is a very important work to which you are this day set apart. I feel the difficulty of your situation. You need both counsel and encouragement; I wish I were better able to administer both. In what I may offer, I am persuaded you will allow me to be free; and understand me, not as assuming any authority or superiority over you, but only as saying that to you which I wish to consider as equally addressed to myself.

Out of a variety of topics that might afford a lesson for a Christian minister, my thoughts have turned, on this occasion, upon that of *example*. Example has a great influence upon the human mind; examples from Scripture especially, wherein characters the most illustrious in their day, for gifts, grace, and

---

[1] This charge was preached by Andrew Fuller at the ordination of Robert Fawkner at Thorn, Bedfordshire, on 31 October 1787. It was published, together with John Ryland's sermon to the church on the same occasion, as Andrew Fuller and John Ryland, *The Qualifications and Encouragements of a Faithful Minister, Illustrated by the Character and Success of Barnabas, and Paul's Charge to the Corinthians Respecting Their Treatment of Timothy, Applied to the Conduct of Churches toward Their Pastors* (London: J. Buckland, 1787), and is in Fuller, *Works*, i.135-144. The published discourses contain a brief description of the ordination service: "divine worship began, as usual, with singing, which was repeated at proper intervals. The Rev. Mr. Cole, of Maiden, prayed, and the Rev. Mr. Pilley, of Luton, made a brief but very suitable introduction to the work of the day, and received from a deacon of the church a short narrative of the leadings of providence which induced them to call the Rev. Mr. Fawkner to become their pastor; which call the whole Church now recognized by lifting up their hands: then after Mr. Fawkner had signified his acceptance of the pastoral office; and delivered his confession of Faith, the Rev. Mr. Sutcliff, of Olney, recommended the Pastor and People unto God by prayer. The Charge and Sermon were next delivered; and the Rev. Mr. Geard, of Hichin, concluded the opportunity in prayer."

usefulness, are drawn with the pencil of inspiration, have an assimilating tendency. Viewing these, under a Divine blessing, we form some just conceptions of the nature and importance of our work, are led to reflect upon our own defects, and feel the fire of holy emulation kindling in our bosoms.

The particular example, my brother, which I wish to recommend to your attention, is that of Barnabas, that excellent servant of Christ and companion of the apostle Paul. You will find his character particularly given in the words I have just read.

Were we to examine the life of this great and good man, as related in other parts of Scripture, we should find the character here given him abundantly confirmed. He seems to have been one of that great company who, through the preaching of Peter and the other apostles, submitted to Christ soon after his ascension; and he gave early proof of his love to him, by selling his possessions, and laying the price at the feet of the apostles for the support of his infant cause. As he loved Christ, so he loved his people. He appears to have possessed much of the tender and affectionate, on account of which he was called "Barnabas—a son of consolation." Assiduous in discovering and encouraging the first dawnings of God's work, he was the first person that introduced Saul into the company of the disciples. The next news that we hear of him is in the passage which I have selected. Tidings came to the ears of the church at Jerusalem of the word of the Lord being prosperous at Antioch, in Syria. The church at Jerusalem was the mother church, and felt a concern for others, like that of a tender mother towards her infant offspring. The young converts at Antioch wanted a nursing father; and who so proper to be sent as Barnabas? He goes; and, far from envying the success of others, who had laboured before him, he "was glad to see the grace of God" so evidently appear; "and exhorted them all that with purpose of heart they would cleave unto the Lord". As a preacher, he does not seem to have been equal to the apostle Paul; yet so far was he from caring about being eclipsed by Paul's superior abilities, that he went in search of him, and brought him to Antioch, to assist him in the work of the Lord. It may well be said of such a character, that he was a "good man, and full of the Holy Spirit, and of faith". Oh that we had more such ministers in the church at this day! Oh that we ourselves were like him! Might we not hope, if that were the case, that, according to God's usual manner of working, more *people would be added to the Lord*?

There are three things, we see, which are said of Barnabas in a way of commendation: he was "a good man, full of the Holy Spirit, and of faith". Thus far he is held up for our example; a fourth is added, concerning the effects which followed; "and much people was added unto the Lord". This seems to be held up for our encouragement. Permit me, my dear brother, to request your candid attention, while I attempt to review these great qualities in Barnabas, and by every motive to enforce them upon you.

I. HE WAS A GOOD MAN. It were easy to prove the necessity of a person being a good man, in order to his properly engaging in the work of the ministry:

Christ would not commit his sheep but to one that loved him. But on this remark I shall not enlarge. I have no reason to doubt, my brother, but that God has given you an understanding to know him that is true, and a heart to love him in sincerity; I trust, therefore, such an attempt, on this occasion, is needless. Nor does it appear to me to be the meaning of the evangelist. It is not barely meant of Barnabas that he was a *regenerate* man, though that is implied; but it denotes that he was *eminently* good. We use the word so in common conversation. If we would describe one that more than ordinarily shines in piety, meekness, and kindness, we know not how to speak of him better than to say, with a degree of emphasis, He is a *good* man. After this eminence in goodness, brother, may it be your concern, and mine, daily to aspire!

Perhaps, indeed, we may have sometimes heard this epithet used with a sneer. Persons who take pleasure in treating others with contempt will frequently, with a kind of proud piety, speak in this manner: Aye, such a one is a *good* man; leaving it implied that goodness is but an indifferent qualification, unless it be accompanied with greatness. But these things ought not to be. The apostle Paul did not value himself upon those things wherein he differed from other Christians; but upon that which he possessed in common with them— charity, or Christian love. "Though I speak with the tongues of men and of angels, and have not charity, I am become as sounding brass, or a tinkling cymbal. And though I have the gift of prophecy, and understand all mysteries, and all knowledge; and though I have all faith, so that I could remove mountains, and have not charity; I am nothing."

My dear brother, *value the character of a good man in all the parts of your employment; and above all, in those things which the world counts great and estimable.* More particularly,

1. Value it *at home in your family.* If you walk not closely with God there, you will be ill able to work for him elsewhere. You have lately become the head of a family. Whatever charge it shall please God, in the course of your life, to place under your care, I trust it will be your concern to recommend Christ and the gospel to them, walk circumspectly before them, constantly worship God with them, offer up secret prayer for them, and exercise a proper authority over them. There is a sort of religious gossiping which some ministers have indulged to their hurt; loitering about perpetually at the houses of their friends, and taking no delight in their own. Such conduct, in a minister and master of a family, must, of necessity, root out all family order, and, to a great degree, family worship; and, instead of endearing him to his friends, it only exposes him to their just censure. Perhaps they know not how to be so plain as to tell him of it at their own houses; but they will think the more, and speak of it, it is likely, to each other, when he is gone. I trust, my brother, that none of your domestic connexions will have to say when you are gone, He was loose and careless in his conduct, or sour and churlish in his temper; but rather, *He was a good man.*

2. Value this character in your *private retirements.* Give yourself up to "the

word of God, and to prayer". The apostle charged Timothy, saying, "Meditate on these things, give thyself wholly to them", or, "be thou *in* them". But this will never be, without a considerable share of the *good man*. Your heart can never be *in* those things which are foreign to its prevailing temper; and if your heart is not in your work, it will be a poor lifeless business indeed. We need not fear exhausting the Bible, or dread a scarcity of Divine subjects. If our hearts are but kept in unison with the spirit in which the Bible was written, every thing we meet with there will be interesting. The more we read, the more interesting it will appear; and the more we know, the more we shall perceive there is to be known. Beware also, brother, of neglecting secret *prayer*. The fire of devotion will go out if it be not kept alive by an habitual dealing with Christ. Conversing with men and things may brighten our gifts and parts; but it is conversing with God that must brighten our graces. Whatever ardour we may feel in our public work, if this is wanting, things cannot be right, nor can they in such a train come to a good issue.

3. Value it in your *public exercises.* It is hard going on in the work of the ministry, without a good degree of spirituality; and yet, considering the present state of human nature, we are in the greatest danger of the contrary. Allow me, brother, to mention two things in particular, each of which is directly opposite to that spirit which I am attempting to recommend. One is, an *assumed earnestness*, or *forced zeal*, in the pulpit, which many weak hearers may mistake for the enjoyment of God. But though we may put on violent emotions—may smite with the hand and stamp with the foot—if we are destitute of a genuine feeling sense of what we deliver, it will be discerned by judicious hearers, as well as by the Searcher of hearts, and will not fail to create disgust. If, on the contrary, we feel and realize the sentiments we deliver, emotions and actions will be the natural expressions of the heart; and this will give weight to the doctrines, exhortations, or reproofs which we inculcate; what we say will come with a kind of Divine authority to the consciences, if not to the hearts of the hearers. The other is, being under the influence of *low and selfish motives* in the exercise of our work. This is a temptation against which we have especial reason to watch and pray. It is right, my brother, for you to be diligent in your public work; to be instant in season and out of season; to preach the gospel not only at Thorn, but in the surrounding villages, wherever a door is opened for you: but while you are thus engaged, let it not be from motives of policy, merely to increase your auditory, but from love to Christ and the souls of your fellow sinners. It is this only that will endure reflection in a dying hour. The apostle Paul was charged by some of the Corinthian teachers with being *crafty*, and with having *caught* the Corinthians *with guile*; but he could say, in reply to all such insinuations, in behalf of himself and his fellow labourers, "Our rejoicing is this, the testimony of our conscience, that in simplicity and godly sincerity, not with fleshly wisdom, but by the grace of God, we have had our conversation in the world."

4. Value it in the *general tenor of your behaviour*. Cultivate a meek, modest,

peaceful, and friendly temper. Be generous and humane. Prove by your spirit and conduct that you are a lover of all mankind. To men in general, but especially to the poor and the afflicted, *be pitiful, be courteous*. It is this, my brother, that will recommend the gospel you proclaim. Without this, could you preach with the eloquence of an angel, you may expect that no good end will be answered.

5. Prize the character of the good man *above worldly greatness*. It is not sinful for a minister, any more than another man, to possess property; but to aspire after it is unworthy of his sacred character. Greatness, unaccompanied by goodness, is valued as nothing by the great God. Kings and emperors, where that is wanting, are but great "beasts, horned beasts", pushing at one another. When Sennacherib vaunted against the church of God, that he would "enter the forest of her Carmel, and cut down her tall cedars", the daughter of Zion is commanded to *despise* him. God speaks of him as we should speak of a buffalo, or even of an ass: "I will put my hook in thy nose, and my bridle in thy lips, and I will turn thee back by the way by which thou camest." Outward greatness, when accompanied with goodness, may be a great blessing; yet, even then, it is the latter, and not the former, that denominates the true worth of a character. Once more,—

6. Value it *above mental greatness*, or greatness in gifts and parts. It is not wrong to cultivate gifts; on the contrary, it is our duty to do so. But, desirable as these are, they are not to be compared with goodness. "Covet earnestly the best gifts," says the apostle, "*and yet show I unto you a more excellent way*"; viz. *charity*, or *love*. If we improve in gifts and not in grace, to say the least, it will be useless, and perhaps dangerous, both to ourselves and others. To improve in gifts, that we may be the better able to discharge our work, is laudable; but if it be for the sake of popular applause, we may expect a blast. Hundreds of ministers have been ruined by indulging a thirst for the character of the *great* man, while they have neglected the far superior character of the *good* man.

Another part of the character of Barnabas was that,

II. HE WAS FULL OF THE HOLY SPIRIT. The *Holy Spirit* sometimes denotes his extraordinary gifts, as in Acts xix, where the apostle Paul put the question to some believers in Christ whether they had received the Holy Spirit; but here it signifies his indwelling and ordinary operations, or what is elsewhere called "an unction from the Holy One". This, though more common than the other, is far more excellent. Its fruits, though less brilliant, are abundantly the most valuable. To be able to surmount a difficulty by Christian patience is a greater thing in the sight of God than to remove a mountain. Every work of God bears some mark of Godhead, even a thistle, or a nettle; but there are some of his works which bear a peculiar likeness to his holy moral character: such were the minds of men and angels in their original state. This will serve to illustrate the subject in hand. The extraordinary gifts of the Holy Spirit are a communication of his *power*; but in his dwelling in the saints, and the ordinary operations of his grace, he communicates his own *holy nature*; and this it was of which Barnabas was full. To be full of the Holy Spirit is to be full of the *dove*, as I may say; or full of those fruits of the Spirit mentioned by the apostle to the Galatians; namely, "love, joy, peace, long-suffering, gentleness, goodness".

To be sure, the term *full* is not here to be understood in an unlimited sense; not in so ample a sense as when it is applied to Christ. He was filled with the Spirit *without* measure, but we *in* measure. The word is doubtless to be understood in a comparative sense, and denotes as much as that he was habitually under his holy influence. A person that is greatly under the influence of the love of this world is said to be *drunken* with its cares or pleasures. In allusion to something like this, the apostle exhorts that we "be not drunken with wine, wherein is excess; but *filled* with the Spirit". The word "filled", here, is very expressive; it denotes, I apprehend, being *overcome*, as it were, with the holy influences and fruits of the blessed Spirit. How necessary is all this, my brother, in your work! Oh how necessary is an "unction from the Holy One!"

1. It is this that will enable you to *enter into the spirit of the gospel, and preserve you from destructive errors concerning it*. Those who have an unction from the Holy One are said to "know all things; and the anointing which they have received abideth in them, and they need not that any man teach them, but as the same anointing teacheth them all things, and is truth, and is no lie". We shall naturally fall in with the dictates of that spirit of which we are full. It is for want of this, in a great measure, that the Scriptures appear strange, and foreign, and difficult to be understood. He that is full of the Holy Spirit has the contents of the Bible written, as I may say, upon his heart; and thus its sacred pages are easy to be understood, as "wisdom is easy to him that understandeth".

It is no breach of charity to say, that if the professors of Christianity had more of the Holy Spirit of God in their hearts, there would be a greater harmony among them respecting the great truths which he has revealed. The rejection of such doctrines as the exceeding sinfulness of sin, the total depravity of mankind, the proper Deity and atonement of Christ, justification by faith in his name, the freeness and sovereignty of grace, and the agency of the Holy Spirit, may easily be accounted for upon this principle. If we are destitute of the Holy Spirit, we are blind to the loveliness of the Divine character, and destitute of any true love to God in our hearts; and if destitute of this, we shall not be able to see the reasonableness of that law which requires love to him with all the heart; and then, of course, we shall think lightly of the nature of those offences committed against him; we shall be naturally disposed to palliate and excuse our want of love to him, yea, and even our positive violations of his law; it will seem hard, very hard indeed, for such little things as these to be punished with everlasting destruction. And now, all this admitted, we shall naturally be blind to the necessity and glory of salvation by Jesus Christ. If sin is so trifling an affair, it will seem a strange and incredible thing that God should become incarnate to atone for it; and hence we shall be very easily persuaded to consider Christ as only a good man, who came into the world to set us a good example; or, at least, that he is not equal with the Father. The freeness and sovereignty of grace also, together with justification by imputed righteousness, will be a very strange sound in our ears. Like the Jews, we shall "go about to establish our own righteousness, and shall not submit to the righteousness of God". It will seem equally strange and incredible to be told that we are by nature utterly unfit for the kingdom of God; that, therefore, we *must* be born again; that we are so bad that we cannot even come to Christ for life, except the Father draw us; yea, and that our best doings after all, are unworthy of God's notice. It will be no wonder if, instead of receiving these unwelcome and humiliating doctrines, we should coincide with those writers and preachers who think more favourably of our condition, and the condition of the world at large; who either deny eternal punishment to exist, or represent men in general as being in little or no danger of it. And having avowed these sentiments, it will then become necessary to compliment their abettors (including ourselves in the number) as persons of a more rational and liberal way of thinking than other people.

My dear brother, of all things, be this your prayer, "Take not thy Holy Spirit from me!" If once we sink into such a way of performing our public work as not to depend on his enlightening and enlivening influences, we *may* go on, and probably *shall* go on, from one degree of evil to another. Knowing how to account for the operations of our own minds, without imputing them to a Divine agency, we shall be inclined, in this manner, to account for the operations in the mind of others; and so, with numbers in the present age, may soon call in question even "whether there be any Holy Spirit".

2. Being full of the Holy Spirit will give *a holy tincture to your meditation and preaching.* There is such a thing as the mind being habitually under the influence of Divine things, and retaining so much of a savour of Christ as that Divine truths shall be viewed and expressed, as I may say, in their own language. Spiritual things will be spiritually discerned, and if spiritually discerned, will be spiritually communicated. There is more in our *manner* of thinking and speaking upon Divine truth than perhaps, at first sight, we are aware of. A great part of the phraseology of Scripture is by some accounted unfit to be addressed to a modern ear; and is, on this account, to a great degree laid aside, even by those who profess to be satisfied with the sentiments. Whatever may be said in defense of this practice, in a very few instances, such as those where words in a translation are become obsolete, or convey a different idea from what they did at the time of being translated, I am satisfied the practice in general is very pernicious. There are many sermons, that cannot fairly be charged with untruth, which yet have a tendency to lead off the mind from the simplicity of the gospel. If such Scripture terms, for instance, as "holiness, godliness, grace, believers, saints, communion with God", &c., should be thrown aside as savouring too much of cant and enthusiasm, and such terms as, *morality, virtue, religion, good men, happiness of mind,* &c., substituted in their room, it will have an amazing effect upon the hearers. If

such preaching is the gospel, it is the gospel heathenized, and will tend to heathenize the minds of those who deal in it. I do not mean to object to the use of these latter terms, in their place; they are some of them Scriptural terms: what I object to is putting them in the place of others, when discoursing upon evangelical subjects. To be sure, there is a way of handling Divine subjects after this sort that is very clever and very ingenious; and a minister of such a stamp may commend himself, by his ingenuity, to many hearers: but, after all, God's truths are never so acceptable and savoury to a *gracious* heart as when clothed in their own native phraseology. The more you are filled, my brother, with an unction from the Holy One, the greater relish you will possess for that savoury manner of conveying truth which is so plentifully exemplified in the Holy Scriptures. Further,

3. It is this that will make the doctrines you preach, and the duties you inculcate, seem *fitted to your lips*. I allude to a saying of the wise man: "The words of the wise are pleasant, if thou keep them within thee; they shall withal be fitted in thy lips". It is expected that there should be an agreement between the character of the speaker and the things which are spoken. "Excellent speech becometh not a fool." Exhortations to holiness come with an ill grace from the lips of one who indulges himself in iniquity. The opposite of this is what I mean by the doctrines and duties of religion being *fitted in your lips*. It is this that will make your face shine, when you come forth in your public labours, like the face of Moses when he had been conversing with God in the holy mount.

4. It is this that will give *a spiritual savour to your conversation in your visits to your friends*. Though religious visits may be abused; yet you know, brother, the necessity there is for them, if you would ascertain the spiritual condition of those to whom you preach. There are many faults also that you may discover in individuals which it would be unhandsome, as well as unfriendly, to expose in a pointed manner in the pulpit, which nevertheless ought not to be passed by unnoticed. Here is work for your private visits; and, in proportion as you are filled with the Holy Spirit, you will possess a spirit of love and faithfulness, which is absolutely necessary to successful reproof. It is in our private visits also that we can be free with our people, and they with us. Questions may be asked and answered, difficulties solved, and the concerns of the soul discussed. Paul taught the Ephesians, not only publicly, but "from house to house". Now it is being full of the Holy Spirit that will give a spiritual savour to all this conversation. It will be as the holy anointing oil on Aaron's garments, which diffused a savour on all around him.

5. This will also teach you *how you ought to behave yourself in every department you are called to occupy*. It will serve instead of ten thousand rules; and all rules without it will be of no account. This it is that will teach you to be of a meek, mild, peaceful, humble spirit. It will make such a spirit be natural to you. "As touching brotherly love", said the apostle to the Thessalonians, "ye need not that I write to you, for ye yourselves are taught of God to love one

another."

6. In short, it is this that will denominate you *the man of God.* Such was Barnabas, and such, my brother, was your predecessor [The Rev. David Evans], whose memory is dear to many of us; and such, according to all that I have heard, was his predecessor [The Rev. William Butfield], whose memory is equally dear to many here present. Each, in his day, was a burning and shining light; but they shine here no more. May you, my brother, and each of us, be followers of them, as they also were of Christ!

Another part of the character of Barnabas is,

III. HE WAS FULL OF FAITH. It may be difficult to ascertain with precision the real meaning and extent of this term; but, I should think, in this connexion it includes, at least, the three following ideas:—having the mind occupied with Divine sentiment; being rooted and grounded in the truth of the gospel, and daily living upon it. The first of these ideas distinguished him from those characters whose minds are void of principle; the next, from such as are always hovering upon the borders of skepticism; and the last, from those who, though they have no manner of doubts about the truth of the doctrines of the gospel, yet scarcely ever, if at all, feel their vital influence upon their hearts and lives. Let us review each of these a little more particularly.

1. His mind was *well occupied, or stored with Divine sentiment.* How necessary is this to a gospel minister! It is to be feared that many young men have rushed into the work of the Lord without any decided principles of their own; yea, and have not only begun in such a state of mind, but have continued so all through their lives. Alas! what can the churches expect from such characters? What can such a void produce? How can we feed others with knowledge and understanding if we ourselves are destitute of them? To say the least, such ministers will be but "unprofitable servants". But this is not all; a minister that is not inured to think for himself is constantly exposed to every false sentiment, or system, that happens to be presented to him. We sometimes hear of a person *changing his sentiments*; and doubtless, in many cases it is just and right he should change them: but there are cases in which that mode of speaking is very improper; for, in reality, some persons have no sentiments of their own to change; they have only changed the sentiments of some one great man for those of another.

2. He had *a firm persuasion of the truth of that gospel which he preached to others*. He was rooted and grounded in the gospel. The great controversy of that day was whether the gospel was true; whether Jesus was the Messiah; whether he, who so lately expired on the cross, was the Son of God; and whether his death was the way to obtain eternal life. There were great temptations for a person who should view these things through a medium of sense to think otherwise. The popular opinion went against it. To the Jews it was a stumbling-block, and to the Greeks foolishness. Those who adhered to the gospel, thereby exposed themselves to cruel persecutions. But Barnabas "was full of faith"; he was decidedly on the Lord's side; he "believed on the Son of God", and had the

"witness" of the truth of his gospel "within himself".

Preaching the gospel is bearing a *testimony* for God; but we shall never be able to do this to any good purpose, if we be always hesitating and indulging a sceptical disposition. There is no need of a dogmatical, overbearing temper; but there is a need of being rooted and grounded in the truths of God. "Be not carried about," said the apostle to the Hebrews, "with strange doctrines: it is a good thing that the heart be established with grace." But he elsewhere condemns the character of those who are "ever learning, and never able to come to the knowledge of the truth".

3. That gospel which he preached to others *he himself lived upon.* "The word preached," we are told, "did not profit some, because it was not mixed with faith in them that heard it." This will equally hold good in the case of the preacher as the hearer. If we mix not faith with the doctrine we deliver, it will not profit us. Whatever abilities we may possess, and of whatever use we may be made to others, unless we can say, in some sort, with the apostle John, "That which we have seen with our eyes, and looked upon, and our hands have handled of the word of life—that declare we unto you", our own souls may, notwithstanding, everlastingly perish! This is a very serious matter, and well deserves our attention as ministers. Professors in the age of Barnabas might be under greater temptations than we are to question whether Jesus was the Messiah: but we are under greater temptations than they were of resting in a mere implicit assent to the Christian religion, without realizing and living upon its important truths.

The studying of Divine truth as *preachers* rather than as *Christians*, or, in other words, studying it for the sake of finding out something to say to others, without so much as thinking of profiting our own souls, is a temptation to which we are more than ordinarily exposed. If we studied Divine truths as Christians, our being constantly engaged in the service of God would be friendly to our growth in grace. We should be "like trees planted by the rivers of waters, that bring forth fruit in their season", and all that we did would be likely to "prosper". But if we study it only as preachers, it will be the reverse. Our being conversant with the Bible will be like surgeons and soldiers being conversant with the shedding of human blood, till they lose all sensibility concerning it. I believe it is a fact that, where a preacher is wicked, he is generally the most hardened against conviction of any character whatever. Happy will it be for us if, like Barnabas, we are "full of faith" in that Saviour whom we recommend—in that gospel which it is our employment to proclaim.

IV. We come now to the last part of the subject, which is held up by way of encouragement: AND MUCH PEOPLE WAS ADDED UNTO THE LORD. When our ministry is blessed to the conversion of sinners, to the bringing them off from their connexion with sin itself to a vital union with Christ; when our congregations are filled, not merely with professors of religion, but with sound believers; when such believers come forward and offer themselves willingly for communion, saying, "We will go with you, for we have heard that God is with you"; then it may be said that "much people is added unto the Lord". The connexion between such additions, and eminency in grace and holiness in a minister, deserve our serious attention.

I think it may be laid down as a rule, which both Scripture and experience will confirm, that *eminent spirituality in a minister is usually attended with eminent usefulness*. I do not mean to say our usefulness depends upon our spirituality, as an effect depends upon its cause; nor yet that it is always in proportion to it. God is a Sovereign; and frequently sees proper to convince us of it, in variously bestowing his blessing on the means of grace. But yet he is not wanting in giving encouragement to what he approves, wherever it is found. Our want of usefulness is often to be ascribed to our want of spirituality, much oftener than to our want of talents. God has frequently been known to succeed men of inferior abilities, when they have been eminent for holiness, while he has blasted others of much superior talents, when that quality has been wanting. Hundreds of ministers, who, on account of their gifts, have promised to be shining characters, have proved the reverse; and all owing to such things as pride, unwatchfulness, carnality, and levity.

Eminency in grace, my brother, will contribute to your success in three ways:—

1. It will fire your soul *with holy love to Christ and the souls of men*; and such a spirit is usually attended with success. I believe you will find that, in almost all the great works which God has wrought in any period of time, he has honoured men of this character, by making them his instruments. In the midst of a sore calamity upon the murmuring Israelites, when God was inclined to show mercy, it was by the means of his servant Aaron running with a censer of fire in his hand, and standing between the living and the dead! The great reformation that was brought about in the days of Hezekiah was by the instrumentality of a man "who wrought that which was good and right and truth before the Lord his God"; and then it follows, "and in every work that he began in the service of the house of God, and in the law, and in the commandments, to seek his God, *he did it with all his heart*, and *prospered*".

There was another great reformation in the Jewish church, about the time of their return from Babylon. One of the chief instruments in this work was Ezra, "a ready scribe in the law of his God"—a man who had "prepared his heart to seek the law of the Lord, and to do it, and to teach in Israel statues and judgments"—a man who "fasted and prayed at the river Ahava", previously to his great undertaking—a man who was afterwards "sorely astonished, and in heaviness, and would eat no meat, nor drink water, but fell upon his knees, and spread out his hands unto the Lord his God, on account of the transgressions of the people". Another great instrument in this work was Nehemiah, a man who devoted himself wholly to the service of God and his people, labouring night and day, and was not to be seduced by the intrigues of God's adversaries, nor yet intimidated by their threatenings; but persevered in his work till it was finished, closing his labours with this solemn prayer and appeal, "Think upon me, O my God, for good, according to all that I have done for this people."

Time would fail me to speak of all the great souls, both inspired and uninspired, whom the King of kings has delighted to honour: of Paul, and Peter, and their companions; of Wickliff, and Luther, and Calvin, and many others at the Reformation; of Elliot, and Edwards, and Brainerd, and Whitefield, and hundreds more whose names are held in deserved esteem in the church of God. These were men of God; men who had great grace, as well as gifts; whose hearts burned in love to Christ and the souls of men. They looked upon their hearers as their Lord had done upon Jerusalem, and wept over them. In this manner they delivered their messages; "and much people were added unto the Lord".

2. Eminency in grace will *direct your ends to the glory of God, and the welfare of men's souls*; and where this is the case, it is usually attended with a blessing. These are ends which God himself pursues; and if we pursue the same, we are "labourers together with God", and may hope for his blessing to attend our labours; but if we pursue separate and selfish ends, we walk contrary to God, and may expect God to walk contrary to us. Whatever apparent success may attend the labours of a man whose ends are evil, all is to be suspected; either the success is not genuine, or, if it be, it is not in a way of blessing upon him, nor shall it turn out, at last, to his account. It must be an inexpressible satisfaction, brother, to be able to say as the primitive ministers and apostles did: "James, a servant of God—Paul, a servant of Jesus Christ—We seek not yours, but you."

3. Eminency in grace will enable you to *bear prosperity in your ministry without being lifted up with it; and so contribute towards it*. It is written of Christ, in prophecy, "He shall build the temple of the Lord, and shall *bear* the glory." He does bear it indeed; but to bear glory without being elated is no easy thing for us. I am often afraid lest this should be one considerable reason why most of us have no more real success in our work than we have; perhaps it is not safe for us to be much owned of God; perhaps we have not grace enough to bear prosperity.

My dear brother, permit me to conclude with a word or two of serious advice. First, "Watch over your own soul, as well as the souls of your people." Do not forget that ministers are peculiarly liable, while they keep the vineyard of others, to neglect their own. Further, "Know your own weakness, and depend upon Christ's all-sufficiency." Your work is great, your trials may be many; but let not your heart be discouraged. Remember what was said to the apostle Paul, "my grace is sufficient for thee, my strength is made perfect in weakness"; and the reflection which he makes upon it, "When I am weak, then am I strong". Finally, *Be often looking to the end of your course, and viewing yourself as giving an account of your stewardship*. We must all appear before the judgment-seat of Christ, and give account of the deeds done in the body. Perhaps there is no thought more solemn than this, more suitable to be kept in view in all our undertakings, more awakening in a thoughtless hour, or more cheering to an upright heart.

I have only to request, my dear brother, that you will excuse the freedom of this plain address. I have not spoken so much to instruct you in things which you know not, as to remind and impress you with things which you already know. The Lord bless you, and grant that the solemnities of this day may ever be remembered with satisfaction, both by you and your people!

APPENDIX 2

Spiritual knowledge and love necessary for the ministry.[1]

"He was a burning and a shining light"—John v.35.

In addressing you, my dear brother, on this solemn occasion, I shall not undertake so much to communicate any thing new as to remind you of what you know, and have felt already. You are aware that there are two main objects to be attained in the work of the Christian ministry—*enlightening the minds* and *affecting the hearts* of the people. These are the usual means by which the work of God is accomplished. Allow me to remind you that, in order to the attainment of these objects, you yourself must be under their influence. If you would enlighten others, you must be "a shining light" yourself. And if you would affect others, you yourself must feel; your own heart must "burn" with holy ardour. You must be "a *burning* and a *shining* light".

It is not enough that you should be what is called a *popular preacher*. A man may have gifts, so as to shine in the eyes of the multitude, almost as bright as he does in his own eyes; and yet possess little or nothing of *spiritual* light— light, the tendency of which is to transform the heart. So also a man may burn with zeal, as Jehu did, and yet have little or no true love to God, or affection for the souls of men. *Spiritual light* and *holy love* are the qualities which Christ here commends.

You will give your candid attention, my dear brother, while I endeavour to remind you of the necessity of each of these, in the different parts of your important work:—in the great work of preaching the gospel—in presiding in the church—in visiting your people—and in your whole demeanour through life.

I. In the great work of PREACHING THE GOSPEL.—O my brother, in this department we had need resemble the living creatures mentioned by Ezekiel, (chap. i.18,) "full of eyes". We had almost need, in one view, to be made up of pure intellect—to be all light. I shall not attempt to decide how much knowledge is necessary, of men and things, of past and present times, of the church and the world; but shall confine myself to two or three particulars, as

---

[1] Fuller, *Works*, i.478-482.

specimens.

1. How necessary is it to understand in some good degree *the holy character of God!*—It is this to which you will find that men in general are blind. They conceive of God as if he were such a one as themselves ... And hence they fancy they are not enemies to him. You will have to point out the true character of God, that the sinner may see his own deformity, and not have the enmity of his heart concealed from his eyes. A just view of the holy character of God will also be one of the best preservatives against error in other respects. Almost all the errors in the world proceed from ignorance of the true character of God. To what else can be attributed the errors of Socinianism, Arianism, and Antinomianism? From degraded views of God's character arise diminutive notions of the evil of sin—of its just demerit—of our lost condition—of our need of a great Saviour—and of the work of the Spirit. O my brother, may you shed abroad this light with unsullied lustre! And, in order to this, commune much with God in private; since there is no way of knowing the true character of another so well as by personal, private intercourse.

2. A knowledge of *Christ, as the Mediator* between God and man, is necessary.—"This is life eternal, to know thee, the only true God, and Jesus Christ whom thou hast sent." Here, also, men are greatly ignorant. He is in the world, and the world knows him not. It must be our concern, as ministers, to know him; and, comparatively speaking, "to know nothing else" ... and this that we may diffuse the knowledge of him to others. The glory of Christ's character is such that if he were but viewed in a true light, and not through the false mediums of prejudice and the love of sin, but through the mirror of the gospel, he must be loved, John iv.29, 39-42. Here, my brother, we need to be intimately acquainted with Christ, that we may be able on all occasions to give him a just character—that we may be able to tell of his dignity, his love, the generous principles of his undertaking, and how nobly he executed the arduous enterprise.

3. A knowledge of *human nature as created* is necessary.—We shall be unskillful workmen, unless we are acquainted with the materials on which we have to work. It is not more necessary for a surgeon or a physician to understand the anatomy of the human body, than it is for ministers to understand what may be called the anatomy of the soul. We had need enter into all the springs of action. In particular, we must be very careful to distinguish between primary and criminal passions. God habitually addresses the former, and so should we, but not the latter; the latter being only the abuse of the principles implanted in our nature. To be more explicit, God has created us with the love of possession, but the excess of this love becomes covetousness and idolatry. God has implanted within us a principle of emulation; but the abuse of this is pride and ambition. God has created us with the love of pleasure; but this indulged to excess becomes sensuality. Now the gospel never addresses itself to our corrupt passions; but the word of God is full of appeals to those principles of our nature with which we are created. For example: in his word, God

addresses himself to our love of possession; and points to "an inheritance, incorruptible, undefiled, and that fadeth not away"—to the principle of emulation; and presents to our view "a crown"—to our love of pleasure; and informs us that "in his presence there is fullness of joy, and at his right hand are pleasures for evermore". And in short, in the same way, he addresses the principles of zeal, love, hatred, shame, fear, revenge, &c. And so must we.

4. A knowledge of human nature *as depraved* is necessary.—Without this knowledge, we shall be unable to trace and detect the workings of a wicked heart. Sin is a deceitful thing, and we are apt to be imposed upon by its specious names. Parsimoniousness is called frugality; prodigality, generosity; bitterness of spirit in reproving, fidelity; and resentment, a becoming spirit. We need therefore to know the root of the disease, and the various ways in which it operates. In order to effect a cure, the knowledge of the disease is indispensable; and in order to attain to this knowledge, we must study the various symptoms by which the disorder may be distinguished.

5. A knowledge of human nature *as sanctified by the Spirit* is necessary.— Without this, we shall be unable to trace the work of God in the soul; and unable to fan the gentle flame of Divine love in the genuine Christian, and to detect and expose the various counterfeits.

You will need also, my brother, a heart *warmed* with Divine things, or you will never be "a burning and a shining light". When we are thinking or preaching, we need to *burn*, as well as shine. When we study, we may rack our brains, and form plans; but unless "our hearts burn within us", all will be a mere skeleton—our thoughts mere bones; whatever be their number, they will be all dry—very dry; and if we do not feel what we say, our preaching will be poor dead work. Affected zeal will not do. A gilded fire may shine, but it will not warm. We may smite with the hand, and stamp with the foot, and throw ourselves into violent agitations; but if we feel not it is not likely the people will—unless, indeed, it be a feeling of disgust. But suppose there be no affectation, nor any deficiency of good and sound doctrine; yet if in our work we feel no inward satisfaction, we shall resemble a mill-stone—preparing food for others, the value of which we are unable to appreciate ourselves. Indeed, without feeling, we shall be incapable of preaching any truth or of inculcating any duty aright. How can we display the evil of sin, the love of Christ, or any other important truth, unless we feel it? How can we preach against sin, without feel a holy indignation against it? It is this that will cause us, while we denounce sin, to weep over the sinner. Otherwise, we may deal in flings and personalities; but these will only irritate; they will never reclaim. O! if ever we do any good in our work, it must be the effect of love to God and love to men— love to the souls of men, while we detest, and expose, and denounce their sins. How could Paul have pursued his work with the ardour and intenseness which he manifested, if his heart had not burned with holy love?

II. Spiritual light and holy love are equally necessary in PRESIDING IN THE CHURCH OF GOD.

Wisdom and love are necessary, calmly to lay down rules of discipline—to solve difficult questions—to prepare and digest, in concurrence with the deacons, such matters as require to be laid before the church—to nip little differences in the bud—to mediate between contending parties, &c. My brother, think of the example of the Lord Jesus, who, in his intercourse with his disciples, saluted them with this benediction—"Peace be with you!" The great art of presiding in a church, so as to promote its welfare, is to be neutral between the members, always on the side of God and righteousness, and to let them see that, whatever your opinion may be, you really love them.

III. These qualities are necessary in the more private duty of VISITING THE PEOPLE.

A considerable part of the pastoral office consists in visiting the people, especially the afflicted. Paul could appeal to the elders of the church at Ephesus, that he had taught them publicly and "from house to house". It is of great consequence that, in your pastoral visits, you should preserve the character of "a burning and a shining light". Pastoral visits should not degenerate into religious gossiping—a practice in which some have indulged to the disgrace of religion. Unused to habits of reflection, they feel no relish for solitude; and therefore, to employ the time which hangs so heavy on their hands, they saunter about to see their friends, and to ask them how they are. Nor is this the worst. Satan promptly furnishes a subject where there is such a dearth; and hence gossiping has generally produced tales of slander, and practices which have proved a scandal to the Christian name! I trust, my brother, you know the preciousness of time too well to squander it away in idle visits. And yet visiting is an essential part of your work, that you may become acquainted with the circumstances, the spiritual necessities of your people. They will be able to impart their feelings freely and unreservedly; and you will be able to administer the appropriate counsel to much better purpose than you possibly can from the pulpit, and with greater particularity than would be becoming in a public address. Only let us burn while we shine. Let a savour of Christ accompany all our instructions. A minister who maintains an upright, affectionate conduct, may say almost any thing, in a way of just reproof, without giving offence.

IV. Spiritual light and holy love are necessary in YOUR WHOLE DEMEANOUR THROUGH LIFE. May you, my brother, shine in holy wisdom, and burn with ardent love. You will need them, wherever you go—in whatever you engage—that you may walk as one of the children of light.

Allow me to point a few things which I have found of use, to conduce to these ends:—

1. *Read the lives of good men*—the lives of such men as God has distinguished for gifts, and graces, and usefulness. Example has a great influence. The scriptures abound with such examples. And, blessed be God, we have some now.

2. *Study the word of God, above all other books, and pray over it.*—It is this

will set our hearts on fire. There are no such motives exhibited any where as there—no such exhibitions of wisdom and love.

3. *Read men*, as well as books, *and your own heart*, in order that you may read others.—Copyists, you know, are generally bunglers. There is nothing that equals what is taken immediately from the life. We need always be making our observations, wherever we are, or wherever we go. If we get a system of human nature, or experience, or any thing else, from books, rather than from our own knowledge, it will be liable to two disadvantages. First, It is not likely to be so near the truth; for systems which go through several hands are like successive copies of a painting, every copy of the preceding one is more unlike the original—or like the telling of a tale, the circumstances of which you do not know of your own personal knowledge: every time it is repeated there is some variation, and thus it becomes further removed from the truth. Thus Agrippa showed his wisdom, when, instead of depending on the testimony of others, he determined to hear Paul himself. Secondly, If it be correct, still it will not be so serviceable to *you* as if it were a system of your own working. Saul's armour might be better than David's sling; but not to him, seeing he had not proved it.

4. *Live the life of a Christian*, as well as of a minister.—Read as one, preach as one, converse as one—to *be profited*, as well as to profit others. One of the greatest temptations of a ministerial life is to handle Divine truth as ministers, rather than as Christians—for others, rather than for ourselves. But the word will not profit them that *preach* it, any more than it will them that hear it, unless it be "mixed with faith". If we study the Scriptures as Christians, the more familiar we are with them, the more we shall feel their importance; but if our object be only to find out something to say to others, our familiarity with them will prove a snare. It will resemble that of soldiers, and doctors, and undertakers with death; the more familiar we are with them, the less we shall feel their importance. See Prov. xxii.17, 18; Psal. i.2, 3.

5. *Commune with God in private*.—Walking with God in the closet is a grand means, with his blessing, of illuminating our minds and warming our hearts. When Moses came down from the mount, his face shone bright, and his heart burned with zeal for the honour of God and the good of his people. Alas! alas! for want of this. ... See Jer. x.21.

6. Hold forth the word of life, not only by precept, but by *a holy practice*.— "Let your light so shine before men, that they, seeing your good works, may glorify your Father who is in heaven." Without this, in vain will be all our pretensions to being "burning and shining lights".

My dear brother, allow me to conclude with an earnest prayer, that you may long continue a "burning and a shining light" to this church; and that, after having "turned many to righteousness", you may shine as a distinguished star in the firmament for ever and ever!

APPENDIX 3

Letter to John Ryland, jun., with advice to ministerial students[1]

I remember my visit to Bristol with pleasure, and the treatment of friends there with gratitude. My love to all who may inquire after me. I hope the students do not smoke more or longer than when I came. I must say, however, that I relished several pipes in their company. I earnestly wish they may steer clear of the ditch and the quagmire. It is of vast importance for a minister to be decidedly on the side of God, against himself as a sinner, and against an apostate world. Nor is it less important that he have an ardent love to Christ, and the gospel of salvation by free grace. I wish they may so believe and feel and preach the truth, as to find their message an important reality, influencing their own souls and those of others. Let them beware of so preaching doctrine as to forget to declare *all* the counsel of God, all the precepts of the Word. Let them equally beware of so dwelling upon the preceptive part of Scripture as to forget the grand principles on which alone it can be carried into effect. We may contend for practical religion, and yet neglect the practice of religion. I should not write thus, if I did not know that they would take kindly the hints I may give of this sort, or any other.

---

[1] Fuller, letter to John Ryland, jun., 5 April 1799, in Ryland, *Life of Fuller*, 234. Ryland was then the principal of the Baptist Academy at Bristol.

APPENDIX 4

Letter to a young minister in prospect of ordination[1]

MY DEAR FRIEND,

As it is very doubtful whether I shall be able to attend your ordination, you will allow me to fill up the sheet with brotherly counsel.

You are about to enter, my brother, on the solemn work of a pastor, and I heartily wish you God speed. I have seldom engaged in an ordination of late in which I have had to address a younger brother, without thinking of the apostle's words in 2 Tim. iv. 5, 6, in reference to myself and others who are going off the stage: "Make full proof of *thy* ministry: for *I* am now ready to be offered, and the time of my departure is at hand!" Your charge at present is small; but if God bless you, it may be expected to increase, and of course your labours and cares will increase with it. If you would preserve spirituality, purity, peace, and good order in the church, you must live near to God yourself, and be diligent to feed the flock of God with evangelical truth. Without these, nothing good will be done. Love your brethren, and be familiar with them; not, however, with that kind of familiarity which breeds disrespect, by which some have degraded themselves in the eyes of the people, and invited the opposition of the contentious part of them; but that which will endear your fellowship, and render all your meetings a delight. Never avail yourself of your independence of the people in respect of support, to carry matters with a high hand amongst them. Teach them so to conduct themselves as a church, that if you were to die, they might continue a wise, holy, and understanding people. The great secret of ruling a church is to convince them that you love them, and say and do every thing for their good. Love, however, requires to be mingled with faithfulness, as well as faithfulness with love. Expect to find defects and faults in your members, and give them to expect free and faithful dealing while connected with you; allow them, also, to be free and faithful towards you in return. There will be many faults which they should be taught and encouraged to correct in one another; others will be proper objects of pastoral admonition; and some must be brought before the church. But do not degrade the dignity of a church by employing it to sit in judgment on the shape of a cap, or a bonnet; or on squabbles between individuals, which had better be healed by the interposition of a common friend. The church should be taught, like a regiment of soldiers, to

---

[1] Andrew Fuller, letter, 30 August 1810, in *The Baptist Magazine* (London), 7 (October 1815), 419-420.

attend to discipline, when called to it, in a proper spirit; not with ebullitions of anger against an offender, but with fear and trembling, considering themselves, lest they also be tempted. Let no one say to another, "overlook my fault today, and I will overlook yours tomorrow"; but, rather, "deal faithfully with me today, and I will deal faithfully with you tomorrow".

I have always found it good to have an understanding with the deacons upon every case before it is brought before the church. Neither they nor the members have always been of my opinion; and where this has been the case I have not attempted to carry a measure against them, but have yielded, and this not merely from prudence, but as knowing that others have understanding as well as I, and may therefore be in the right. In this way I have been pastor of the church, which I now serve [Kettering], for nearly thirty years without a single difference.

A young man in your circumstances will have an advantage in beginning a church on a small scale. It will be like cultivating a garden before you undertake a field. You may also form them, in many respects, to your own mind; but if your mind be not the mind of Christ, it will, after all, be of no use. Labour to form them after Christ's mind, and you will find your own peace and happiness in it.

Mercy and truth attend you and the partner of your cares! I am, &c.,

A.Fuller

Bibliography

1. Manuscripts

Angus Library, Regent's Park College, Oxford

Fawcett, John, Andrew Fuller, J.W. Morris, and John Ryland. Correspondence to Rev. John Sutcliff. 1773-1811. Bound signed autograph letters. Baptist Missionary Society Home—Correspondence.

Fuller, Andrew. Signed autograph letters to Carey, Ward, Marshman and others in Serampore, India. 1796-1815. Baptist Missionary Society—Home. Officers: Letters and Papers.

— Letters, in typewritten transcription by Ernest A. Payne and Joyce A. Booth.

Soham Baptist Church Book. 1752-1868. Typewritten transcription by L. Grimshaw.

Bristol Baptist College

Ryland, John. "Autograph Reminiscences". 1807. Bound autograph manuscript.

Fuller Baptist Church, Kettering, Northamptonshire

"A brief history of the Baptist Church at Kettering". ca. 1820. Autograph manuscript. Gotch Papers.

Brown, John, and Andrew Fuller, Narrative notes on the history of the Kettering Baptist Church. ca. 1788. Bound autograph manuscript.

Church Book. ca. 1768-1815. Bound autograph manuscript.

Fuller, Andrew. Bound autograph volumes of transcribed correspondence. Compiled by A.G. Fuller. 2 Volumes.

— Sermon outlines and exegetical notes, largely in shorthand. "XXX. From August 26th to Dec. 19, 1813". Autograph notebook.

Hall, Robert, jun. "A Charge Delivered by the Revd R. Hall, Leicester, at the Ordination of His Nephew, the Revd J.K. Hall at Kettering, 1815". Autograph notebook.

Pew subscriptions. (1815?) Autograph notebook.

Wallis, George. "Memoirs, etc, of State of Mind, continued". March 15, 1805 - June 1, 1817. Autograph diary.

Northamptonshire Record Office

Northamptonshire Baptist Association. Bound autograph annual letters from the churches.

Ryland, John. "History of the Baptist Church at Northampton". ca. 1793. Autograph notebook. College Street Baptist Church Records.

Soham Baptist Church / County Records Office, Cambridge

Church Book. 1752-1868. Bound autograph manuscript.

Fuller, Andrew. "A narration of the dealings of God in a way of Providence with the Baptist Church of Christ at Soham, from the year 1770, as Containing its dissolution, replantation, and progression". 1782. Autograph notebook.

The History of Soham Baptist Church. n.d. Typewritten manuscript.

2. Printed Primary Sources

Ash, John. *The Perfection of the Saints for the Work of the Ministry. A Sermon Preached in Broad-Mead, Bristol, before the Bristol Education Society*. Bristol: W. Pine, 1778.

Aspland, Robert. *Bigotry and Intolerance Defeated; or, an Account of the Late Prosecution of Mr. John Gisburne, Unitarian Minister of Soham, Cambridgeshire: With an Exposure and Correction of the Defects and Mistakes of Mr. Andrew Fuller's Narrative of That Affair: In Letters to John Christie, Esq.* Harlow: B. Flower, 1810.

The Baptist Magazine. Vol 7. London: J. Barfield, 1815.

Baxter, Richard. *The Reformed Pastor*. Edited by William Brown. 1656. Reprint, Edinburgh: Banner of Truth Trust, 2001.

Bicheno, James. *A Glance at the History of Christianity, and of English Nonconformity*, 2nd ed. Newbury, 1798.

Blackmore, Richard. *The Accomplished Preacher: Or, an Essay Upon Divine Eloquence*. London: J. Downing, 1731.

Booth, Abraham. *Pastoral Cautions: An Address to the Late Mr. Thomas Hopkins, When Ordained Pastor of the Church of Christ, in Eagle Street, Red Lion Square, London, July 13, 1785. Now Published and Greatly Enlarged.* London: C. Whitingham, 1805.

— *The Works of Abraham Booth*. 3 volumes. London: J. Haddon, 1813.

Brine, John. *A Refutation of Arminian Principles, Delivered in a Pamphlet, Intitled, the Modern Question Concerning Repentance and Faith, Examined with Candour, &c., in a Letter to a Friend*. London: A. Ward, 1743.

Brown, John. *The Love of God Inseparable from His People. A Sermon Preached at the Interment of Mr. William Wallis, at Kettering, in Northamptonshire, Who Died October the 12th, 1757, in the Fifty-Fifth Year of His Age.* London: George Keith, 1758.

Brown, Rev. John, ed. *The Christian Pastor's Manual: A Selection of Tracts on the Duties, Difficulties, and Encouragements of the Christian Ministry*. 1826. Reprint, Ligonier, PA: Soli Deo Gloria Publications, 1991.

Bunyan, John. *Grace Abounding to the Chief of Sinners*. Edited by W.R. Owens. London: Penguin, 1987.

— *The Miscellaneous Works of John Bunyan*. Vol. 12. Edited by W.R. Owens. Oxford: Clarendon Press, 1994.

Burnet, Gilbert. *A Discourse of the Pastoral Care*, 4th ed. Dublin: J. Hyde and R. Gunne, 1726.

Carey, William. *An Enquiry into the Obligations of Christians to Use Means for the Conversion of the Heathens*. 1792. Reprint, London: Carey Kingsgate Press, 1961.

Claude, Jean. *Essay on the Composition of a Sermon*, 3rd ed. Translated by Robert Robinson. 2 volumes. London: Scollick, Wilson & Spence, 1788.

Collins, Hercules. *The Temple Repair'd: Or, an Essay to Revive the Long-Neglected Ordinances, of Exercising the Spiritual Gift of Prophecy for the Edification of the Churches; and of Ordaining Ministers Duly Qualified*. London: William and Joseph Marshal, 1702.

Crisp, Tobias. *Christ Alone Exalted*, 4th ed. London: R. Noble, 1791.

Crosby, Thomas. *History of the English Baptists from the Reformation to the Beginning of the Reign of King George I*. London: J. Robinson, 1738-1740.

Davis, Richard. *Hymns Composed on Several Subjects, and on Divers Occasions*, 7th ed. Edited by John Gill. London, 1748.

— *A Vindication of the Doctrine of Justification and Union before Faith*. London, 1698.

Day, Robert. *The Labor and Fruits of a Christian Husbandman. A Sermon Preached before the Bristol Education Society*. Bristol: W. Pine, 1779.

Doddridge, Philip. *Lectures on Preaching, and the Several Branches of the Ministerial Office*. Boston: Manning and Loring, 1808.

— *The Miscellaneous Works of Philip Doddridge, D.D.* London: Joseph Ogle Robinson, 1830.

[Dutton, Anne]. *A Brief Account of the Gracious Dealings of God with a Poor, Sinful, Unworthy Creature*. London: J. Hart, 1750.

Edwards, Jonathan. *Freedom of the Will*. Edited by Paul Ramsey. Vol. 1 of *The Works of Jonathan Edwards*, edited by J.E. Smith. New Haven: Yale University Press, 1957.

— *The "Miscellanies. 501-832*. Edited by Ava Chamberlain. Vol. 18 of *The Works of Jonathan Edwards*, edited by Harry Stout. New Haven: Yale University Press, 2000.

— *Sermons and Discourses, 1730-1733*. Edited by Mark Valeri. Vol. 17 of *The Works of Jonathan Edwards*. edited by Harry Stout. New Haven: Yale University Press, 1999.

— *Treatise Concerning the Religious Affections*. Edited by J.E. Smith, Vol. 2 of *The Works of Jonathan Edwards*, edited by Perry Miller. New Haven: Yale University Press, 1959.

Erskine, Ralph. *Gospel Sonnets, or Spiritual Songs*, 8th ed. London: Dilly, 1762.

The Evangelical Magazine. Vol. 3. London: T. Chapman, 1795.

Evans, Caleb, and Hugh Evans. *A Charge and Sermon Delivered at the Ordination of the Rev. Thomas Dunscombe, at Coate, Oxon*. Bristol: W. Pine, 1773.

Evans, Hugh. *The Able Minister: A Sermon Preached in Broadmead before the Bristol Education Society*. Bristol: W. Pine, 1773.

— *Ministers Described, under the Characters of Fathers and Prophets, and Their Death Improved. A Sermon Preached to the Ministers and Messengers of Several Associated Churches at Bethesda, near Newport, in the County of Monmouth*. Bristol: W. Pine, 1773.

Fawcett, John. *The Constitution and Order of a Gospel Church Considered*. Ewood Hall, 1797.

Fuller, Andrew. *The Complete Works of Rev. Andrew Fuller with a Memoir of His Life by Andrew Gunton Fuller*. Edited by Joseph Belcher. 3 vols. Philadelphia: American Baptist Publications, 1845.

— *The Diary of Andrew Fuller*. Edited by Michael M. McMullen. Vol. 1 of *The Complete Works of Andrew Fuller*, edited by Michael A.G. Haykin. Carlisle: Paternoster Press, forthcoming.

— "Essay on the Composition of a Sermon: Or, Plain and Familiar Thoughts, Addressed to a Young Minister, from His Pastor". In *The Preacher; or Sketches of Original Sermons, Chiefly Selected from the Manuscripts of Two Eminent Divines of the Last Century for the Use of Lay Preachers and Young Ministers*, Vol. 1, 13-21. Philadelphia: J. Whetham & Son, 1842.

— *The Last Remains of the Rev. Andrew Fuller*. Edited by Joseph Belcher. Philadelphia: American Baptist Publication Society, 1856.

— "Preface". In *Thornton Abbey: A Series of Letters on Religious Subjects*, by John Satchel. Philadelphia and Richmond: Johnson and Warner, 1811.

Fuller, Andrew, and John Ryland. *The Qualifications and Encouragements of a Faithful Minister, Illustrated by the Character and Success of Barnabas, and Paul's Charge to the Corinthians Respecting Their Treatment of Timothy, Applied to the Conduct of Churches toward Their Pastors*. London: J. Buckland, 1787.

Fuller, Andrew Gunton. *Andrew Fuller*. Men Worth Remembering. London: Hodder and Stoughton, 1882.

Fuller, Thomas Ekins. *A Memoir of the Life and Writings of Andrew Fuller*. The Bunyan Library. London: J. Heaton & Son, 1863.

Gibson, Edmund. *Codex Juris Ecclesiastici Anglicani: Or, the Statutes, Constitutions, Canons, Rubricks and Articles, of the Church of England*. London, 1713.

Gill, John. *A Collection of Sermons and Tracts*. 2 vols. London: George Keith, 1773.

— *A Complete Body of Doctrinal and Practical Divinity or a System of Evangelical Truths Deduced from the Sacred Scriptures*. 2 vols. Tegg & Co., 1839. Reprint, Grand Rapids: Baker Book House, 1978.

— *An Exposition of the New Testament*. 3 vols. Philadelphia: William W. Woodward, 1811.

Hall, Robert. *The Works of Robert Hall*. Edited by Olinthus Gregory. 6 Vols. London: Holdsworth and Ball, 1832.

Hall, Robert, sen. *Help to Zion's Travellers: Being an Attempt to Remove Various Stumbling Blocks out of the Way, Relating to Doctrinal, Experimental, and Practical Religion*. Bristol: William Pine, 1781.

Haykin, Michael A.G., ed. *The Armies of the Lamb: The Spirituality of Andrew Fuller*. Dundas: Joshua Press, 2001.

— ed. *"Pure Religion and Undefiled": Spiritual Letters of Andrew Fuller*. Dundas: Joshua Press, 1999.

Hussey, Joseph. *God's Operations of Grace, but No Offers of His Grace*. London: D. Bridge, 1707.

Jenkins, Joseph, et al. *A Charge Delivered at the Ordination of Mr. John Rogers, at Eynsford, in Kent, September 29, 1802, by Joseph Jenkins, D.D. Together with a Sermon to the Church, by James Upton; and Introductory Discourse by John Stanger, and Mr. Rogers's Confession of Faith. Published at the Request of the Church and Congregation*. London: C. Whittingham, 1802.

Keach, Benjamin. *The Glory of a True Church, and Its Discipline Display'd*. London, 1697.

Lumpkin, William L. *Baptist Confessions of Faith*, rev. ed. Valley Forge: Judson Press, 1969.

Maurice, Matthias. *A Modern Question Modestly Answered*. London, 1737.

Morris, J. W. *Memoirs of the Life and Writings of the Rev. Andrew Fuller*. Edited by Rufus Babcock. Boston: Lincoln & Edmands, 1830.

Nuovo, Victor, ed. *John Locke: Writings on Religion*. Oxford: Clarendon Press, 2002.

Owens, W.R., ed. *The Miscellaneous Works of John Bunyan*. Vol. 12. Oxford: Clarendon Press, 1994.

Periodical Accounts Relative to the Baptist Missionary Society. Vol. 1. Clipstone: J.W. Morris, 1800.

Perkins, William. *The Art of Prophesying, with the Calling of the Ministry*. 1606. Reprint, Edinburgh: Banner of Truth Trust, 2002.

Rippon, John. *The Baptist Annual Register*. 4 vols. London, 1790-1802.

— "A Brief Memoir of the Life and Writings of the Reverend and Learned John Gill, D.D." In John Gill. *An Exposition of the Old Testament*. Vol. 1, ix-xxxvi. London: City Press, 1852.

— *Selection of Hymns from the Best Authors, Intended to Be an Appendix to Dr. Watts's Psalms and Hymns*, 10th ed. London: J. Bateson, 1800.

Robinson, Robert. *A Sermon Preached at the Ordination of the Rev. Mr. George Birley*. N.p., 1786.

Ryland, John. *A Candid Statement of the Reasons Which Induce the Baptists to Differ in Opinion and Practice from Their Christian Brethren*, 2nd ed. London: Wightman and Cramp, 1827.

— *Christianæ Militiæ Viaticum: Or, a Brief Directory for Evangelical Ministers*, 2nd ed. London: W. Button, 1799.

— *The Earnest Charge and Humble Hope of an Affectionate Pastor: Being the Substance of Three Discourses, Addressed to the Church, and Congregation, in College Lane, Northampton*. Bristol: W. Pine, 1793.

— *The Indwelling and Righteousness of Christ No Security against Corporeal Death, but the Source of Spiritual and Eternal Life. A Sermon Preached at Kettering, in Northamptonshire, at the Funeral of the Rev. Andrew Fuller*. London: W. Button & Son, 1815.

— *Memoirs of the Rev. Robert Hall of Arnsby; with a Brief History of the Baptist Church, at Arnsby, Leicestershire*, 2nd ed. Revised by J.A. Jones. London: James Paul, 1850.

— [Agnostos]. *Remarks Upon the Notion of Extraordinary Impulses and Impressions on the Imagination, Indulged by Many Professors of Religion; Contained in a Letter to a Friend*, rev. ed. Bristol, 1804.

— *The Work of Faith, the Labour of Love, and the Patience of Hope, Illustrated; in the Life and Death of the Rev. Andrew Fuller*, 2nd ed. London: Button & Son, 1818.

Ryland, John, Andrew Fuller, John Sutcliff, and Thomas Morgan. *The Difficulties of the Christian Ministry, and the Means of Surmounting Them; with the Obedience of Churches to Their Pastors Explained and Enforced ... Delivered ... At the Ordination of Thomas Morgan, to the Pastoral Office*. Birmingham: J. Belcher, 1802.

Ryland, John, and James Hinton. *The Difficulties and Supports of a Gospel Minister; and the Duties Incumbent on a Christian Church ... at the Ordination of Thomas Coles, A.M. To the Pastoral Care of the Baptist Church at Bourton-on-the-Water, Gloucestershire*. Bristol: Harris and Bryan, 1801.

Ryland, John, and Samuel Pearce. *The Duty of Ministers to Be Nursing Fathers to the Church; and the Duty of Churches to Regard Ministers as the Gift of Christ ... At the*

Ordination of the Rev. W. Belsher. London: Button, 1796.

Ryland, John Collett. *The Beauty of Social Religion; or, the Nature and Glory of a Gospel Church, Represented in a Circular Letter ...* Northampton: T. Dicey, 1777.

— *The Christian Preacher Delineated.* London: D. Nottage, 1757.

— *The Student and Preacher; or Advice to Students of Divinity and Young Ministers of the Gospel, by John Ryland, A.M., Master of a Boarding School in Northampton.* London: John Wheeler Pasham, 1770.

— *The Wise Student and Christian Preacher: A Sermon Preached at Broad-Mead, August 28, 1780, Being the Day of the Annual Meeting of the Bristol Education Society.* Bristol: W. Pine, 1780.

— ed. *Dr. Cotton Mather's Student and Preacher. Intituled, Manuductio Ad Ministerium; or, Directions for a Candidate of the Ministry.* London: Charles Dilly, 1781.

Ryland, Jonathan Edwards, ed. *Pastoral Memorials: Selected from the Manuscripts of the Late Revd. John Ryland, D.D. Of Bristol.* London: B.J. Holdsworth, 1828.

Smalley, John. *The Consistency of the Sinner's Inability to Comply with the Gospel, with His Inexcusable Guilt in Not Complying with It, Illustrated and Confirmed in Two Discourses on John vi^{th}, 44th.* Hartford: Green & Watson, 1769.

Spurgeon, Charles H. *An All-Round Ministry: Addresses to Ministers and Students.* 1900. Reprint, London: The Banner of Truth Trust, 1972.

— *The Autobiography of Charles H. Spurgeon.* Edited by Susannah Spurgeon and W.J. Harrald. 4 vols. Philadelphia: American Baptist Publication Company, ca. 1897-1900.

— *Lectures to My Students.* Grand Rapids: Zondervan, 1954.

Steadman, William. *The Salvation of Men, the Desire and Prayer of Every Faithful Minister.* Bristol: J. Rose, 1797.

Stennett, Joseph. *The Complaints of an Unsuccessful Ministry. A Sermon Preached to the Ministers and Messengers of Several Churches in the West of England, Met Together in Association.* London: J. Ward, 1753.

— *The Works of the Late Reverend and Learned Mr. Joseph Stennett.* Vol. 2. London, 1731.

Taylor, Dan. *The Faithful and Wise Steward, Being the Substance of a Discourse Delivered by Way of Address to Young Ministers, at an Association of Ministers and Others.* Leeds: Griffith Wright, 1766.

Toller, Thomas N. *Sermons on Various Subjects.* London: B.J. Holdsworth, 1824.

Tommas, John. *Serious Advice to Students and Young Ministers: A Sermon Preached at Broadmead, Bristol, before the Education Society.* Bristol: W. Pine, M. Ward, and T. Cadell, 1774.

Turner, Daniel. *A Compendium of Social Religion; or the Nature and Constitution of Christian Churches, with the Respective Qualifications and Duties of Their Officers and Members,* 2nd ed. Bristol: W. Pine, 1778.

— *The Divine Appointment, and Great Importance of the Christian Ministry Considered, in a Sermon Preached before the Bristol Education Society.* Bristol: W. Pine, T. Cadell, M. Ward, 1774.

Turner, Daniel, and Caleb Evans. *A Charge and Sermon, Delivered at the Ordination of the Rev. Mr. Job David.* Bristol: W. Pine, 1773.

Watts, Isaac. *Discourses of the Love of God and the Use and Abuse of the Passions in Religion, with a devout Meditation suited to each Discourse. To which is prefix'd, A plain and particular Account of the Natural Passions, with Rules of the Government of them.* London, 1729.

Westminster Confession of Faith. Glasgow: Free Presbyterian Publications, 1985.

Whitfield, Charles. *The Form and Order of a Church of Christ.* Newcastle Upon Tyne: Robson and Angus, 1775.

Wilkins, John. *Ecclesiastes: Or, a Discourse Concerning the Gift of Preaching, as It Falls under the Rules of Art*, 7th ed. London, 1693.

Williams, Edward. "An Introductory Discourse on the Nature of an Ordination". In *Three Discourses Delivered at the Ordination of the Rev. Daniel Fleming; at Nuneaton, in Warwickshire, August 6, 1793.* Coventry: M. Luckman, 1793.

— ed. *The Christian Preacher, or, Discourses on Preaching, by Several Eminent Divines, English and Foreign.* Philadelphia: William W. Woodward, 1810.

— *The Works of the Rev. Edward Williams, D.D.* Edited by Evan Davies. 4 Vols. London: James Nisbet and Co., 1862.

Wilson, Samuel. *The Duties of a Pastor and Deacons: Recommended in a Sermon Preach'd at the Ordination of the Rev. Mr. Thomas Flower, Jun.* London: John Wilson, 1736.

3. Secondary Sources

Abbey, C.J., and J.H. Overton. *The English Church in the Eighteenth Century*, 2nd ed. London: Longmans, Green, and Co., 1906.

Auksi, Peter. *Christian Plain Style: The Evolution of a Spiritual Ideal.* Montreal and Kingston: McGill-Queen's University Press, 1995.

Barrett, Gladys M. *A Brief History of Fuller Church, Kettering.* St. Albans, Hertfordshire: Parker Brothers, ca. 1945.

Bebbington, David W. *The Dominance of Evangelicalism: The Age of Spurgeon and Moody.* Vol. 3 of *A History of Evangelicalism: People, Movements and Ideas in the English-Speaking World.* Downers Grove: InterVarsity Press, 2005.

— *Evangelicalism in Modern Britain: A History from the 1730s to the 1980s.* Grand Rapids: Baker Book House, 1989.

— "Revival and Enlightenment in Eighteenth-Century England". In *Modern Christian Revivals*, ed. Edith L. Blumhofer and Randall Balmer, 17-41. Urbana and Chicago: University of Illinois Press, 1993.

Brachlow, Stephen. *The Communion of Saints: Radical Puritan and Separatist Ecclesiology, 1570-1625.* Oxford: Oxford University Press, 1988.

Brackney, William H. *Christian Voluntarism: Theology and Praxis.* Faith's Horizons, edited by Ronald E. Valet. Grand Rapids: Eerdmans, 1997

— "Ordination in the Larger Baptist Tradition". *Perspectives in Religious Studies* 29, no. 3 (Fall 2002): 225-239.

Bradley, James E. *Religion, Revolution, and English Radicalism: Nonconformity in Eighteenth-Century Politics and Society.* Cambridge: Cambridge University Press, 1990.

Bradshaw, Paul F. *The Anglican Ordinal: Its History and Development from the Reformation to the Present Day.* Alcuin Club Collections. London: SPCK, 1971.

Brauer, Jerald C. "Conversion: From Puritanism to Revivalism". *Journal of Religion* 58, no. 3 (1978): 227-243.

Brewster, Paul L. "Andrew Fuller (1754-1815): Model Baptist Pastor-Theologian", Ph.D. diss., Southeastern Baptist Theological Seminary, 2007.

Brown, Kenneth D. *A Social History of the Nonconformist Ministry in England and Wales 1800-1930*. Oxford: Clarendon Press, 1988.

Brown, Raymond. "Baptist Preaching in Early 18th Century England". *Baptist Quarterly* 31 (January 1985): 4-22.

— *The English Baptists of the Eighteenth Century*. Vol. 2 of *A History of the English Baptists*, edited by B.R. White. London: The Baptist Historical Society, 1986.

Bull, Frederick William. *A Sketch of the History of the Town of Kettering, Together with Some Account of Its Worthies*. Kettering: Northamptonshire Printing and Publishing, 1891.

— *Supplement to the History of the Town of Kettering, Together with a Further Account of Its Worthies*. Kettering: Northamptonshire Printing and Publishing Co., 1908.

Caldwell, Patricia. *The Puritan Conversion Narrative: The Beginnings of American Expression*. Cambridge: Cambridge University Press, 1983.

Campbell, Ted A. *The Religion of the Heart: A Study of European Religious Life in the Seventeenth and Eighteenth Centuries*. Columbia: University of South Carolina Press, 1991.

Champion, L.G. "Evangelical Calvinism and the Structures of Baptist Church Life". *Baptist Quarterly* 28 (January 1980): 196-208.

— *Farthing Rushlight: The Story of Andrew Gifford, 1700-1784*. London: Carey Kingsgate Press, 1961.

— "The Theology of John Ryland: Its Sources and Influences". *Baptist Quarterly* 28 (1979): 17-29.

Charry, Ellen T. *By the Renewing of Your Minds: The Pastoral Function of Christian Doctrine*. New York and Oxford: Oxford University Press, 1997.

Child, Robert L. "Baptists and Ordination: A Comment Upon *Church Relations in England*". *Baptist Quarterly* 14 (1952): 243-251.

Chrysostom, John. *Treatise on the Priesthood*. In *A Select Library of the Nicene and Post-Nicene Fathers of the Christian Church*, edited by Philip Schaff, Vol. 9, 31-83. Grand Rapids: Eerdmans, 1979.

Chun, Chris. "'Sense of the Heart': Jonathan Edwards' Legacy in the Writings of Andrew Fuller". *Eusebeia*. 9 (Spring 2008): 117-134.

Clark, J.C.D. *English Society 1660-1832*, 2nd ed. Cambridge: Cambridge University Press, 2000.

— *The Language of Liberty, 1660-1832: Political Discourse and Social Dynamics in the Anglo-American World*. Cambridge: Cambridge University Press, 1994.

Clebsch, William A., and Charles R. Jaekle. *Pastoral Care in Historical Perspective: An Essay with Exhibits*. Englewood Cliffs, NJ: Prentice-Hall, 1964.

Clifford, Alan C. *Atonement and Justification: English Evangelical Theology 1640-1790: An Evaluation*. Oxford: Clarendon Press, 1990.

Clipsham, E.F. "Andrew Fuller and Fullerism: A Study in Evangelical Calvinism". *Baptist Quarterly* 20, nos. 1-4 (1963-1964): 99-114; 147-154; 215-225; 269-276.

— "Andrew Fuller and the Baptist Mission". *Foundations* 10 (January-March 1967): 4-18.

Collinson, Patrick. "Shepherds, Sheepdogs, and Hirelings: The Pastoral Ministry in Post-Reformation England". In *The Ministry: Clerical and Lay*, ed. W.J. Sheils and Diana Wood. 185-220. Studies in Church History, no. 26. Oxford: Basil Blackwell,

1989.

Copson, Stephen. "Two Ordinations at Bridlington in 1737". *Baptist Quarterly* 33 (1989): 146-149.

Cox, F.A. *History of the English Baptist Missionary Society, 1792-1842*. Boston: William S. Damrell, 1845.

Culross, James. *The Three Rylands: A Hundred Years of Various Christian Service*. London: Elliot Stock, 1897.

Daniel, Curt. "Hyper Calvinism and John Gill". Ph.D. diss., University of Edinburgh, 1983.

Davies, Horton. *Worship and Theology in England: From Watts and Wesley to Martineau, 1690-1900*. Vol. 3. Grand Rapids, MI: Eerdmans, 1996.

— *The Worship of the English Puritans*. Westminister: Dacre Press, 1948.

Delattre, Roland André. *Beauty and Sensibility in the Thought of Jonathan Edwards: An Essay in Aesthetics and Theological Ethics*. New Haven: Yale University Press, 1968.

Dixon, Thomas. *From Passions to Emotions: The Creation of a Secular Psychological Category*. Cambridge: Cambridge University Press, 2003.

— "Theology, Anti-theology and Atheology: From Christian Passions to Secular Emotions". *Modern Theology*, 15 (July 1999) 3: 297-330.

Downey, James. *The Eighteenth Century Pulpit*. Oxford: Clarendon Press, 1969.

Dreyer, Frederick. *The Genesis of Methodism*. Bethlehem: Lehigh University Press, 1999.

Ella, George M. *Law and Gospel in the Theology of Andrew Fuller*. Durham: Go Publications, 1996.

Elwyn, Thornton. *The Northamptonshire Baptist Association*. London: Carey Kingsgate Press, 1964.

— "Particular Baptists of the Northamptonshire Baptist Association as Reflected in the Circular Letters, 1765-1820". *Baptist Quarterly*. Part 1, 36 (1996): 368-281; Part 2, 37 (1997): 3-19.

Erdt, Terrence. *Jonathan Edwards, Art and the Sense of the Heart*. Amherst: University of Massachusetts Press, 1980.

Evans, G.R., ed. *A History of Pastoral Care*. London and New York: Cassell, 2000.

Fiering, Norman. *Jonathan Edwards's Moral Thought and Its British Context*. Chapel Hill: University of North Carolina Press, 1981.

Ford, James Thomas. "Preaching in the Reformed Tradition". In *Preachers and People in the Reformations and Early Modern Period*, ed. Larissa Taylor, 65-88. Boston and Leiden: Brill, 2003.

George, A. Raymond. "Ordination". In *A History of the Methodist Church in Great Britain*, edited by Rupert Davies, A. Raymond George, and Gordon Rupp, Vol. 2, 143-160. London: Epworth Press, 1978.

George, Timothy, and David S. Dockery, eds. *Theologians of the Baptist Tradition*. Nashville: Broadman and Holman, 2001.

Gilbert, A.D. *Religion and Society in Industrial England: Church, Chapel and Social Change 1740-1914*. Themes in British Social History, edited by J. Stevenson. London: Longman, 1976.

Goldie, Mark, "John Locke, Jonas Proast and Religious Toleration, 1688-1692". In John Walsh, Colin Haydon, and Stephen Taylor, eds. *The Church of England, c.1689-c.1833: From Toleration to Tractarianism*. Cambridge: Cambridge University Press,

1993.

Goodman, Frank C. *The Great Meeting: The Story of Toller Congregational Church, Kettering, Founded in 1662.* Kettering: Toller Congregational Church, 1962.

Gordon, Grant. "The Call of Dr. John Ryland Jr." *Baptist Quarterly* 34 (1992): 214-227.

Greaves, Richard L. "The Ordination Controversy and the Spirit of Reform in Puritan England". *Journal of Ecclesiastical History* 21, no. 3 (July 1970): 225-241.

Greenall, R.L. *A History of Northamptonshire.* The Darwen County History Series. London: Phillimore, 1979.

— ed. *The Kettering Connection: Northamptonshire Baptists and Overseas Missions.* Leicester: Department of Adult Education, University of Leicester, 1993.

Gregory the Great. *Pastoral Care.* Translated by Henry Davis. Ancient Christian Writers. New York and Mahwah: Newman Press, 1978.

Gribben, Crawford. "Lay Conversion and Calvinist Doctrine During the English Commonwealth". In *The Rise of the Laity in Evangelical Protestantism*, ed. Deryck W. Lovegrove, 36-46. London: Routledge, 2002.

Hall, David D. *The Faithful Shepherd: A History of the New England Ministry in the Seventeenth Century.* Chapel Hill: University of North Carolina Press, 1972.

Hamlin, Gordon. "Two Baptist Pamphlets". *Baptist Quarterly* 16 (1956): 328.

Harris, Frederic William. "Ordination among Dissenters of the Early Eighteenth Century". *Baptist Quarterly* 24 (1971): 126-129.

Hayden, Roger. "Evangelical Calvinism among Eighteenth-Century British Baptists, with Particular Reference to Bernard Foskett, Hugh and Caleb Evans, and the Bristol Baptist Academy, 1690-1791". Ph.D. diss., University of Keele, 1991.

Haykin, Michael A.G. "The Baptist Identity: A View from the Eighteenth Century". *Evangelical Quarterly* 67, no. 2 (1995): 137-152.

— "'A Habitation of God, through the Spirit': John Sutcliff (1752-1814) and the Revitalization of the Calvinistic Baptists in the Late Eighteenth Century". *Baptist Quarterly* 34 (1992): 304-319.

— "'Hazarding All for God at a Clap': The Spirituality of Baptism among British Calvinistic Baptists". *Baptist Quarterly* 38 (1999): 185-195.

— "Jonathan Edwards and His Legacy". *Reformation and Revival* 4, no. 3 (1995): 65-86.

— "'The Oracles of God': Andrew Fuller and the Scriptures". *Churchman* 103, no. 1 (1989): 60-76.

— "John Sutcliff and the Concert of Prayer". *Reformation and Revival* 1, no. 3 (1992): 65-88.

— *One Heart and One Soul: John Sutcliff of Olney, His Friends and His Times.* Darlington: Evangelical Press, 1994.

— ed. *'At the Pure Fountain of Thy Word': Andrew Fuller as an Apologist.* Studies in Baptist History and Thought. Carlisle: Paternoster Press, 2004.

— ed. *The British Particular Baptists, 1638-1910.* Springfield, Missouri: Particular Baptist Press, 1998, 2000, 2003.

— ed. *The Life and Thought of John Gill (1697-1771): A Tricentennial Appreciation.* Leiden: Brill, 1997.

Hempton, David. *Religion and Political Culture in Britain and Ireland: From the Glorious Revolution to the Decline of Empire.* Cambridge: Cambridge University Press, 1996

Higgs, Lionel F. "The Calling and Ordination of Ministers in the Eighteenth Century".

Baptist Quarterly 16 (1956): 277-279.

Hindmarsh, D. Bruce. *The Evangelical Conversion Narrative: Spiritual Autobiography in Early Modern England*. Oxford: Oxford University Press, 2005.

— *John Newton and the English Evangelical Tradition between the Conversions of Wesley and Wilberforce*. Oxford: Clarendon Press, 1996.

— "The Reception of Jonathan Edwards by Early Evangelicals in England". In *Jonathan Edwards at Home and Abroad: Historical Memories, Cultural Movements, Global Horizons*, ed. David W. Kling and Douglas A. Sweeney, 201-221. Columbia: University of South Carolina Press, 2003.

Hinson, E. Glenn. "Ordination in Christian History". *Review and Expositor* 78 (Fall 1981): 485-496.

Hole, Robert. *Pulpits, Politics and Public Order in England, 1760-1832*. Cambridge: Cambridge University Press, 1989.

Hudson, Winthrop S., ed. *Baptist Concepts of the Church*. Philadelphia: Judson Press, 1959.

Jacob, J.M. *The Clerical Profession in the Long Eighteenth Century, 1680-1840*. Oxford: Oxford University Press, 2007.

Jenson, Robert W. *America's Theologian: A Recommendation of Jonathan Edwards*. Oxford: Oxford University Press, 1998.

Kimnach, Wilson H. "General Introduction to the Sermons: Jonathan Edwards' Art of Prophesying". In Jonathan Edwards, *Sermons and Discourses 1720-1723*, edited by Wilson H. Kimnach. Vol. 10 of *The Works of Jonathan Edwards*, edited by Harry Stout. New Haven: Yale University Press, 1992.

Kirkby, Arthur H. "Andrew Fuller–Evangelical Calvinist". *Baptist Quarterly* 15 (1954): 195-202.

Laws, Gilbert. *Andrew Fuller: Pastor, Theologian, Ropeholder*. London: The Carey Press, 1942.

Lee, Sang Hyun, ed. *The Princeton Companion to Jonathan Edwards*. Princeton: Princeton University Press, 2005.

Lessenich, Rolf P. *Elements of Pulpit Oratory in Eighteenth-Century England (1660-1800)*. Köln: Böhlau-Verlag, 1972.

Lovegrove, Deryck W. *Established Church, Sectarian People: Itinerancy and the Transformation of English Dissent, 1780-1830*. Cambridge: Cambridge University Press, 1988.

— "Idealism and Association in Early Nineteenth Century Dissent". In *Voluntary Religion*, ed. W.J. Sheils and Diana Wood, 303-317. Studies in Church History. Oxford: Basil Blackwell, 1986.

— "Lay Leadership, Establishment Crisis and the Disdain of the Clergy". In *The Rise of the Laity in Evangelical Protestantism*, ed. Deryck W. Lovegrove. London and New York: Routledge, 2002.

Manley, Ken R. "John Rippon, D.D. (1751-1836) and the Particular Baptists". D.Phil. diss., Regent's Park College, Oxford University, 1967.

— "Pattern of a Pastorate: John Rippon at Carter Lane, Southwark (1773-1836)". *Journal of Religious History* 11, no. 2 (1980): 269-288.

— *'Redeeming Love Proclaim': John Rippon and the Baptists*. Studies in Baptist History and Thought. Carlisle: Paternoster Press, 2004.

Marsden, George. *Understanding Fundamentalism and Evangelicalism*. Grand Rapids: Eerdmans, 1991.

— ed. *Evangelicalism and Modern America*. Grand Rapids: Eerdmans, 1984.

McGrath, Alister. *Iustitia Dei: A History of the Christian Doctrine of Justification*. Vol. 2, *From 1500 to the Present Day*. Cambridge: Cambridge University Press, 1986.

McKibbens, Thomas R. "Disseminating Biblical Doctrine through Preaching". *Baptist History and Heritage* 19, no. 3 (1984): 42-52.

— *The Forgotten Heritage: A Lineage of Great Baptist Preaching*. Macon: Mercer, 1986.

McKim, Donald K. "The Functions of Ramism in William Perkins' Theology". *The Sixteenth Century Journal* 26, no. 4 (1985): 503-517.

McLoughlin, William G., ed. *Isaac Backus on Church, State, and Calvinism: Pamphlets, 1754-1789*. Cambridge, Mass.: Harvard University Press, 1968.

McNeill, John T. *A History of the Cure of Souls*. New York: Harper & Row, 1977.

Miller, Perry. "Jonathan Edwards on the Sense of the Heart". *Harvard Theological Review* 41 (April 1948) 2: 123-145.

— *The New England Mind: The Seventeenth Century*. New York: Macmillan, 1939.

Mitchell, Louis J. *Jonathan Edwards on the Experience of Beauty*. In Studies in Reformed Theology and History. Princeton: Princeton Theological Seminary, 2003.

Mitchell, W. Fraser. *English Pulpit Oratory from Andrewes to Tillotson: A Study of Its Literary Aspects*. London: SPCK, 1932.

Moorman, John R.H., ed. *The Curate of Souls: Being a Collection of Writings on the Nature and Work of a Priest from the First Century after the Restoration 1660-1760*. London: SPCK, 1958.

Morden, Peter J. *Offering Christ to the World: Andrew Fuller (1754-1815) and the Revival of Eighteenth Century Particular Baptist Life*. Studies in Baptist History and Thought. Carlisle: Paternoster Press, 2003.

Morgan, Edmund S. *Visible Saints: The History of a Puritan Idea*. Ithica: Cornell University Press, 1963.

Naylor, Peter. *Calvinism, Communion and the Baptists: A Study of English Calvinistic Baptists from the Late 1600s to the Early 1800s*. Studies in Baptist History and Thought. Carlisle: Paternoster Press, 2003.

— *Picking up a Pin for the Lord: English Particular Baptists from 1688 to the Early Nineteenth Century*. London: Grace Publications, 1992.

Nazianzen, Gregory. "Oration 2: In Defense of His Flight to Pontus". In *A Select Library of Nicene and Post-Nicene Fathers of the Christian* Church, 2nd Series, edited by Philip and Henry Schaff, Vol 2, 204-227. Grand Rapids: Eerdmans, 1974.

Nettles, Thomas J. *By His Grace and for His Glory: A Historical, Theological, and Practical Study of the Doctrines of Grace in Baptist Life*. Grand Rapids: Baker Book House, 1986.

Newman, William. *Rylandiana: Reminiscences Related to the Rev. John Ryland, A.M. Of Northampton*. London: George Wightman, 1835.

Niebuhr, H. Richard, and Daniel D. Williams, eds. *The Ministry in Historical Perspectives*. New York: Harper & Brothers, 1956.

Noll, Mark. *The Rise of Evangelicalism: The Age of Edwards, Whitefield and the Wesleys*. Vol. 1 of *A History of Evangelicalism: People, Movements and Ideas in the English-Speaking World*. Downers Grove: InterVarsity Press, 2003.

Nuttall, Geoffrey F. "Calvinism in Free Church History". *Baptist Quarterly* 22 (1968): 418-428.

— "Northamptonshire and the Modern Question: A Turning Point in Eighteenth-

Century Dissent". *Journal of Theological Studies* n.s. 16, no. 1 (1965): 101-123.

— *Visible Saints: The Congregational Way, 1640-1660*. Oxford: Basil Blackwell, 1957.

Oden, Thomas C. *Pastoral Theology: Essentials of Ministry*. San Francisco: Harper & Row, 1983.

Old, Hughes Oliphant. *The Reading and Preaching of the Scriptures in the Worship of the Christian Church*. Vol. 5 of *Moderatism, Pietism, and Awakening*. Grand Rapids: Eerdmans, 2004.

Oliver, Robert William. "The Emergence of a Strict and Particular Baptist Community among the English Calvinist Baptists, 1770-1850". Ph.D. diss., London Bible College, 1986.

Owen, W.T. *Edward Williams, D.D., 1750-1813: His Life, Thought and Influence*. Cardiff: University of Wales Press, 1963.

Packer, J.I. *A Quest for Godliness: The Puritan Vision of the Christian Life*. Wheaton: Crossway, 1990.

Parsons, Kenneth A.C., ed. *The Church Book of the Independent Church (Now Pound Lane Baptist) Isleham, 1693-1805*. Cambridge: Cambridge Antiquarian Records Society, 1984.

Payne, Earnest A. "Andrew Fuller as Letter Writer". *Baptist Quarterly* 15 (1954): 290-296.

— *The Prayer Call of 1784*. London: Baptist Laymen's Missionary Movement, 1941.

— "Baptists and the Laying on of Hands". *Baptist Quarterly* 15 (1954): 203-215.

Petersen, William H. "On the Pattern and in the Power: A Historical Essay of Anglican Pastoral Care". In *Anglican Theology and Pastoral Care*, ed. James E. Griffiss, 5-40. Wilton, CT: Morehouse-Barlow, 1985.

Pettit, Norman. *The Heart Prepared: Grace and Conversion in Puritan Spiritual Life*. New Haven: Yale University Press, 1966.

Puglisi, James F. *The Process of Admission to Ordained Ministry: A Comparative Study*. Translated by Michael S. Driscoll and Mary Misrahi. 3 vols. Collegeville, MN: Pueblo, 1996.

Purves, Andrew. *Pastoral Theology in the Classical Tradition*. Louisville: Westminster John Knox Press, 2001.

Rivers, Isabel. "Dissenting and Methodist Books of Practical Divinity". In *Books and Their Readers in Eighteenth-Century England*, ed. Isabel Rivers, 127-164. Leicester: Leicester University Press, 1982.

— *Reason, Grace, and Sentiment: A Study of the Language of Religion and Ethics in England, 1660-1780*. Vol. 1 of *Whichcote to Wesley*. Cambridge: Cambridge University Press, 1991.

Robison, Olin C. "The Legacy of John Gill". *Baptist Quarterly* 24 (1971): 111-125.

— "The Particular Baptists in England, 1760-1820". D.Phil. diss., Oxford University, 1963.

Rupp, Gordon. *Religion in England, 1688-1791*. Oxford History of the Christian Church, edited by Henry Chadwick and Owen Chadwick. Oxford: Clarendon Press, 1986.

Russell, Anthony. *The Clerical Profession*. London: SPCK, 1980.

Sell, Alan P.F. "*The Gospel Its Own Witness*: Deism, Thomas Paine, and Andrew Fuller". In *"You Will Be My Witnesses": A Festschrift in Honor of the Reverend Dr. Allison Trites on the Occasion of His Retirement*, ed. Glenn R. Wooden, et al., 188-229. Macon: Mercer University Press, 2003.

— *The Great Debate: Calvinism, Arminianism and Salvation.* Studies in Christian Thought and History. Worthing, West Sussex: H.E. Walter, 1982.

— *John Locke and the Eighteenth-Century Divines.* Cardiff: University of Wales Press, 1997.

— *Saints: Visible, Orderly and Catholic. The Congregational Idea of the Church.* Allison Park: Pickwick Publications, 1986.

Serjeantson, R.M., and W. Ryland D. Adkins. "Ecclesiastical History". In *The Victoria History of the County of Northampton*, edited by R.M. Serjeantson and W. Ryland D. Adkins, Vol. 2, 1-78. London: James Street, 1906.

Shaw, Ian J. *High Calvinists in Action: Calvinism and the City: Manchester and London, c. 1810-1860.* Oxford: Oxford University Press, 2002.

Smith, John E. *Jonathan Edwards: Puritan, Preacher, Philosopher.* Notre Dame: University of Notre Dame Press, 1992.

Smyth, Charles. *The Art of Preaching: A Practical Survey of Preaching in the Church of England, 747-1939.* London: SPCK, 1953.

Spaeth, Donald A. *The Church in an Age of Danger: Parsons and Parishioners, 1660-1740.* Cambridge: Cambridge University Press, 2000.

Spurr, John. "From Puritanism to Dissent, 1660-1700". In *The Culture of English Puritanism, 1560-1700*, ed. Christopher Durston and Jacqueline Eales, 234-265. New York: St. Martin's Press, 1996.

Stackhouse, John G., Jr. "Defining 'Evangelical'". *Church & Faith Trends* (The Centre for Research on Canadian Evangelicals) 1, no. 1 (2007): 1-5.

— ed. *Evangelical Ecclesiology: Reality or Illusion?* Grand Rapids: Baker Academic, 2003.

Stanley, Brian. *The History of the Baptist Missionary Society, 1792-1992.* Edinburgh: T & T Clark, 1992.

Stein, Stephen J., ed. *The Cambridge Companion to Jonathan Edwards.* Cambridge: Cambridge University Press, 2007.

Stoeffler, F. Ernst. *The Rise of Evangelical Pietism.* Studies in the History of Religions. Leiden: E. J. Brill, 1965.

Sykes, Norman. *Church and State in England in the 18th Century.* New York: Octagon Books, 1975.

Taylor, Larissa, ed. *Preachers and People in the Reformations and Early Modern Period.* Boston and Leiden: Brill, 2003.

Tidball, Derek. *Skilful Shepherds: Explorations in Pastoral Theology.* Leicester: Apollos, 1997.

Toon, Peter. *The Emergence of Hyper-Calvinism in English Nonconformity, 1689-1765.* London: The Olive Tree, 1967.

— "John Brine, 1703-1765". *Free Grace Record* 3, no. 12 (1965): 557-571.

Tull, James E. *Shapers of Baptist Thought.* Macon: Mercer University Press, 1984.

Underwood, A.C. *A History of the English Baptists.* London: The Kingsgate Press, 1947.

Virgin, Peter. *The Church in an Age of Negligence: Ecclesiastical Structure and Problems of Church Reform 1700-1840.* Cambridge: James Clark & Co., 1989.

von Rohr, John. *The Covenant of Grace in Puritan Thought.* American Academy of Religion Studies in Religion, Vol. 45, edited by Charles Hardwick and James O. Duke. Atlanta: Scholars Press, 1986.

Wainwright, William J. *Reason and the Heart: A Prolegomenon to a Critique of*

Passional Reason. Ithaca: Cornell University Press, 1995.

Wakefield, Gordon S. *Puritan Devotion: It's Place in the Development of Christian Piety*. London: Epworth Press, 1957.

Walker, Michael J. *Baptists at the Table: The Theology of the Lord's Supper Amongst English Baptists in the Nineteenth Century*. Didcot: Baptist Historical Society, 1992.

Walsh, John. "Origins of the Evangelical Revival". In *Essays in Modern Church History in Memory of Norman Sykes*, ed. G.V. Bennett and J.D. Walsh, 132-162. London: Adam and Charles Black, 1966.

— "Religious Societies: Methodist and Evangelical 1738-1800". In *Voluntary Religion*, ed. W.J. Sheils and Diana Wood, 279-302. Studies in Church History. Oxford: Basil Blackwell, 1986.

Walsh, John, Colin Haydon, and Stephen Taylor, eds. *The Church of England, c.1689-c.1833: From Toleration to Tractarianism*. Cambridge: Cambridge University Press, 1993.

Walton, Brad. *Jonathan Edwards, Religious Affections and the Puritan Analysis of True Piety, Spiritual Sensation and Heart Religion*. Studies in American Religion. Lewiston: Edwin Mellen Press, 2002.

Ward, W.R. "The Baptists and the Transformation of the Church, 1780-1830". *Baptist Quarterly* 25 (October 1973): 167-184.

— *Early Evangelicalism: A Global Intellectual History, 1670-1789*. Cambridge: Cambridge University Press, 2006.

— "Pastoral Office and the General Priesthood in the Great Awakening". In *The Ministry: Clerical and Lay*, ed. W.J. Sheils and Diana Wood. Studies in Church History. Oxford: Basil Blackwell, 1989.

— *Religion and Society in England 1790-1850*. London: B.T. Batsford, 1972.

Watts, Michael R. *The Dissenters*. 2 vols. Oxford: Clarendon Press, 1978, 1995.

Webster, Tom. *Godly Clergy in Early Stuart England: The Caroline Puritan Movement, C. 1620-1643*. Cambridge: Cambridge University Press, 1997.

Wheeler, Nigel. "Eminent Spirituality and Eminent Usefulness: Andrew Fuller's (1754-1815) Pastoral Theology in his Ordination Sermons", Ph.D. diss., University of Pretoria, 2009.

White, B.R. *The English Baptists of the Seventeenth Century*. Vol. 1 of *A History of the English Baptists*, edited by B.R. White. London: The Baptist Historical Society, 1983.

— *The English Separatist Tradition: From the Marian Martyrs to the Pilgrim Fathers*. Oxford: Oxford University Press, 1971.

Whitley, W.T. *A History of British Baptists*. London: Charles Griffin & Co., 1923.

Wolffe, John. *The Expansion of Evangelicalism: The Age of Wilberforce, More, Chalmers and Finney*. Vol. 2 of *A History of Evangelicalism: People, Movements and Ideas in the English-Speaking World*. Downers Grove: InterVarsity Press, 2007.

Woodward, James, and Stephen Pattison, eds. *The Blackwell Reader in Pastoral and Practical Theology*. Oxford: Blackwell, 2000.

Young, Doyle L. "Andrew Fuller and the Modern Mission Movement". *Baptist History and Heritage* 17, no. 4 (1982): 17-27.

— "The Place of Andrew Fuller in the Developing Modern Missions Movement". Ph.D. diss., Southwestern Baptist Theological Seminary, 1981.

Index

Aberdeen 71
Act of Toleration 63
Act of Uniformity 18
activism 1, 3, 31, 107, 109-110
Adkins, W. Ryland 18
affections
  and assurance 15, 35-36, 39
  and church discipline 104
  and doctrine 12, 14-15, 100-103
  and emotions 9-10, 99
  and evangelicalism 9-15, 100-104, 107, 109
  integrating mind and heart 9-10, 12-14, 99, 101-103, 108
  and ministers' spirituality 96-100, 108
  personal experience 9, 12, 69, 96-100, 108-109
  and Puritans 10
  and preaching 95-103, 107-108
  vocabulary 9
  and voluntarism 12, 107-109
Alleine, Joseph 33
Andrewes, Lancelot 80
antinomianism 26, 27, 40, 42, 48
Arminianism 26, 48, 91
assurance 23, 25, 28, 30, 38-40, 47, 109
  and scripture impressions 15, 31-37, 47
Auksi, Peter 80
Backus, Isaac 55-56
baptism 16-17, 19, 72-73, 75
Baptist Annual Register 60
Baptist Itinerant Society 78
Baptist Missionary Society 1, 20, 25, 61, 88, 109
  see also missions
Baptists, *see* Particular Baptists
Barrett, Gladys 18
Barrow, Isaac 103
Baxter, Richard 26, 100, 103

Bebbington, David
  on assurance 31
  on defining evangelicalism 3-4, 92-94, 109
  on Fuller as evangelical 24, 94-95
Belcher, Joseph 81, 103
Beza, Theodore 27
biblicism 3, 93, 109
Bolton, Robert 38
Brachlow, Stephen 63, 67
Bradley, James 63
Bradshaw, Paul 69
Brainerd, David 6
Brine, John 18, 27, 44-45, 47
Bristol Academy 6, 27, 96
Bristol Education Society 6
Broadmead Baptist Church (Bristol) 27
Bull, Frederick 18-19
Bunyan, John 29, 37, 39, 49
Burnet, Gilbert 5, 55, 68
Burroughs, Joseph 59
Caldwell, Patricia 29
Calvin, John 26
  see also Calvinism
Calvinism 10, 18, 26, 91, 103, 109
  see also evangelical Calvinism, high Calvinism
Campbell, Ted 10
Carey, William 17, 61, 95, 107
Catholicism 69
Champion, L. G. 1
Charry, Ellen 24
Chun, Chris, 14
church discipline 42, 104
church membership 57, 73
Church of England
  and conversionism 54
  and ecclesiology 53-54, 74-75
  as Established Church 63-64, 69

evangelicalism in 4-5, 54, 68-69, 74-75
ordination 55-56, 64, 66, 69-70
pastoral neglect 64
pastoralia 4-5
religious societies in 53-54, 68-69, 74-75, 107
Claude, Jean 79-85, 103
Clipsham, E. F. 1, 24
Coles, William 93
Collins, Hercules 58, 64, 98
communion, *see* Lord's Supper
Congregationalists 18
see also Independents
congregationalism
and associationalism 65-72
and conversionism 53-54, 107
ecclesiology 53-54, 63, 65-75, 108
and evangelicalism 4, 8, 64-65, 74-75, 107-108, 109-110
and ordinations 58-62, 64-72
and pastoral call 54-58
and voluntarism 53-54, 65-72, 107
conversion, conversionism 45-49, 64
and affections 100-104, 107-108
as characteristic of evangelicalism 3, 109
and congregationalism 53-54
in Fuller's pastoral theology 23-50, 94-95, 109
narratives 25, 28-31, 57
and preaching 94-95, 107-108
presumption as obstacle to 37-49
theme of *Gospel Worthy of All Acceptation* 8
Cornick, David 5
Crisp, Tobias 26-28, 38, 40
Crosby, Thomas 59
crucicentrism 3, 92-95, 104, 107, 109
Culy, David 16
Daniel, Curt 26, 28, 33, 38, 40, 44
Davies, Horton 60-61
Davis, Richard 16, 18, 26-28, 43-44
Deism 20, 91

Delattre, Roland 13
Dissent
and affections 10-12
and ecclesiology 53, 62-65
and evangelicalism 1-3, 8, 12, 77, 110
ordinations 59, 63
preaching 98, 108
and rationalism 10-12
Dixon, Thomas 9-10, 99
doctrine
and affections 12, 14-15, 100-103, 108
pastoral implications of 7-8, 24
Doddridge, Philip 12, 18, 19, 59, 70, 77
Donne, John 80
Downey, James 87, 98
Dreyer, Frederick 54, 68
Driver, Joseph 55
Dutton, Anne 39
Eaton, John 26
ecclesiology
Baptist 62, 63, 110
and church membership 73
Dissenting 62-65
expressed in ordination services 7, 58-62
and ordinances 72-75
and pastoral theology 7-8, 107
and priesthood of all believers 72-75
see also congregationalism
Edinburgh 73
Edwards, Jonathan 6
on affections 12-14, 96-97, 101, 108
on assurance 36
influence upon Fuller 12-14, 45, 48, 81, 109-111
on moral and natural ability
preaching 81, 86, 96-97
on scripture impressions 34-37
on the "sense of the heart" 12-14
emotions 9-10, 99
see also affections
enthusiasm 9, 12, 55, 63-64
see also affections, passions
epistemology 101-102

Erdt, Terrence 10, 13
Erskine, Ralph 29-31
Established Church, *see* Church of
England
evangelical, evangelicals, evangelicalism
activist signs of 1-3
and affections 9-15, 68-69, 100-104,
108-109
and congregationalism 4, 8, 107, 109-
110
conversion narratives 28-31, 57
definition of 3-4, 92-94, 109-110
and Dissent 1-3, 8, 10-12, 77
and preaching 91-95, 98-104, 108
transdenominationalism 4, 109
and voluntarism 53-54, 107-108
see also conversionism, crucicentrism
evangelical Calvinism 1, 6-7, 20, 23, 27,
45-49, 91, 107, 109
see also Fuller, *Gospel Worthy*
Evangelical Magazine 60
Evangelical Revival 27, 53, 77, 108, 110
see also evangelicals
Evans, Hugh 96
Eve, John 16, 26, 28, 41-43
Fawcett, John 88-89
Fiering, Norman 10
Flavel, John 103
Fuller, Andrew
as apologist 20
baptism 16-17
and Baptist Missionary Society 1-3,
20, 88
confession of faith 95
conversion 23, 25, 28, 37-38
as evangelical 3-4, 45-49, 109-110
as evangelical activist 1-3
ordination 17, 59-62
ordination sermons 7
pastoral call 55-58, 59
pastorates 2, 15-21
as preacher 81, 87-90
sermon notebook 89-90
significance and influence 1, 6-7, 24

as village preacher 1-2, 77, 95, 107,
109
Fuller, Andrew, writings
"The Affectionate Concern of a
Minister for the Salvation of His
Hearers" 100
"The Conversion of Sinners" 78, 94
"Essay on the Composition of a
Sermon" 79
*Expository Discourses on the Book of
Genesis* 85
Gospel Worthy of All Acceptation 8,
17, 23-25, 45-49, 78, 94, 107
"The Nature and Importance of an
Intimate Knowledge of Divine Truth"
14, 102
"The Nature of the Gospel and the
Manner in Which It Ought to Be
Preached" 92
"The Reward of a Faithful Minister"
86-87
"The Satisfaction Derived from Godly
Simplicity" 82
"The Uniform Bearing of the
Scriptures on the Person and Work of
Christ" 93
Fuller, Andrew Gunton (son) 20, 88
Fuller Baptist Church, *see* Kettering
Baptist Church
Fullerism 1
see also evangelical Calvinism
Geard, John 96
George, Timothy 70
Gibson, Edmund 55
Gill, John 39, 49
and free offers 43-45
and high Calvinism 27
on independency 67
and Kettering 18
on ordination 55, 70, 74
pastoral theology 24
Glasgow 66, 71-72
Goldie, Mark 5
Great Awakening 12

Greaves, Richard 64
Gregory, Jeremy 68
Gregory Nazianzan 56
Gregory the Great 56
Greenall, R. L. 18-19
Gunton, Philippa (Fuller's grandmother) 16
Gurney, W. B. 90-91
Hall, David 80
Hall, John Keen 73
Hall, Robert, jun. 19, 44
Hall, Robert, sen. 17, 34-35, 38, 59
Hayden, Roger 6, 27, 44, 58
Haykin, Michael 1, 17, 61, 96
high Calvinism 6, 16, 20, 23, 25
    and assurance 31-37
    and eternal decrees 28, 47
    and free offers, *see under* preaching
    origins of 26-28
    and preaching 28, 91, 109
    and presumption 25, 37-40
    and spiritual ability 25, 41-43, 47-48, 94, 104, 109
    see also justification, Modern Question, scripture impressions
Hiltner, Seward 7
Hindmarsh, Bruce
    on conversion narratives 29-31, 57
    on defining evangelicalism 4
    on evangelical ecclesiology 110
    on Fuller as evangelical 3
    on moderate Calvinism 1
    on religious societies 54, 68
    on varieties of eighteenth-century theology 26
Holcroft, Francis 16
Hole, Robert 63
Hooker, Thomas 67
Hume, David 10
Hussey, Joseph 27, 39-40, 43
Hutcheson, Francis 10
hyper Calvinism, *see* high Calvinism
independent, *see* congregationalism
Independents 16, 18, 48, 66, 69

see also Congregationalists
individualism 64
Isleham Independent Church (Cambridgeshire) 16
itinerancy 95
    as expression of evangelical activism 1-3, 107, 109
    and social order 64
    and transformation of pastoral ministry 2, 77
Ivimey, Joseph 81
Jacob, W. M. 5
Jackson, Alvery 27
Jones, Edmund 40
justification 25
    eternal 26, 28, 38, 44, 47
Keach, Benjamin 67, 74
Kettering, Northamptonshire (town) 2, 19
Kettering Baptist Church 2, 3, 17-21, 27, 90, 94
Kimnach, Wilson 79, 81, 84, 86, 96-97
latitudinarianism 5, 68
Law, William 18
lay ordination controversies 64
Leland, John 96
Lessenich, Rolf 80-81, 85, 92, 98
Locke, John 67
Lollards 18
London 6, 27, 59
London Baptist Confession of Faith 27
Lord's Supper 72-75, 104
    open communion 19
Lovegrove, Deryck
    on associationalism 65
    on itinerancy 1-3, 64, 77
Manley, Ken 58, 87, 98
Marsden, George 4
Martin, John 45
Mather, Cotton 6
Maurice, Matthias 27
McGrath, Alister 33
McKim, Donald 80
Methodism
    connexion 53-54, 68, 74-75, 107

conversion narratives 57
ecclesiology 53-54, 68, 74-75
and expressions of evangelicalism 4
preachers 57
preaching 98
and voluntarism 68, 74-75, 107
Miller, Perry 13, 80, 86, 88
missions 74
commissioning services 61-62
as expression of evangelical activism
1-3, 107
see also Baptist Missionary Society
Mitchell, Fraser 79, 81
Mitchell, Louis 13
Modern Question, The 26-27, 43-45
see also high Calvinism
Morden, Peter 3-4, 44, 94
Morgan, Edmund 29
Morris, J. W. 7, 24, 79, 83, 88
Murray, Iain 96
mysticism 33
Nettles, Thomas 81
Newton, John 68-69
Noll, Mark 3, 24, 68
Northamptonshire 17-18, 26, 77
see also Kettering
Northamptonshire Particular Baptist
Association 1, 17, 27, 97
Nuttall, Geoffrey
on congregationalism 62, 67, 69
on high Calvinism 16, 26-27
on moderate Calvinism 1
Oden, Thomas 5, 8
Olsen, Roger 110
ordinances 72-75, 104
see also baptism, Lord's Supper
ordinations
and associationalism 65-72
congregational affirmation 56-58
congregational ecclesiology 58-62, 64
episcopal 64, 69
Fuller's 17, 59-62
inner call 55-56, 64
lay ordination controversies 64

laying on of hands 61, 65, 69-72
and missionary commissioning
services 61
morphology of 58-62
as orderly 62-65
and voluntarism 65-72
see also pastoral call
ordination sermons
Fuller's 7
ordo salutis 29, 31, 37, 94, 109
Owen, John 6-7, 47-48, 93, 103
Particular Baptists
and conversionism 53
ecclesiology 53, 59-62
and evangelicalism 1-3, 6-7, 25, 27,
91, 110
ordinations 59-62
pastoral theology 6-7
and social order 63
see also Northamptonshire Particular
Baptist Association
Particular Baptist Society for the
Propagation of the Gospel Among the
Heathen, *see* Baptist Missionary
Society
passions 9, 12, 14, 102
see also affections, enthusiasm
pastoral call
congregational context 56-58
inner call 54-56, 64
narratives 57-58
see also ordination
pastoral theology
classical tradition 5
definition of 7-8
and evangelicalism 2, 4-6, 107-109
expressed in ordination service 58-62
Gospel Worthy as 23-25
see also ecclesiology, preaching
pastoral visiting 104
Pattison Stephen 7, 24
Payne, Ernest 61
Pearce, Samuel 80
Perkins, William 28, 31, 80-81

Pettit, Norman 29
plain style, *see* preaching
Pound Lane Particular Baptist Church
     (Cambridgeshire) 16
preaching
     and affections 95-103, 107-108
     and conversionism 23, 94-95, 107,
     109
     and crucicentrism 92-95, 104, 107,
     109
     as evangelical 5, 77, 91-95, 98, 109
     delivery 87-90, 98-100, 107-108
     free offers of the gospel 20, 24-25, 27,
     39-40, 43-50, 94, 99, 107, 109
     goals of 5
     genres of sermons 84-87
     plain style 70-84, 86, 103, 107
     sermon composition 78-84, 102-103
professions 66
Puglisi, James 56, 59, 62, 69
Puritans 45, 109
     and affections 10
     and assurance 36-37, 109
     conversion narratives 25, 28-31, 38
     covenant theology 27, 37
     devotional writing 28-31
     and high Calvinism 26-28
     in Northamptonshire 18
     and plain style 80-81, 86, 103
     preaching 81, 86
Purves, Andrew 5, 56
Quakers 72
radicalism 63-64
Ramism 80-81, 86
Ramus, Peter, *see* Ramism
rationalism 10-12, 109
religious societies 54, 68-69, 107
     see also voluntarism, voluntary
     societies
Rippon, John 18, 40, 60
Rivers, Isabel 69
     on affections 10-12, 96, 104
     on devotional books 28-29
Robinson, Robert 80-82

Robison, Olin 1, 6, 60
Rogers, John 6
Rupp, Gordon 3
Rushdon, Northamptonshire 20
Russell, Anthony 71, 83, 87, 92
Ryland, John, jun. 6-7, 17, 25, 32-35, 93
Ryland, John Collett (senior) 59, 98, 102
Saltmarsh, John 26
sanctification 48
Sandemanianism 20
scripture impressions 15, 31-37, 39
Sell, Alan 67
sense of the heart 12-14, 110
Serjeantson, R. M. 18
Separatism, *see* Dissenters
sermons, *see* preaching
Shaftesbury, Third Earl of 10
Simeon, Charles 80
Smalley, John 27
Smith, John 9, 12
Socinianism 20
Soham Baptist Church 2, 16-17, 26, 28,
     41-43, 55-58, 59, 65
Spurgeon, Charles 16, 70
Stackhouse, John G., Jr. 4
Stoeffler, Ernst 4, 109
Stuart, Charles 25
supralapsarianism 28
Sutcliff, John 17, 66-67, 70, 96
Taylor, Abraham 27, 45
Taylor, Stephen 4-5, 68
Tidball, Derek 7-8, 24
Tillotson, John 87
Toller, Thomas 19
Toon, Peter 26, 28, 33, 38, 42, 44
Turner, Daniel 64-65, 67
Unitarianism 91
Universalism 20, 92
Virgin, Peter 66
voluntarism
     and affections 12, 108-109
     and congregational ecclesiology 53-
     54, 65-72, 75, 108-109
     and evangelicalism 53-54, 107-109

and Methodist connexion 53-54, 74-75
and ordination 65-72
and pastoral reform 5, 68
see also religious societies, voluntary
  societies
voluntary societies 1-3, 54, 68-69, 74-
  75, 107
see also religious societies
von Rohr, John 26, 27, 36, 38
Wakefield, Gordon 31
Walker, Michael 63, 69, 73
Wallis, Beeby 20
Wallis, George 3, 9-10, 21, 73, 77, 104
Wallis, Thomas 18
Wallis, William 18
Walsh, John
  on evangelical pastoralia 4-5
  on devotional books and the revival 28
  on religious societies 68, 74
  on voluntarism 54, 68, 74

Walton, Brad 10
Ward, W. R. 1-3, 6, 8, 66, 72
Ward, William 71
Watts, Isaac 12, 83, 100, 108
Watts, Michael 29, 67, 87, 98
Wayman, Lewis 27
Wesley, John 54, 68, 74, 110
  see also Methodism
Western Particular Baptist Association 6,
  27
Westminster Assembly 26
Westminster Confession of Faith 27, 33
Wheeler, Nigel 60
White, B. R. 72
Wicken, Cambridgeshire 16
Wilkins, John 87
Williams, Edward 48, 66, 69, 80
Wolffe, John 4
Woodward, James 7, 24